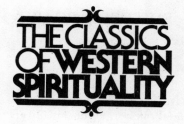

Emanuel Swedenborg
The Universal Human and Soul-Body Interaction

EDITED AND TRANSLATED BY
GEORGE F. DOLE

INTRODUCTION BY
STEPHEN LARSEN

PREFACE BY
ROBERT H. KIRVEN

PAULIST PRESS
NEW YORK • RAMSEY • TORONTO

Cover Art:
LIZ BRADLEY is an artist from northern New Jersey. In this original portrait of Swedenborg she captures the bearing and depth of the famous Swedish seer.

Contents

Editor of this Volume

GEORGE F. DOLE received his B.A. (Classics) from Yale, his M.A. (Hebrew) from Oxford, and his Ph.D. (Assyriology) from Harvard. He is currently a member of the faculty of the Swedenborg School of Religion in Newton, Massachusetts. He and his wife, Lois, are the parents of five children.

Author of the Introduction

STEPHEN LARSEN received his B.A. from Columbia College, his M.A. from Columbia University, and his Ph.D. from the Union Graduate School, all in psychology. Trained as a behavioral psychologist, he nonetheless reverted to a specialization in the psychology of religion, mythology, and symbolism. His book *The Shaman's Doorway* (Harper & Row 1976) analyzes the shaman's role as visionary psychologist. A later study on Emanuel Swedenborg, "Swedenborg and the Visionary Tradition," shows Swedenborg's life and ideas also to relate closely to this prototypic pattern.

Dr. Larsen is in private practice in psychotherapy in Kingston, N.Y., and teaches psychology at Ulster County Community College. He also serves on the board of directors of The Swedenborg Foundation, New York City.

Author of the Preface

ROBERT H. KIRVEN, Ph.D. is a graduate of the University of Chicago, Andover Newton Theological School, Swedenborg School of Religion, and Brandeis University. He was raised in St. Louis and has lived in Boston since 1958. Twelve years a writer of radio and television commercials and documentary films, he has taught at the Swedenborg School of Religion since 1962 and been president of that institution since 1979.

to Wilson Van Dusen
*"The tablets . . . were the work of Moses,
but the writing was still the writing of God."*
A.C. 10453[3]

Preface

Before he began having the spiritual experiences that led to the writings from which these translations are drawn, Emanuel Swedenborg was involved with mining, commerce, and other practical affairs of the Swedish government. He wrote and published widely in these fields, and also in a special interest of his—physiological research on the problem of locating or defining the human soul. These technical and scientific works almost equal the volume of his spiritual writings in Biblical interpretation and theology.

This earlier literary output is relevant to the material translated here for at least two reasons. For one thing, analysis of the method that characterizes his scientific work shows much in common with modern scientific method. For example, I have found many similarities between his explanations in this area and those of Darwin. Since there is much evidence of continuity in his methods before and after his intensive and ongoing spiritual experiences, this suggests the validity of approaching his descriptions of spirituality with the expectation of encountering a relatively modern, scientific mind at work.

A second implication is related to the first. Swedenborg's interests and experience, as well as his methodology, led him to a profound respect for physical reality. Therefore, his awakening perceptions of spiritual reality did not bring him to a radical subordination of matter, nor even a dualistic construct, but rather produced a vastly enlarged whole of reality.

This holistic approach to traditional spirit/matter and mind/body dichotomies is one of Swedenborg's major contributions to the thought and literature of spirituality. It also presents a serious obstacle to comprehension by minds schooled in the predominantly Aristotelian traditions of Western language and logic. Repeatedly, Swedenborg resolves long-standing metaphysical dilemmas by replac-

PREFACE

ing *either/or* alternatives of categorical thought with *both/and* constructions, which are inherent in the physical-and-spiritual wholeness of his reality.

This is why an adjective, such as "human," can be attributed to creation and creator alike, and both material substance and spiritual substance can exist in the same form. This transcendence of categorical dichotomies may be more difficult for new readers of Swedenborg than management of his somewhat specialized vocabulary or his occasional redefinition of traditional terms. That transcendence is rewarded, however, by a comprehensive view of reality as whole—reality in which the distinctions between matter and spirit are never blurred, but in which the inherent and consistent interconnections that unite them are never forgotten.

Foreword

The material here presented under the title *The Universal Human* has been extracted from Swedenborg's *Arcana Coelestia* (referred to herein as *A.C.*), his first and largest theological publication. The *Arcana* proceeds chapter by chapter and verse by verse through Genesis and Exodus, giving what we might refer to as the outline of spiritual or symbolic exegesis.

Perhaps to ease the strain of such a sustained presentation (twelve volumes in the current English translation), Swedenborg began at the second chapter appending material on particular theological topics, beginning with life after death. At the close of Chapter 23, he turned to the subject of the general nature of "correspondence," and followed this theme through a systematic treatment of the spiritual connections and significance of the human body and its parts. This treatment closes with a discussion of diseases at the end of Chapter 43.

For present purposes, some slight adjustments have been made. For example, promises to continue the subject "at the close of the next chapter" have been omitted, and references to the location of previously presented material have been altered to fit the present arrangement. Swedenborg's paragraph numbers, however, have been left intact, having proved invaluable in simplifying references to a work that has appeared in numerous editions. References to material in the *Arcana* but not in the present volume have been retained.

Soul-Body Interaction is, in contrast to the *Arcana*, a complete work. The version presented here is revised from my translation in *Studia Swedenborgiana* (2, nos. 1–3; January 1976–January 1977).

The *Arcana* was published betwen 1747 and 1753 and *Soul-Body Interaction* in 1769, by which time Swedenborg was eighty-one. The material in this volume presents him in different ways—as the empiricist in the *Arcana* material and as the philosopher in *Soul-Body Interaction*.

At the close of paragraph 475 of *The Word Explained* (an editorial title for the massive precursor to the *Arcana*, left in manuscript by Swedenborg) is the following statement.

> As to what I have written about myself, I cannot yet be so sure of it that I can swear to it in God's name, because I cannot know whether the particular words of the description are proper and precise enough to be absolutely right. So they need to be improved at some later time, God willing— improved to the point that I seem to myself to be telling the truth absolutely.

For the rest of his career, Swedenborg remained aware of the inadequacy of language, and was under no illusion that he had managed to construct a consistent terminological system (cf. n. 4658 in "The Universal Human"). The translator's effort, then, has been to identify the core meaning and semantic range of the words, and to reflect their contextual variations in translation.

In the area of syntax, the effort has been to find English structures that are structurally and stylistically equivalent to Swedenborg's Latin ones. The "literalism" of previous translations has tended to misrepresent the fundamental simplicity of the original. If there is obscurity in the present version, the reader may suspect that the fault lies in the English rather than in the Latin.

I wish to express my gratitude to Mary Bryant for her cheerful competence at the typewriter. I am also most grateful to the Paulist Press, and to Richard Payne as originator of this series. I profoundly hope that the final product adequately rewards their encouragement and support.

Introduction

In the inventory of human passions none is more mysterious than the desire to know. It seems to defy reduction to biogenic or behavioristic sources, and often carries the would-be knower far from the familiar evolutionary paths of mere survival and adaptation. Where it penetrates furthest into the universe that is the object of its knowing, it may isolate the questing individual on a lonely and socially misunderstood way, far from the normal human byways that lead to personal social power or the procreation of the species.

The need to understand and "know" the living essence of this universe we inhabit was earliest formulated by the classical Greeks. For them the wisdom path of *gnosis* was the pinnacle of human endeavor and a motive beyond ordinary concerns. But the quest for knowing has in fact proven self-validating. The cumulative yield of this otherworldly-seeming process has been the best and highest fruits of civilization. And we are all the beneficiaries of the human quest for knowledge by dedicated men and women who pursued it beyond the personal, into the realm of transpersonal experience, relevant to us all.

The Man Who Had to Know

This notion that a motive might be teleological rather than derivative, forward-pointing rather than emergent, is very close to the heart of Emanuel Swedenborg's philosophy. Swedenborg was to come to perceive an interconnectedness betweens goals and motives, effects and causes, natural world and spiritual reality, that was profoundly purposeful. And science, his first love, was to become ever more religious for him as he increasingly intuited a unitive Presence behind the multiplicity of phenomena. But Swedenborg did not just

1

pursue this *gnostic* motive intellectually, this need "to know." In the broad outlines of his life, he came to live it. His personal story, then, tells of this motive; and as we consider his biographical data, as well as his revelatory insights, we find the same theme recurring at every level. Swedenborg was "the man who had to know."

Born two centuries earlier than Teilhard de Chardin, Swedenborg was also a scientist who devoted his life to the search for a spiritual principle within the material universe. Like de Chardin, he sought to do this within the framework of a deeply felt Christianity, and like de Chardin, he was an archaeologist of the Spirit, ever seeking and sifting through the meticulously collected data of science for evidence of spiritual consciousness invisibly at work within the processes of the physical world.

Swedenborg was a truly modern thinker in that he insisted that his inherited theistic concept of the universe be brought into relationship with empirical science. He may have been incapable of that cognitive segregation which allows many people to keep their commonsense knowledge and felt beliefs apart. But in the attempt to reconcile these opposing poles of power, he stepped into the field of the very Energy he sought to know, and underwent the ordeal of personal metamorphosis that often comes to those who so do. One may not seek for ultimate knowledge, it seems, without the readiness to be transformed in the process.

It is this personal journey of change over a lifetime, a kind of living answer to a passionately asked question, that has fascinated me as a psychologist looking at Swedenborg's biography. I see a transformation from extroversion (of a scientific, intellectual sort) to introversion (of a yogic, contemplative sort). He moves from a Freudian fascination with the fair sex to a Jungian encounter with the *anima* as spirit-guide. His writings begin with the technological and move to the psychological and then the theological. His spiritual crisis (which might nowadays be called an adult developmental crisis) is fascinatingly documented with dreams abounding in mythological symbols.[1]

While Swedenborg must be of great interest to the transpersonal psychologist, his is also a personal story, set in a particular time and place, surrounded by specific historic and cultural conditions, and these we shall consider as well: how did the religious attitudes of his time influence Swedenborg and, in turn, how did he subsequently influence religion in Europe and America? How did the academics, philosophers, and theologians of his time receive Swedenborg? In

INTRODUCTION

what ways was his influence felt in other areas such as literature and the arts?

In the following few pages I shall try to introduce the reader to a vast subject. If it seems but a partial treatment, I acknowledge ahead of time that this is so, but this Introduction will have served its purpose if it provides the reader some basics for entering the pages that follow. We shall first examine biography and history, later to move into a consideration of psychological and spiritual issues.

Early Life and Family

Emanuel Swedenborg was born in 1688 of Swedish parents of well-to-do status. His father, Jesper Swedberg, was an upwardly mobile cleric of the Swedish Lutheran Church. From chaplain of the King's Guard he rose to rector, professor of theology, and dean of Uppsala University, and finally was appointed Bishop of Skara. Bishop Swedberg is described as a self-righteous man, somewhat pompous and self-important, but a persuasive orator and good storyteller. He was certainly a "good" man according to public morality of his time, leading a life he himself was aware of as "exemplary," and personally in favor with the Swedish King, Charles XII. He left each of his children and the Uppsala Library a copy of his thousand-page autobiography, "for needed instruction in how to pass well through this world."[2]

Swedenborg's mother, Sara Behm, was an heiress of a mining family, and her considerable personal wealth, along with Jesper's power, made the family one of the more important around Uppsala (site of the university) and Stockholm. She appears to have been a gentle soul with an introspective cast. She was to die when Emanuel was eight. Within a year, Jesper had remarried another woman of some wealth, Sara Bergia. Sara was unable to conceive children of her own, and unlike the barren stepmothers of fairy tale, loved her adopted brood of seven children as if they were her very own. Her favorite was reportedly Emanuel.

In this well-to-do and thoroughly religious household young Emanuel grew up. In later life he would dream again of his father's house in Uppsala, such was its atmosphere. Bishop Swedberg well exemplified the all-powerful *pater familias* of his day, whose values were as law, and whose unquestionable wielding of authority bespoke an unconscious *imitatio Dei.* But Swedberg's universe went deeper than the Christian overlay, and still teemed with the primeval spirit forms of the Nordic imagination. He had a literal belief in good and evil spirits and in the Devil, and he was not above invoking these in his florid way from the pulpit, a practice also very popular among his contemporaries. Congregations were expected to need some frightening, along with the inevitable moral exhortation.

Scandinavia was the last sector of Europe to be Christianized, and it is evident that it was no easy graft, for the Middle-Eastern religion with its crucified Savior was bonded to a stock of ancient and potent mythology. Particularly a visionary-shamanistic mode had prevailed, which actually had less trouble with the concept of a dying-and-reborn God than with some of the other doctrines and dogmas of the church. As the shaman must die to receive initiation and the power to heal men, even so Great Odin, the High God, hung on "the windy tree" nine days and nights to receive the runes of power. (I will discuss Swedenborg's own lived-through version of this rite of transformation—the sacrifice of self to gain knowledge—later in the Introduction.) The *Kalevala*, the national epic of Finland, well portrays this magical pre-Christian world of the Northern collective unconscious. But in Swedenborg, the magic of the woods, the waters, and the mountains was to be reclaimed in the service of a human mystery.

Jesper Swedberg was a Christian shaman who healed, not only by prayer, but by the laying on of hands and even casting out spirits. He well believed in his own (God-given, to be sure) personal power. The presence of other worlds was taken for granted in the Swedberg household. When Emanuel said he was with other children but was obviously alone, it was thought he played with angelic companions; and when out of his mouth came very precocious sayings, his parents thought angels must be speaking through him.[3] But perhaps his pre-Christian ancestors might have thought him fey and companioning with the elves.

Emanuel was not the typical son we might expect extraverted Jesper to have been hoping for. Lacking his father's skill in oratory, he was shy and throughout his life had a slight stutter while speaking. Though later he would dive headlong into the domain of what must be considered religion, as a youth he shared no bent toward theology, nor toward the ministry, as was naturally expected of his father's son. The sciences and mathematics were to claim his attention until his fifty-fifth year. At Uppsala University he studied philosophy, natural sciences, and mathematics (or "mathesis" as the combination was called).

Now the Cartesian world view with its secular and scientific universe had entered Sweden with Descartes himself in 1650. The great scholar and rationalist had been invited for a visit by Queen Christina, but after a few months in Sweden's hibernal climate he died of pneumonia, to the grief and consternation of the learned world. Nonetheless, his coming had lit the torch of academic freedom at Uppsala University. There was the inevitable clash between the faculties of Natural Science and Theology.

Such was Descartes's influence that within fifty years Uppsala was to rule that while Cartesian thought might be taught in relation to science and philosophy, it must not cross the *temenos* (boundary circle dividing the sacred from the secular) into the sphere of theology and religion. While the efficacy of natural science was increasingly obvious to the eighteenth-century mind, it was still held to be a mode of knowing qualitatively different from the Faith appropriate to things of the Spirit, which Luther had so emphasized. King Charles XI ruled that "the doctrines of the Christian faith may not be subjected to philosophical criticism but for the rest, philosophy shall be free, in practice and discussion."[4]

Young Emanuel was soon to show a precocity in natural science and mathematics that rivaled his father's genius in theology and politics. And perhaps we would not have been surprised to hear the older man admonish his son along with his students: "I beg you most earnestly that you fear and love God above all else, for without this fear of God all other training, all study, all learning, is of no account, indeed quite harmful."[5]

We may think of this admonition as going deep within the young man, emerging only much later, in the latter half of his life, at the pinnacle of his scientific erudition, when indeed he says, "From that time I put away natural things and labored in what is Spiritual."

Scientific Studies and Travels

But this was not to be for thirty-five years. In the meantime, Swedenborg had a world to explore, and much nontheological learning to accomplish. In Carl Jung's schema of life-development, the proper pursuit of the first half of life is indeed to throw oneself into it fully, to master life on its terms, to pursue "worldly" goals and to develop the ego (the psychic organ of relationship to life) to its fullest extent. Only when this phase has been fully accomplished is a slow shift of emphasis to occur, which, in the second half of life, disengages the ego from the world and orients it toward more ultimate things. In a profoundly paradoxical way, the ego, which has been the object of so much attention and education in the prior stage, will now have to be "given up."

Swedenborg's life-myth, as we look at its broad outlines, follows this pattern of deep engagement in life before disengagement. He was an apprentice to Christopher Polhem, an inventor and mechanical genius, the "Daedalus Hyperboreus" for whom Swedenborg would later name a scientific journal. Swedenborg himself would bear the same association with the mythic Greek master of inventive arts. If Jung had analyzed Swedenborg at this point, he would clearly have labeled his dominant functions[6] *thinking-sensation.* He would with good reason have believed a man so involved in thinking and reality testing (*sensation*) less capable of feeling or intuition, his inferior or "shadow" functions. (Paradoxically, after his life crisis and illumination, feeling and intuition were to become dominant in Swedenborg.) I refer the reader to Wilson Van Dusen's excellent discussion of this process of Swedenborg's psychological *enantiodromia* (exchange of opposites) in *The Presence of Other Worlds* (especially chapters 3 and 5).[7]

Swedenborg not only acquired the languages of the many places to which his European travels took him; while there he would board with master craftsmen to learn their trades. In this way, he learned lens grinding, watchmaking, even the delicate and demanding skill of marble inlay. He brought back to Sweden new methods of mining, smelting, and ore processing, as well as new concepts in mathematics (leading some to label him Sweden's foremost mathematician at the time). He was, in short, unlike many geniuses, able to learn something from almost anyone.

Swedenborg journeyed through France and finally to Italy: Venice, Florence, Rome. One might have expected a Northern Protestant to rail against the decadencies of Southern Catholicism (like his father, who deplored the French customs popular in Sweden), but on Swedenborg's encounter with the religious culture and iconography of the Mediterranean he was enraptured: "In the Uffizi Gallery [Florence] are the most magnificent objects in Europe, rarities old and new ... impossible to describe." He was able to admire the paintings of Raphael, the Vatican with its Great Library, even some ancient masks of the Classical Mysteries, and the statue of a satyr, for which he expressed admiration.[8]

Eventually the number of cognitive systems Swedenborg had assimilated was staggering. They include most of the modern European languages, as well as Greek, Latin, Hebrew; mathematics, physics, and chemistry, optics, metallurgy, and astronomy. He also studied anatomy and the nervous system, proposed a coherent and pioneering theory of cerebral functioning, and wrote on psychology. He was a competent organist who liked the music of J. S. Bach (his close contemporary, born in 1685).

It is this massive erudition in fields scientific, technical, and practical that would seem to make Swedenborg such an unlikely candidate for a mystical experience. The entire momentum of such accumulated experience compels away from the One (and the utter simplicity of the mystic revelation) and into the many, the world of theory and knowledge.

For years Swedenborg served as assessor on the Swedish Board of Mines. The assessors were obliged to determine legal matters as well as scientific; to make judgments in difficult cases, to set policy, and so forth. Swedenborg is reported to have been an unusually valuable and respected member of this board, continuing to serve on it even after his "opening to the spirit world," and able to continue making sound judgments (Jung's sensation function).

Far from otherworldly, this solid scientist of the eighteenth century studied chemistry, not alchemy; astronomy, not astrology. He used the microscopes and telescopes that were available at the time. He visited smelting houses and foundries and entered deep and dangerous mines, matter's very "heart of darkness." He sought for the basic building blocks of matter, in fact the brute stuff of *physis*, in his work the *Principia*, only to come up with the radical proposition that the basis of matter is motion (energy). (Most of Swedenborg's contemporaries, believing atoms to consist of tiny irreducible particles of matter, ridiculed this theory.)

But Swedenborg had studied crystallography and magnetism. He thought that the principle that formed the crystals, and so fascinatingly arranged the iron filings in a magnetic field, was the same as the structuring field of matter itself (an early version of "field theory"). A point, the origin of all things, he thought, enters into a spiral motion producing "the smallest thing in nature" (the atom). Swedenborg noted that nature is alike in large and small, and often compared the elementary particles and the solar system.

Before Immanuel Kant and Pierre LaPlace (to whose names, for history, the Nebular Hypothesis is formally attached), he postulated that the planets had emerged from the solar mass. He thought that the stars were suns and were arranged along the axis of the Milky Way, and that there are even systems of galaxies, of which our own is just a part. These observations seem commonplace in our day, but it took an amazingly advanced mind and eye to make them then; especially amidst the tangle of medieval thinkers inhabiting the academies, who were ready to denounce one's thinking, either from the viewpoint of Holy Writ or the golden light of reason (as they saw it, of course). *Empiricism*, in science or in life, was still a dirty word (representing a way of knowing unreliant on either learned philosophy or scriptural authority).

Deism had portrayed a kind of *Deus Absconditus* who set His Great Machine in motion, and then abandoned the field to its own mechanical laws, which for men might be known only by the laws of the reasonable mind. Pietism, on the other hand, held to the letter of Scripture, from which deviation might not be allowed. Neither of these views allowed for direct knowing, either of *phenomena* or *noumenon*, and it was this kind of knowing that appealed to Swedenborg. (Like all well-educated people of his time he had read the classics: Plato and Aristotle and, perhaps more importantly, Plotinus, whose Neoplatonism he had encountered at Oxford.)[9]

Swedenborg, like a good Neoplatonist, was to pursue his search for *nous* ever deeper into the heart of *physis*. Finally this was to crystallize into a central life study; the search for the seat of the soul, which he thought must be the binding place of spirit and matter. He was not content with the (mystical) reassurances of his scientific colleagues that it dwelt in the pineal gland (or perhaps the liver, at night). He sought a more precise knowledge, devoting thousands of hours to anatomical studies, even in the dissecting rooms of Paris (where this still abhorred and novel science was allowed to flourish as nowhere else in Europe). It has taken two centuries of physiological research to show how "unprejudiced, acute and deep an anatomical thinker Swedenborg was."[10] Here we may wonder at the depth Swedenborg explored, simply to know. He determined to rely heavily on the researches of others, because

INTRODUCTION

I found, when intently occupied in exploring the secrets of the human body, that as soon as I discovered anything that had not been observed before, I began—seduced probably by self-love—to grow blind to the ... researches of others. I therefore laid aside my scalpel and, restraining my desire for making observation, determined rather to rely on the researches of others than trust to my own.[11]

It was this kind of dedicated objectivity that allowed the Swedish seer to see so profoundly and ultimately into areas beyond the physical. Among his conclusions: that the blood contains the entire spectrum of nutrients for survival of the body; that the red blood, through the lungs, takes in "atmospheric salts and other substances, borne on the bosom of the air" (Sigstedt notes that this was fifty years before the discovery of oxygen)[12]; that there is a "purer blood" that nourishes the brain and nerves (cerebrospinal fluid); that the cerebral cortex is the seat of higher faculties, and regulates sensorimotor functions (this from studying the effects on behavior of brain lesions, as modern physiological psychologists do); that the left and right cerebral hemispheres differ in their functioning.[13] He also anticipated the discovery of brain cells (he hypothesized tiny oval bodies), long before microscopy developed to the point of making cellular structure visible.

Informing this synthetic and inductive hypothesizing, which now has proven to be so accurate, was one central belief, impossible to prove in and of itself: that this great spectacle of nature, which surrounds us and in which we partake, is in and of itself dead, all life coming from the transpersonal source, the Lord Himself. Nature herself carries this image as a great metaphor: the sun, which warms and energizes earthly life, is a mere physical symbol of the Lord who as a kind of Spiritual Sun sustains all things. Hence Swedenborg concentrated on the blood and the nervous system as the likely portals of energy or inflow of Divine Life into the biological body. As we shall see, this search for the seat of the soul, which Swedenborg began as one kind of quest (scientific), was to continue in another modality: direct visionary experience, the first-hand witnessing of that most intimate kind of intercourse between soul and body. What is truly astonishing about Swedenborg's later chronicles of the spirit worlds and heaven and hell is that such high-flown mysteries are really out of character for him as a scientist, and yet he reports his conversation with angels and spirits of the deceased with as much matter-of-factness as if he were delivering an anatomical discourse or a mining report.

The Crisis Period

The period of Swedenborg's life often referred to as his "crisis" was 1743–1745, beginning in his fifty-fifth year.[14] He was living in Holland during this time, studying anatomy at the university at Leiden, working on his *Regnum Animale* (*The Animal Kingdom*), and seeking publishers for his scientific works. Much of his time was spent alone in his rooms, or in libraries. The psychic life of the genteel, aristocratic scholar seemed to be invaded from within. His dreams became carnivalesque and nightmarish, he experienced extremes of mood from ecstasy to depression, his thoughts were fragmented. He experienced waking visions. His body vibrated, and he describes being flung about his rooms in Den Haag (The Hague) by psychical forces.[15]

Swedenborg later referred to this as a time of temptation, "vastation," and preparation for his mission in the second half of life as *amanuensis* or instrument of the Lord. It clearly does follow the archetypal sequence of the dark night of the soul before rebirth and illumination. After many grueling months of this inner struggle came a crucial night in which Swedenborg retired at about ten o'clock. He heard a noise and . . .

> Straightaway there came over me a shuddering, so strong from the head downwards and over the whole body, with a noise of thunder, and this happened several times. I found that something holy was upon me.[16]

After this Swedenborg was able to sleep, but later that night he awakened to find himself again shuddering and with a . . . "thundering noise as if many winds beat together." He found himself prostrate and praying aloud to Christ to make him "worthy of His grace. . . . I held together my hands, and prayed, and then came forth a hand, which squeezed my hands hard."

Swedenborg acknowledged his sinfulness, calling on the Lord's mercy, and then came the experience that made him star this entry in his *Journal of Dreams* with three "N.B.'s."

INTRODUCTION

At that same moment, I sat in his bosom, and saw him face to face; it was a face of holy mien, and in all it was indescribable, and he smiled so that I believe that his face had indeed been like this when he lived on earth. He spoke to me and asked if I had a clean bill of health. I answered 'Lord, thou knowest better than I.'[17]

Swedenborg had, in 1710, as a young man, naively broken a smallpox quarantine in England and narrowly escaped hanging. For him a "bill of health" held a life versus death personal association.

It was after this great vision that Swedenborg's spiritual sight began gradually to be opened. The writings penned by him concerning these experiences for the next three years (until 1748) are recorded in the first 4104 numbers of *The Spiritual Diary*. Swedenborg felt the Lord had chosen him to explain the Scriptures, and would permit him to travel freely through the spirit worlds, heaven and hell. We begin to find passages like the following for the first time in his work:

> This morning it was clearly shown to me how spirits operate upon man, that is, how God Messiah leads man by means of spirits and angels.[18]

Swedenborg here was describing things "seen and heard" with inner faculties. Much of this he claimed to experience in states of consciousness not drastically different from his ordinary one. Only on a few occasions, such as his clairvoyant witnessing of the Stockholm fire (in company at the house of Mrs. William Castell in Gothenberg) did visions disrupt his ordinary social composure.

From this period onward the subject matter of Swedenborg's intensive concentration was no longer mathematics, physics, archaeology, or anatomy. He began to study only the Sacred Scriptures. He set himself to learning Hebrew, and by 1748 had begun the most meticulous and ambitious project of Biblical exegesis ever attempted by a single scholar. He wrote on the opening page, paragraph number 2 of the first volume of *Arcana Coelestia*:

> The Christian world however is as yet profoundly unaware of the fact that all things in the Word both in general and in particular, nay, the very smallest particulars down to the

11

most minute iota, signify and unfold within them heavenly things . . .[19]

It was not until eight years later that Swedenborg finished the last volume of the series.

One of the world's deepest mysteries is this of the transformation of personality, of ego death and spiritual rebirth. In Christianity it is symbolized in the crucifixion and resurrection of Christ and also in the mystery of the Virgin Birth (conception not by an earthly father but a spiritual one). Iconographically, the miraculous conception takes place through no physical generative organ, but by means of a beam of light or a dove (symbolic of the Holy Spirit). The soul, which has looked into its own depth, now is quickened with a new life, an illumination within, qualitatively different from the motives and energy of the three-dimensional world. Such was Swedenborg's "enlightenment." He writes:

I have been elevated into the light, which sparkled like the light radiating from diamonds; and while I was kept in it I seemed to myself to be withdrawn from corporeal ideas and let into spiritual ideas.[20]

In the hierarchy of human motives, the spiritual quest, especially in its newly awakened form, may overcome and relativize all other motives—hence its dangerous side, as well as its positive and life-transforming one. In the relatively unconscious "mythic seizure," previous successful life adaptation may be thrown out, and there is a loss of relationship and ego skills. One may join a cult, become a fanatical evangelist, or (if the adaptation to the mythic world view is too autistic) be institutionalized.[21] This is the dark side of the meaning-bestowing, life-enriching, and more coherent transformation of the truly evolving soul.

It is worthwhile, then, for the psychologically oriented scholar of religion to compare the pre- and post-"awakening" life of the visionary or religious reformer. Who was he before as well as after? Was the life change a radical reversal (or *enantiodromia*)? What was lacking? What was added? What was sacrificed to gain something else? And what would be the sociocultural view of the sanity of the mystic before and after his revelation? We also know that worldly "sanity" might not be spiritual "sanity"; thus it is interesting to look at the tension between personal and transpersonal orientations.

Swedenborg's Sanity

Swedenborg has been a controversial figure for psychologists. The transformation of a respectable assessor of mines into a visionary seemed to some more like regression than growth; more like schizophrenia than a high and holy seership. His contemporary, the philosopher Immanuel Kant, portrayed him as mad in *Dreams of a Spirit Seer:* he is "the arch-visionary among all visionaries;" and said of *Arcana Coelestia* (Heavenly Secrets): "Eight Quarto volumes full of nonsense."[22] Kant's book circulated widely during Swedenborg's lifetime and undoubtedly was damaging to his reputation in German academies and elsewhere. Kant here was clearly aligned with the thrust of a skeptical rationalism that was to lead to our prevailing contemporary world view.

But in this study Kant fails to give honest voice to his own ambivalence about Swedenborg. For example, it is known that he sent a highly educated friend, to whom he often entrusted the task of critiquing his own writing, an Englishman named Green, to call on Swedenborg and interview him. The watchful Green, expecting a strange fanatic, reported to Kant "a reasonable, polite, and open-hearted man." He does not mention any of this in his book.

In a little-known document which is still preserved, Kant's *Letter to Fraulein von Knobloch* (presumably written in 1763, three years earlier than *Dreams of a Spirit-Seer,* and which was a reply to the Fraulein's genuine questions over the mysteries surrounding Swedenborg), Kant shows himself far more respectful. He had investigated the three famous anecdotes: Swedenborg's clairvoyant seeing of the Stockholm fire (two hundred miles away, in Gothenberg, recorded by a number of witnesses); "the missing receipt," which involved communication from a woman's deceased husband over a large debt (through Swedenborg's intervention the receipt was found and the debt shown to have been paid already); and the "queen's secret," which later will be told herein, in more detail.[23] In the *Letter,* Kant records precise details of his investigations. He shows himself open to the veracity of the anecdotes and cites Green's personal impressions, which were very positive. None of this honest searching shows up, unfortunately, in his *Dreams*, the tone of which is openly derisive.

John Wesley, the founder of Methodism, openly held to Swedenborg's insanity, until an unusual personal communication with the seer shook him in his conviction. His earlier reaction to Swedenborg's writing was that the author was "one of the most ingenious, lively, entertaining madmen that ever set pen to paper." He believed that it must have been a fever that induced Swedenborg's delusions, because his character references previous to his spiritual awakening had been so excellent. The story goes that in February 1772, Wesley was in the company of some of his preachers, including one Samuel Smith, when a letter was delivered to him from Swedenborg. The letter stated that Swedenborg had been informed in the world of spirits that Reverend Mr. Wesley asked to speak with him. Wesley read the letter aloud, appearing astonished, and admitted he had been having a desire to meet Swedenborg. "How he came to know it I have not an idea, as I never told any creature I have such a desire."

Wesley wrote an answer to Swedenborg, explaining he was preparing for a six-month journey, but would be glad to meet with him soon after his return to London. Swedenborg's reply came back that the date proposed by Wesley would be too late as he (Swedenborg) was to die and enter the world of spirits on the twenty-ninth of the next month (March). This event was profoundly impressive to Samuel Smith, who had been present when Wesley received the letter. Smith was later to become a Swedenborgian minister, and Wesley was said to have pondered deeply over the incident. His final judgment still was to be that the implications of Swedenborg's writings were heretical, and that he had become disordered through a fever.[24]

There are a number of early twentieth-century psychiatric studies of Swedenborg, which, judging a visionary of the eighteenth century by the psychoanalytic revelations of the nineteenth, have him among the paranoids, hysterics, and repressed homosexuals of their post-Victorian consulting rooms. These studies may themselves by now be considered curiosa in the museum of psychohistory, and are damaging to Swedenborg only if one accepts psychiatric diagnosis as fact rather than symbolic behavior. To the sophisticated modern reader in the social sciences, aware of the fallibility of diagnostic systems and the poor reliability between independent diagnosticians using them, such terms as *paranoia tardiva expansiva religiosa* (Emil

Kleen's diagnosis) represent (creative) fictions rather than facts about the man. We have become aware of the fantastic relativity of "models" for behavior, and realize that not only are there no absolutes in this field, but that each system, perforce, contains its own self-fulfilling prophecies.

Karl Jaspers, professor of philosophy and medicine at the University of Heidelberg, diagnosed Swedenborg as schizophrenic, and in a psychiatric study put him in with strange (but creative) bedfellows: August Strindberg, Johann Holderlin, and Vincent van Gogh.[25] This study generalizes "schizophrenia" to an absurd degree, and involves comparisons of people whose personal differences far outweigh similarities (membership in a diagnostic category).

Signe Toksvig, in her biography *Swedenborg*, written in 1948, did a nice job of showing his experiences as consistent with the findings of parapsychology rather than psychopathology.[26] There is a contemporary renaissance in disciplines such as "the psychology of consciousness" and "transpersonal psychology," which include the study of altered states of consciousness, mental imagery, visionary narratives, spiritual disciplines, meditative practices, and so forth. These approaches would confirm the nonpathological and universal character of some of the experiences Swedenborg recorded.[27] After all, Freud never got to read Maslow nor was there even in the beginnings of psychoanalysis an appreciation of the adult midlife crisis, nor the trials and glories of self-actualization as the major quest of adult life. There was no understanding of the altered state of consciousness as a creative as well as pathological event.

The Jungian analyst Kristine Mann's contention that Swedenborg did not actualize his self-development (Jungian *individuation*), but lived through it only symbolically, perhaps needs to be taken more seriously.[28] For we see Swedenborg clearly embarked throughout his life on a particular course of self-actualization (or individuation) and it is an important question how authentic his journey is. I have elsewhere described Swedenborg's life-myth as curiously appropriate to the astrological reading of his sun sign, Aquarius.[29] Edward Whitmont, also a Jungian analyst, has read this symbol as the dialogue between spirit and matter, or in Swedenborg's own words, "Soul-Body Interaction." The problem for some people has been that Swedenborg attempted to solve this riddle "respectably" (from the physical, scientific viewpont) in the first half of his life, but after his *metanoia* (change of mind), through the "suspicious" process of direct

15

visionary experience (from the viewpoint of the spirit) in the second half. It is interesting to note that for either deterministic or psychoanalytic psychology this is clearly regression, while from the perspective of transpersonal psychology it is a positive (and inevitable) stage of evolution: the abandonment of a linear, verbal, cognitive mode of perception and the opening to an imagistic, visionary mode. In Swedenborg's case, the contact with the visionary dimension seems not to have interfered with his "reality function" or common sense.

The clinical psychologist Wilson Van Dusen thinks that there is much valuable depth psychology in Swedenborg, which may in fact be used to help understand pathological experience but is not itself pathological.[30] Van Dusen has replied to Kristine Mann's analysis that Swedenborg was not really trying to *individuate* in Jung's sense of the term. He was not just seeking human wholeness, but ultimate knowledge. Nonetheless, Swedenborg's biography must be seen as one of the world's most interesting chronicles of self-actualization. Few lives, even great ones, have articulated themsleves with such an unremitting yet open sense of creative purpose.

Jung himself (also unfairly diagnosed "schizophrenic" by his detractors) read Swedenborg early in his career and must have been subliminally influenced by him, though he does not give overt credit for the following concepts: the "objective" nature of the psyche; the concept of a psychospiritual developmental process of the adult psyche, *individuation*, which closely resembles Swedenborg's *regeneration* process; the terms *animus* and *anima* to describe psychological functions; and the notion that dreams contain spiritual guidance, the so-called anagogic function. "Every dream is stimulated by some sensation," Swedenborg says (agreeing with the psychologist Christian Wolff), "yet we may notice they tend to a definite end ... as though they were directed by one of whose origin we are ignorant." Here we may see the essential germs of the psychologies of Freud *and* Jung in a single sentence.[31]

It would be unfair to Swedenborg to conclude this discussion without allowing him to give his own definition of insanity:

The reflections of thought are the source of melancholy ... debilities of the mind ... deliriums ... also insanities and fantasies; for they who are thus kept in thought about spiritual things ... have many things which are of their memories poured into them by spirits; and they hold them long in them, even to insanities and fantasies.

He adds, agreeing with modern sensory deprivation theory:

Therefore they who are in solitude of life easily fall into such things; for they are dispelled by variety and society. The more solicitude of the love of self . . . of gain, reflection on the future, or the occurrence of some misfortune, the more easily into fantasies and at last into insanities.[32]

Not a few critics have tried to convict or diagnose Swedenborg out of his own mouth so to speak: The Anglican Reverend G. Beaumont[33] took the former approach while Kristine Mann took the latter in her aforementioned essay. Both use paragraphs like the above as self-description on the part of Swedenborg. But it seems important to the present writer to make the observation that few delusional people have such penetrating insights into their own dynamics (unless coached by their psychoanalysts) as did Swedenborg.

Swedenborg notes, as did Jung, Freud, and others, that solitude and religious speculations may induce madness, as does an extreme self-preoccupation, but this may be compensated by "variety and society" (a healthy balance between introversion and extraversion). Even in an early essay written in his school-days on the aphorisms of Mimus and Seneca, Swedenborg voices a formula for mental health: "Exercise and meditation, therefore, is like food to the mind, and unless it is continually nourished and sustained it will deteriorate."[34] He seems to have followed this holistic prescription into his still alert and nimble old age.

Jung mentions in his autobiography that during his own adult crisis period (he refers to it as "confrontation with the unconscious," analogous to Swedenborg's "opening to the spirit world"), one of the main things that allowed him to maintain his stability was the very ordinary human contact with his family.[35] Swedenborg had no nuclear family, but many friends, and hobbies such as gardening and music. Perhaps even more important than these were his dedication to writing down the things "seen, heard and felt" and his ability to maintain an inner distance (his trained scientific objectivity) from the visionary process. He was able to use discrimination in judging both the inhabitants of the spirit world and their revelations, taking not very much for granted. As many recent visionary narratives have shown, the spirit world (or the unconscious, if you will), is full of half-baked metaphysics, cosmic revelations, dramatic prophecies. If these are simply uttered rather than examined, the mystic may start a cult, but probably fail to enlarge his personal wisdom.[36] But Swedenborg was always willing to dialogue with, even theologically cross-examine, the denizens of the world of spirits. Thus he maintained his objectivity and, for me, his sanity.

A very telling fact that argues against charges of megalomania is that Swedenborg published his "theological" works for fifteen years anonymously, before publicly acknowledging himself as their author. It is clear he was far more interested in having his writings circulate on their own account than in acquiring personal renown on account of them.

Responses during Swedenborg's Lifetime

Having considered the reactions of Kant and Wesley, which focused on questioning the seer's sanity, we may be less surprised by the theological attacks by churchmen of Swedenborg's own time. One important and outspoken such critic was Dr. Johan August Ernesti, professor of eloquence, later of theology, at the University of Leipzig. He was said to have been singularly lacking in eloquence, in fact, except on his favorite subject: those who try to find meaning in the Scripture other than the literal letter of it. Swedenborg became for Ernesti an arch-example of those wicked ones who seek to elucidate a spiritual sense to Holy Writ: "Because he [Swedenborg] abuses and perverts the Sacred Scriptures by the pretense of an inner sense, [he] is in the highest degree worthy of punishment."[37]

Ernesti was later to spearhead the heresy trials in Germany against two academics who dared to say positive things about Swedenborg in print. The first of these was Prelate F. C. Oetinger, a scholar and writer who had read Swedenborg's scientific works for many years before encountering his theological works. Oetinger was a student of Jakob Boehme and other European mystics as well, and had an open mind to the idea of mystical revelation. In 1765 he had published *The Earthly and Heavenly Philosophy of Swedenborg and Others*.[38] The Consistory of Wurttemberg, probably goaded by Ernesti, censured Oetinger, forbade his publication of any further works, and in 1766 confiscated the entire edition of Oetinger's work and put him on trial. He wrote to Swedenborg: "But my dear Sir, you will hardly be willing to believe how much I had to suffer on your account, merely for having translated the 'things seen' recorded in the first volume of your work."[39]

Oetinger's son-in-law, H. W. Clemm, professor of theology at Tubingen, was editor of a serial publication called *Complete Introduction to Theology and The Whole of Religion*, in which he discussed the Swedenborgian issue. The wrath of Ernesti, "The Bear," was now to fall on Clemm, who had counseled an open-minded attitude to Oetinger and Swedenborg. Said Ernesti: "God has spoken to us the last time through his Son and the Apostles. The world-order which he established in place of the Mosaic Law is to last until the end of the world."[40] This for the "new Jerusalem" of Swedenborg, which the Swedish seer had envisioned as a worldwide New Christian attitude. And for Dr. Clemm, veiled medieval threats: "If Clemm had said such things as these a hundred years ago, what would not have happened to him?"[41]

Ernst Benz, a more recent scholar of Swedenborg, hypothesized that these deathblows to Swedenborgian ideas in the academy caused them to "go underground" into the tradition of literature, the arts, theosophy, and the Romantic movement. As we shall see later, this influence permeated many visionary and spiritual revitalizations in European painting, sculpture, and poetry.[42]

Meanwhile, back in Sweden there was no less uproar over the now-publicized spiritual revelations of a native son. As we have seen throughout, the problem seemed to be the possibility of empirical revelation[43] in one's own time, and Swedenborg's remarkable claims of daily visits to the spirit world and heaven and hell, especially as recounted in his *Memorable Relations,* interspersed among the theological writings of the *Arcana.* These were much like the "memorabilia" published by literate travelers of the time, but unlike them in that Swedenborg's travelogues described places, people, and events not of this world. Swedenborg's out-of-body journeys took him to the "land of the dead," his "world of spirits" where previously living folk continued an existence midway between earthly life and the more finally polarized and purely spiritual states of heaven and hell.

In this middle zone were to be encountered the shades of all recently dead, and not only these, but the luminaries of history from all of time, from Plato and Aristotle to Luther and Leibniz. These

INTRODUCTION

Swedenborg matter-of-factly reported encountering, and even conducted debates and dialogues on learned subjects with them—a reportage that strained the credulity of many of his readers.

People were often willing, however, to put Swedenborg to the test his miraculous assertions would seem to invite. Queen Lovisa Ulrika was one such, whose first reaction to tales of Swedenborg's powers was quite skeptical. She described herself as "hard to fool." During a visit of Swedenborg to the Royal Palace, when he had requested to make a gift of some of his books to their majesties, she asked him, "by the way" in case in his otherworldly journeys he met her brother, no less a personage than Frederick the Great of Prussia, to give him greeting and bring her word from him. One imagines this often happened publicly to Swedenborg; after all, it cost the asker or challenger nothing, and put the visionary on the spot—but also could satisfy a secret curiosity.

Swedenborg assented, and some two to three weeks later visited the palace to deliver the books. He requested a private audience with the queen, who went aside with him and a few moments later visibly blanched and seemed to be overcome. The visionary was embarrassed and apparently quite apologetic for having been so direct. Swedenborg had greeted her from her brother, who sent his own apology for not having answered her last letter and then went on to reveal something known only to the two of them, of which the queen later said that other than they, "only God could have known that."[44] Count Tessin described the effect on the queen as "terrifying," so he was hesitant to bring the incident up with her until several weeks had passed. The extremely delicate nature of the alleged communication should be noted as due to the fact that during much of the adult lives of the two sibling sovereigns, Sweden and Prussia were at war, or at least involved in competitive international intrigues. The information would have been highly "classified" in military language.

Swedenborg seems to have frequented this mental zone of world politics of his own time often, and was said to have witnessed clairvoyantly the death of Emperor Peter of Russia in prison. This farseeing event was itself observed by the German physician Jung-Stilling at a social gathering in which Swedenborg's composure became visibly altered for a while; when he recovered, after being questioned, he told those assembled not only of the death, which he claimed to have witnessed, but its manner, by strangulation. He is reported to have said afterward: "Gentlemen, will you please make a note of this day in order to compare it with the account which will appear in the newspapers."[45] In this and some other instances he behaved like a modern parapsychology researcher. Of course, however, it is hard to be both experimental scientist and clairvoyant subject at once! When asked how he could obtain such specific knowledge of those living or dead, he is reported by Tuxen to have said:

> I cannot converse with all, but with such as I have known in this world, with all regal or princely persons, with all renowned heroes or great and learned men, whom I have known either personally or from their actions or writings; consequently, of all of whom I could form an idea, for it may be supposed that a person whom I never knew or of whom I could form no idea I neither could nor would wish to speak with.[46]

Perhaps more characteristic of the mature Swedenborg, though, and especially indicative of his poise and humor, is the following anecdote. Archbishop Samuel Troilus was inordinately fond of the three-player card game Tresett, which he used to play with the worldly Erland Broman, president of the Board of Trade, and another friend. Not long after Broman's death, the archbishop met Swedenborg at a large gathering and wished to make sport of him. "By the way, Assessor, tell us something about the spirit world. How does my friend Broman spend his time there?" he asked. Swedenborg is said to have replied immediately, "I saw him but a few hours ago shuffling his cards in the company of the Evil One, and he was only waiting for your worship to make up a game of Tresett."[47] There is no doubt as to who became the object of the company's merriment, but it is equally true that Swedenborg may have been about as popular in Sweden as Dante a few centuries earlier in Italy, at least in certain circles. Both writers were to place many of their historical contemporaries in hell. Swedenborg, too, would remind the world of an abstract principle of justice in the universe, beyond the little view of social convention.

It is no wonder Swedenborg's "theological" works were denounced as heretical in Sweden (he often had to go abroad to more liberal Paris or Amsterdam to publish). The medieval thinkers of his day were simply not ready for this fresh breath of the perennial philosophy. He alarmed both the theologians and the Cartesian scientists by his matter-of-fact acceptance of the reality of the spiritual dimension; but he frightened them most by his accounts of journeying there.

The Lasting Influence of Swedenborg's Life and Work

I shall try in this section to summarize some of the larger implications of Swedenborg's ideas and of his life. We find evidence of his subsequent influence not only in religious thought but in the creative life as well, even in concepts related to health, and personal and spiritual values in many areas.

The Swedish seer's postillumination insights are, in fact, very practical and down to earth when one looks into them. Like his hard-working father, he emphasized deeds and social good, and that faith without works was valueless. (This disputed a well-accepted canon of Luther that Faith by itself was sufficient to receive Grace.) He is striking in the continuity of his purposefulness. He was "the man who had to know" in the first half of his life and the "knower" in the second half. His goal did not change, but the psychological mechanism (Jungian *function*) through which he apprehended it did. He discontinued the prevailing Western mode of *gnosis* (the burgeoning scientific methodology of the eighteenth century, to which, as we have seen, he was a major contributor), and moved into unknown territory: a more Eastern, intuitive mode of knowing. We can see that while a single person may not know all that is to be "known" (the universe) through the first modality (science), he may come to "know" the universe as a whole through the second (mystical knowledge).

The developmental stages of life, like a series of Zen *koans*, present us their riddles, which each must encounter in his own way. Swedenborg's life *koan* lay in the gulf between science and religion, and we see him "answering" it in different ways in each half of life. Through his midlife crisis he moved from the religious study of science to the scientific study of religion. What occurred in Swedenborg resembles other human creative breakthroughs in response to passionately asked questions (especially those that partake in the vital, paradoxical quality of life itself). The question is not "answered" on the level it was originally posed; instead, a transformation takes place within the questioner, which shows the limitations of the previous point of view, from which the question was asked. The problem is not

INTRODUCTION

resolved in its original terms, but a more valuable thing has occurred to the psyche: it has enlarged its vision and learned a new way of seeing (Jung's *transcendent function*).

Swedenborg's primary role then was that of seer or visionary (though he himself was not at all sure he approved of visionaries or mystics). The prototype of this figure is the shaman, which I have elsewhere studied.[48] Human communities seem to require the services of mediator between this world and that other, the separate reality hovering always so close to us. The shaman's role includes the functions of healer, clairvoyant, visionary leader, and traveler to the spirit world. He brings back what is otherwise unobtainable for us earthly folk: the breath of the Spirit Realm. His "medicine," at essence, is the reawakening to the spiritual life. When the human sufferer lays down his problem, the shaman is not to "solve it" at the earthly level, but to put it into a new context; to invite him to share a different perception of it at the spiritual level. We will see that later Swedenborg's visionary world view became seminal in a number of healing systems, from Christian Science to homeopathy, all of which emphasize the dependence of physical health on the inner or causal level of spiritual well-being.

What of Swedenborg's ideas on human relations, especially those between man and woman? We know that sexuality might have been an area of some tension for Swedenborg, as he remained unmarried and kept no mistress and was probably celibate after his illumination. But he did not resist his imagination nor his dreams, and wholly failed to make sex the psychological monster it has been for so many Christian mystics.[49] He knew he dreamt of women (but did not think them succubi, come to tempt his immortal soul). Actual women seemed to like and befriend Swedenborg socially. He is described as "gallant" and "charming," but was probably not even terribly flirtatious in our modern view. Swedenborg asserted that when married partners enter the spiritual world they may potentially gravitate toward other partners for whom they are more psychologically and spiritually appropriate.[50] This is accomplished by means of the principle of affiliation mentioned earlier. Swedenborg was to systematize this principle in his concept "Ruling Love."

A person spiritually affiliates with whom or what he is drawn to most. But Ruling Love shows that a person's loves may come ultimately to dominate that person. Your Ruling Love rules you in the end. In the spiritual condition, free of the body, one's inner affectional or motivational state becomes an irresistible determinant. As Swedenborg said "that after death a man is his own love, that is his own will."[51] Compare the following from the *Chandogya Upanishad:* "Man is a creature of will, as his will is in this world, so is he hereafter."

The soul is the living boundary of the physical with the Divine (compare the deepest insights of Vedantism and Buddhism). Heaven and hell are not "places" to which one "goes" but states of the soul. One may experience either state psychologically (as we all know) while right here in the body. One is not saved or damned by a Divine fiat (a political act, consistent with the "kingship" model of the Divine) but by spiritual affiliation. Those who recognize the other as spiritually equivalent to oneself (*Tat tvam asi*, "Thou art That," or Buber's "I-Thou") are in a heavenly state; those caught in selfish desire and the struggle against others, in a hellish state.[52]

For Swedenborg, the human is ever a receptacle of divine energy. In fact, he stressed that man of himself is devoid of life. What animates us flows in through the deepest wellsprings of the psyche. This energy assumes a twofold form, part entering the will (or intention) and part the understanding (or discernment). We see here both the affective-behavioral and cognitive sides of human experience. True human life lies in the interface of these two. If a man or woman loves without understanding, or understands without loving, he or she is incomplete. When one in fact looks at Swedenborg's "theological" ideas such as this, one finds a system primarily psychological in nature.

The theologians of Swedenborg's time, following Luther, had portrayed man as foolishly sinful, sadly out of touch with his Creator, and so unworthy as to require a boundless and merciful divine grace for Salvation. Swedenborg's portrayal of the human soul's relationship to God was far more intimate and personal and less categorically negative than all of this. For Swedenborg, our very life-principle is to be discerned as the indwelling presence of God. He is clearly aligned here with a principle of religious vitalism and a Lord who is immanent rather than transcendant. Good health and the poetry in one's own soul are the *vox Dei*, rather than (necessarily) the voice of the clergy. (Swedenborg was not known to be overly fond of churchgoing.) Here we also see a similarity to early Christian Gnostic values, which found daily sacrament in the spontaneous life of the soul—as expressed through poetry, sacred song, art, or iconography. The church of the "Fathers" and bishops, such as the third-century Irenaeus, had declared such spontaneous worship heretical: formal religious ceremony administered by an ordained priest was to be the only acceptable form of worship.[53]

Swedenborg's revelation of a creative and personal spirituality informed and permeated the arts of Europe, from William Blake's visionary prints and poetry to Baudelaire's *Correspondences*, with its "forests of symbols." Blake was stimulated and empowered in his own visionary mode by Swedenborg's example. (He was taken by the correspondence between his own date of birth—1757—and Swedenborg's vision of Christ's "Second Coming" in the spiritual world in that year.) His own *The Marriage of Heaven and Hell* was borrowed from Swedenborg's title, but he detested what he felt were the orthodox elements in Swedenborg. Nonetheless his own visions teem with angelic and demonic forms, new theological ideas, and many symbolic themes he originally found in Swedenborg. The visionary painters of nineteenth-century France also found illumination from this northern seer: Odilon Redon, Pierre Bonnard, and others of the *Nabis* looked for the same luminous transparency in life and nature he had envisioned. And one may trace Swedenborg's influence into the New World and up the Hudson River with her visionary painters, and into spiritual communities both Quaker and Shaker, who kept spiritual diaries and painted their dreams and visions.[54] His view of the essential nobility and spirituality of human nature informed Utopian ideals and penetrated the American wilderness in the person of the wilderness-wiseman John Chapman (Johnny Appleseed), who sowed the seeds of health-bestowing apples along with the life-giving spiritual ideas he found in Swedenborg.[55]

The medical philosophy that developed in the nineteenth century also had a Swedenborgian emphasis, and much in homeopathy has to do with his "Doctrine of Correspondences." An idea that probably originated with Paracelsus in the sixteenth century, the "Doctrine of Signatures" found resonance in Swedenborg's later "Doctrine of Correspondences," and was further elaborated by Samuel Hahnemann, founder of homeopathy, in his work in the early nineteenth century. This notion held that the Creator in his divine providence, while allowing sickness and the multitude of human ills, yet provided for their cure by concealing remedies within the world of nature. The domains of mineral, vegetable, and animal substances thus held an important symbolism for the wise eye of the physician. For example, a kidney remedy might be found winking shyly out from a plant with kidney-shaped leaves, whose very form hinted at its therapeutic use Swedenborg writes,

> Whatever is seen anywhere in the universe is representative of the Lord's Kingdom, and . . . there is not anything in the atmosphere or starry universe, or in the earth and its three kingdoms which is not in its own manner representative. (A.C. n. 3483)

Compare this with the following quote from James Tyler Kent, an important late nineteenth-century homeopathic physician, whose work abounds in Swedenborgian ideas:

> All cureable maladies have signs and symptoms in order to make themselves known; their purpose is to shadow forth the disorderly conditions of the vital force or interior of man, so that the physician may read it and understand its nature. This imaging forth when the human race is in a state of ignorance or materialism, is like seeds sown upon stony ground; there is no man to understand them, to apprehend their meaning. The images of sickness are continually being formed, and only wait for a man intelligent enough to observe them, to understand their meaning, to translate them, and it is possible for men, by the doctrines of Homeopathy, to become wise and intelligent enough to be conversant with these signs.[56]

We find here a philosophical basis for holistic medicine, as well as, in the larger theater, for a sacred ecology. The universe with all its contents is a vast intelligible metaphor. For what? Swedenborg's answer is, for its creator and sustainer, the Lord Himself. And this is true of human nature no less than the outer world of nature. (See the concept of the "Grand Man" or "Universal Human" in the text that follows.)

This same sentiment naively informs the religious world view of most preliterate traditional societies. We may think of it in its simple form as the primordial religion, Swedenborg's "Most Ancient Church," on the foundation of whose fundamental truths all the later varieties of religious experience have been differentiated and elaborated.[57] We may feel our more historically recent religions have gone beyond the primitive in spiritual values, yet hear the essential wisdom in this prayer offered by the great American Indian visionary Black Elk:

> Grandfather, *Wakan Tanka* (Great Spirit), you have always been and always shall be. You have created everything— there is nothing which does not belong to You ... You have given us knowledge that we may know all things. We know that it is Your light which comes with the dawn, and we know that it is the Morning Star who gives us wisdom. You have given us the power to know the four Beings of the universe and to know that these four are really one. We see always the sacred heavens, and we know what they are and what they represent.[58]

Swedenborg's Doctrine of Correspondences contains within it, then, this same call to awaken one's own symbolic consciousness, to perceive in every event in life—sickness, psychological discomfort, "accidental event"—the potential meaning. Life is to be experienced transparently, as a waking dream. And if as the poet Calderon says, "La vida es sueño" (life is a dream), then each of its situations may be read (symbolically) as the "somnia a Deo missa," the dreams sent by God. For these the mystic must ever be awake on one level and not asleep. Only in this manner may one come to understand the divine providence of the Creator.

This spiritually informed cosmology, like the *Tao* concept of ancient China, educates us to be aware of the totality of things and our relationship to this whole. But our encounter with this intelligible *Mysterium Tremendum* is not simply to provoke overwhelming awe, nor a quietist withdrawal into nature. It is a call to master life in its symbolic aspect. This means nothing less than a willing participation in a living spiritual continuum to which we are all intimately connected. "Everything in heaven, in the world and in the human body, both great and small, was created from use, in use, and for use," writes Swedenborg, "a part in which ... its being for use, ceases, is separated as harmful."[59] But if this principle of spiritual correspondence is found in human life and the world of nature, reasoned Swedenborg, how much more must it not be found in the sacred Scripture, the living Word of God?

Modern thinkers may balk at the idea of consistent "internal sense" to the Scriptures. Those were events spanning millennia, they say, and those are different texts with many authors. How could there be a consistent internal sense? But for Swedenborg and his contemporaries, the quest was a burning one: how to extract psycho-spiritual widsom from a historical text. The absoluteness and unique-ness of the Judeo-Christian Scripture was not at question; how to make it relevant to life was.

We know that Swedenborg used the Latin Bible translations of Sebastian Castellio, a Christian Neoplatonist. In his preface, as Toks-vig describes it, Castellio expressed

> an idea that may have been the spark to Swedenborg's tin-der. Castellio said "only the person who has in himself the illumination of the same spirit that gave the original revela-tion can see through the garment of the letter to the eternal message, the ever-living word hidden within."[60]

Whether we can accept the Bible and its two thousand years of history as enacted and written for this supreme spiritual revelation, as do some Swedenborgians, or whether we see in his years of profound concentration on the Scriptures a personal creative act of high quality, productive of its own revelatory insights, we may agree on Swedenborg's perseverance and integrity in his hermeneutic task. Out of it were to come the twelve volumes (in the English translation) of the *Arcana Coelestia* and the eight volumes of *Apocalypse, Explained and Revealed*, in which from a single scriptural sentence or passage Swedenborg elucidates many pages of interpretation.

The sampling of Swedenborg's writing included in this volume is a varied and interesting one. The reader will benefit from the clear and accurate translations by George Dole. The writings of Sweden-borg have felt to some like a maze of doctrines and archaic terms, but the Dole translation shows this to be a fault more of the translators than Swedenborg's own. In the following pages the reader of English will find a close approximation of Swedenborg's matter-of-fact Latin, resembling the original in semantic and spirit. Coming from a distin-guished family of Swedenborgian scholars, Dr. Dole nonetheless has missed the orthodox translator's worst pitfall: theologized versions of the writings with a heavy emphasis on doctrine. Often there has been

INTRODUCTION

a tendency to translate Swedenborg's Latin into a somewhat stilted and pedantic style of English that the author never intended. After all, Swedenborg in his later writings was usually simply describing things he experienced.

I find myself in agreement with Castellio in his advice to readers of the Bible, but would suggest it to readers of Swedenborg as well, that if they will but awaken the illumination of their own spirits, they may see through the letter to the "ever-living word hidden within."

NOTES

1. Emanuel Swedenborg, *Swedenborg's Journal of Dreams* (Woofenden, William R., ed. New York: Swedenborg Foundation, 1977).
2. See Signe Toksvig's excellent *Emanuel Swedenborg: Scientist and Mystic* (New Haven: Yale University Press, 1948), chap. 3, for additional details. Toksvig is not very sympathetic to Jesper, clearly identifying him with the type that would later be called "male chauvinist." It should also be noted here the name *Swedenborg* was given to the family only after they were ennobled. *Swedberg* is the correct name for Jesper.
3. Cyriel Odhner Sigstedt, *The Swedenborg Epic: The Life and Works of Emanuel Swedenborg* (New York: Bookman Association, 1952; London, 1981) and Toksvig, *Emanuel Swedenborg* for further details on early life.
4. Quoted in Sigstedt, *The Swedenborg Epic*, p. 9 (from *Grundrage av Swedenborgs lif* [Stockholm, 1908], pp. 14ff.).
5. Ibid.
6. Jung's fourfold function scheme is a holistic model of psychological types. See Carl Jung, *Psychological Types*, Bollingen series, vol. 6 (Princeton: Princeton University Press, 1971).
7. Wilson Van Dusen, *The Presence of Other Worlds: The Psychological/Spiritual Findings of Emanuel Swedenborg* (New York: Harper & Row, 1974 and New York: The Swedenborg Foundation, 1981).
8. Sigstedt, *The Swedenborg Epic*, p. 147.
9. This is described in some detail in Toksvig, *Emanuel Swedenborg*, pp. 48, 49. Also see her discussion of Swedenborg's physics, p. 71.
10. Gustav Retzius, speaking to an international congress of anatomists in Heidelberg in 1903. The Swedish source is cited in Toksvig, *Några*

vittnesbörd om vetenskapsmannen Swedenborg, Samlade af A. H. Stroh (Stockholm, 1909), p. 98, note 7.

11. Swedenborg, *Economy of the Animal Kingdom* (London: W. Newbery, 1844), Introduction, vol. I. Also Sigstedt, *The Swedenborg Epic,* p. 152.

12. Sigstedt, *The Swedenborg Epic,* p. 152. This discovery usually is ascribed to Joseph Priestley, 1774, with his "dephlogystinated air," and to Antoine Lavoisier, 1779, its name "oxygen." In 1780 LaPlace, with Lavoisier, proposed respiration as a kind of combustion. Swedenborg's hypothesis was probably formulated about 1740.

13. Swedenborg should probably be credited with discovering the dual functioning of the cerebral hemispheres (customarily ascribed to Hughlings Jackson, in 1864). He writes: "The intellectual things . . . flow into the left side of the brain; and the voluntary things into the right side" A. C., nn. 641, 644.

14. See Swedenborg, *Journal of Dreams,* kept during this period. The interested reader is also referred to the accounts in Sigstedt, *The Swedenborg Epic;* Toksvig, *Emanuel Swedenborg;* Van Dusen, *The Presence of Other Worlds;* George Trobridge, *Swedenborg, Life and Teaching* (New York: The Swedenborg Foundation, Inc., 1949) (3rd reprint of the 1935 4th ed. of the Swedenborg Society of London); and Kristine Mann, "The Self-Analysis of Emanuel Swedenborg," in *Review of Religion,* vol. X, no. 3 (March 1940). This last reference is a Jungian analysis of some of his dreams. See also Stephen Larsen, "Swedenborg and the Visionary Tradition," in *Studia Swedenborgiana,* vol. 3, no. 4 (June 1980). *Studia Swedenborgiana* is published intermittently by the Swedenborg School of Religion, Newton, Massachusetts; it is also available from the Swedenborg Foundation, Inc., New York.

15. His accounts of psychophysical phenomena during this phase are very similar to shamanistic reports, showing disorganization of the psyche in the early stages, followed by a creative reintegration with the acquisition of clairvoyant powers.

16. Swedenborg, *Journal of Dreams,* p. 16, par. 51.

17. Swedenborg, *Journal of Dreams,* pp. 16 pp. 16–17, par. 54. It should be noted that this account was never intended by Swedenborg for publication. It was written in Swedish, not Latin, in his personal notebook. It was only later discovered by scholars.

18. Swedenborg, *The Spiritual Diary,* 5 vols. (London: The Swedenborg Society, 1962). First published in note form by Im. Tafel, 1843–1846, as memorabilia.

19. Swedenborg, *Arcana Coelestia,* trans. J. F. Potts, 12 vols. (New York: The Swedenborg Foundation, 1978) (vol. 1, p. 1, par 2).

20. Ibid., n. 4413.

21. See Stephen Larsen's discussion of this in *The Shaman's Doorway* (New York: Harper & Row, 1976), chap. 2.

22. Immanuel Kant, *Traume Eines Geistersehers* [Dreams of a Spirit-Seer], (1766) 2nd ed., trans. Em. Goerwitz, ed. Frank Sewall (London: New Church Press Ltd., 1915).

23. See also Robert Kirven, "Emanuel Swedenborg and the Revolt against Deism" (doctoral diss., Brandeis, 1965, available through The Swedenborg School of Religion, Newton, Massachusetts).

24. R. L. Tafel, *Documents Concerning the Life and Character of Emanuel Swedenborg*, 3 vols. (London: Swedenborg Society, 1875–1877). We owe all of the preceding to B. Harford's report of Samuel Smith's testimony (vol. 2, p. 567). Through another source, however, Swedenborg's housekeeper, Elizabeth Reynolds, we hear that the sage well knew the exact date of his death, "as pleased as if he were going to have a holiday, and go to some merrymaking" (vol. 2, p. 546).

25. Karl Jaspers, *Strindberg und Van Gogh* (Berlin: Springer, 1926).

26. See especially chap. 15, "Swedenborg's Clairvoyance," and chap. 16, "Automatic Writing."

27. R. W. Emerson wrote of Swedenborg in *Representative Men* (ed. Myron Simon [Joseph Simon: Malibu, Calif., 1980]) that he began in his own life "what phenomenology and introspection would later do." He also practiced yogic breathing, inner concentration, trance, and dream interpretation, anticipating much of humanistic and transpersonal psychology.

28. Mann, "The Self-Analysis of Emanuel Swedenborg," op. cit., no. 14.

29. See Larsen, "Swedenborg and the Visionary Tradition," op. cit., no. 14, p. 51.

30. See Van Dusen, *The Presence of Other Worlds;* idem, *The Natural Depth in Man* (New York: The Swedenborg Foundation, 1981).

31. Toksvig, *Emanuel Swedenborg*, p. 87.

32. Rev. John Faulkner Potts, comp., ed., and trans., *Swedenborg Concordance: A Complete Work of Reference to the Theological Writings of Emanuel Swedenborg Based on the Original Latin Writings of the Author* (London: The Swedenborg Society, 1888) (reprinted 1948), p. 691, "insane."

33. G. Beaumont, *The Anti-Swedenborg: Or Declaration of the Principal Errors and Anti-Scriptural Doctrines of Emanuel Swedenborg* (London, 1824).

34. *Select Sentences from Publius Syrus Mimus and L. Annaeus Seneca* (Uppsala, 1709 and Skara, 1709). English translation by Rev. J. H. Smithson, *Intellectual Repository*, New Series, vol. III (London, 1842). See also Tafel, *Documents*.

35. Carl Jung, *Memories, Dreams, Reflections* (New York: Pantheon, 1963).

36. For a contemporary account that calls into question the integrity of a visionary founder, see Walter T. Rea, *The White Lie* (Turlock, Calif.: M&R

Publications, 1982), which accuses Adventist founder Ellen G. White not only of unexamined visions, but of actual plagiarism.

37. *New Theological Library*, ed. J. A. Ernesti, 1760. Also see Sigstedt, *The Swedenborg Epic*, p. 305.

38. See Tafel, *Documents.*

39. Letter from Oetinger to Swedenborg in Tafel, *Documents.* The Swedish followers Dr. S. Beyer and Rosen were put on trial for their livelihoods for having taught Swedenborg's ideas in classroom as well. Their persecutor was the ruthless Dean Ekebom of Uppsala. (See Sigstedt's *The Swedenborg Epic;* Toksvig, *Emanuel Swedenborg*).

40. See account in Sigstedt, *The Swedenborg Epic.*, p. 419.

41. Ibid.

42. Ernst Benz, "Swedenborg as the Spiritual Pioneer of German Idealism and German Romanticism," in *Deutsche Vierteljahrschrift fur Literatur wissenschaft und Geistes geschichte Jahrg. XIX Heft 1.* See Kirven, "Emanuel Swedenborg and the Revolt against Deism."

43. See this as discussed by Kirven, "Emanuel Swedenborg and the Revolt against Deism."

44. The accounts on this are drawn from the diaries of Count Tessin, and the account to General Tuxen corroborated by Swedenborg. See Tafel, *Documents.*

45. Ibid.

46. Quoted in Toksvig, *Emanuel Swedenborg*, pp. 192–193. This is consistent with Swedenborg's idea that one moves in the spiritual dimension through affiliation, or similarity. And this last may give some comfort to those who credit Swedenborg's visionary status, yet wonder why his view of the spirit world differs from that of some mystics, and fails to include any idea of reincarnation or soul transmigration, so abundant in other mystical accounts, often but not always Eastern.

47. Ibid., p. 326. See also Tafel, *Documents*, p. 291.

48. See Larsen, *The Shaman's Doorway.*

49. See frequent references in Swedenborg, idem, *The Spiritual Diary.*

50. Wesley (among others) was scandalized by this concept, and referred to Swedenborg's concept of heaven as "Mohammedan." Swedenborg's book on marriage, *Conjugal Love* (in more recent translations, it is entitled *Marital Love*, trans. W.F. Wunsch (New York: The Swedenborg Foundation, 1975), is anything but erotic, however, and depicts marriage as a psychological relationship, a theme Jung was later to explore in his writing (see "Marriage as a Psychological Relationship," *The Collected Works of Carl G. Jung*, vol. 17, *The Development of Personality* (Princeton: Princeton University Press, 1954).

51. Emanuel Swedenborg, *Heaven and Hell* (New York: The Swedenborg Foundation, 1852, 1964), no. 479, p. 297.

INTRODUCTION

52. The hellish state would seem to rsemble Sartre's *Huit Clos,* the existential "No Exit," induced by the wholly self-preoccupied life.
53. See Elaine Pagel's excellent discussion of this whole early controversy in *The Gnostic Gospels* (New York: Random House, 1979). Irenaeus was orthodox Bishop of Lyons, ca. A.D. 180, who was incensed by the Gnostic claims to daily personal spiritual revelation.
54. See J. H. Noyes, *Strange Cults and Utopias of 19th Century America* (New York: Dover Publications, 1966). Also Nathaniel Kaplan and Thomas Katsaros, *The Origin of American Transcendentalism in Philosophy and Mysticism* (New Haven: College and University Press, 1975), especially pp. 228–245, on Swedenborg's influence in many divergent community, philosophical, and intellectual movements. See also Emerson, *Representative Men* and Henry James, Sr., *The Secret of Swedenborg* (Boston: Houghton Mifflin, 1869); idem, *The Literary Remains of Henry James,* ed. William James (Boston: Houghton Mifflin, 1897 and Cambridge: The Riverside Press, 1897).
55. Chapman's earthly along with spiritual nourishment accorded well with Swedenborg's doctrine of *uses,* that the essence of the spiritual life was not only to think but to do good, of a very practical sort. See Robert Price, *Johnny Appleseed: Man and Myth* (Gloucester, Mass.: Peter Smith, 1967).
56. James Tyler Kent, *Lectures on Homeopathic Philosophy* (Richmond, Calif.: North Atlantic Books, 1971 [original 1900]), pp. 86–87.
57. Swedenborg, *Arcana Coelestia,* vol. I. pars. 530, 1083.
58. Black Elk, *The Sacred Pipe,* recorded and ed. Joseph Epes Brown (New York: Penguin Books, 1971), p. 129.
59. *The Apocalypse Explained,* trans. J. Whitehead, 6 vols. (New York: The Swedenborg Foundation, 1982), n. 1194.
60. Toksvig, Ch. XII, "The Great Vision" p. 151.

The Universal Human

PART 1

REPRESENTATIONS AND CORRESPONDENCES

2987.

What are "representations" and "correspondences"? Few people know; and no one can know what they might be unless he knows that there is a spiritual world and that it is distinct from the world of nature. For correspondences occur between spiritual phenomena and natural ones; and things from spiritual sources that come into being in natural phenomena are representations. They are called correspondences because they are completely responsive, and representations because they portray.

2988.

To gain some image of representations and correspondences, we need only consider processes of the mind—of thinking and intent, that is. These tend so to radiate from the face that they can be seen in its expression, especially affections, with the more inward ones visible in and from the eyes. When facial elements are acting as one with mental ones, we say they are being completely responsive, and are correspondences. The actual facial expressions portray and are representations.

The same holds true for things done by means of bodily behavior—all actions produced using muscles, for example. We recognize that they are done in accord with what a person is thinking and intending. The behavior and actions themselves, which are bodily, portray elements of the mind, and are representations. Instances of complete agreement are correspondences.

2989.

We can also know that within the mind there do not occur appearances of the kind presented in facial expression. It is simply affections that are imaged in this way. Further, in the mind there do not occur the kinds of act that are presented by bodily actions. It is thoughts that are thus given form. Mental things are spiritual; bodily things are natural. So we can see that correspondence occurs *between* spiritual and natural phenomena, and that representation is *of* spiritual phenomena *in* natural ones. Or, in other words, when elements of the inner person are imaged in the outer, then things visible in the outer are representative of the inner, and the ones that are in harmony are corresponding.

EMANUEL SWEDENBORG

2990.

We also recognize (at least we can) that there is a spiritual world and a natural world. In their most inclusive forms, the spiritual world is where spirits and angels are and the natural world is where people are before death. In their limited forms, there is a spiritual and a natural world for each individual. Our inner person is our spiritual world, while our outer person is our natural world. Things that flow in from the spiritual world and are presented in the natural are in general representations, and to the extent that they are suitable, they are correspondences.

2991.

There is another basis for knowing that natural phenomena portray spiritual ones and that they are wholly responsive, namely that nothing can come into being except from a cause prior to itself. Its cause comes from the spiritual level: no natural phenomenon occurs that does not find its cause there. Natural forms are effects, which cannot be seen as causes, still less as the causes of causes or fundamentals. Rather, they receive their forms in accord with their function in their situation. Still, the forms of these effects do portray aspects of their causes, which in turn even portray aspects of their fundamentals. So all natural phenomena portray aspects of the spiritual things to which they are responsive, and these spiritual things too portray elements of the heavenly things they come from.

2992.

From an abundance of experience, I have been granted the knowledge that there is not the least thing in the natural world and its three kingdoms that does not portray something in the spiritual world, or that does not have something there to which it is responsive. I have been able to determine this from the following experience, among others. Several times, while I was talking with someone about organs of the body, following their connections from things in the head through the chest to the abdominal region, angels above me led my thoughts through the spiritual phenomena to which the physical ones were responsive, in such a way that there was no discrepancy whatever. They were not thinking at all about the bodily organs that I was thinking about, only about the spiritual phenomena to which the bodily organs were responsive.

THE UNIVERSAL HUMAN

Angelic intelligence is of such nature that angels know on spiritual grounds each and every detail of the body, even the most obscure, that could never come through to human thought. In fact, they know each and every thing in the whole world without error, because they are where the causes are, and the fundamentals of causes.

2993.

The same holds true for things in the vegetable kingdom, where there is not the least element that does not portray something in the spiritual world and respond to it. This I have often been taught by a similar interaction with angels. I have also been told the reasons, namely that the causes of all natural phenomena are from spiritual sources, and the fundamentals of those causes from heavenly sources. Or, in other words, everything in the natural world finds its cause in something true that is spiritual and its fundamental in something good that is heavenly. Further, natural phenomena follow from these sources according to all the varieties of the true and the good that occur in the Lord's kingdom. So they come from the Lord Himself, who is the source of everything good and true. These matters must necessarily seem outlandish, especially to people who are unwilling or unable to rise in thought beyond the realm of nature, and who, not knowing what the spiritual is, do not acknowledge it.

2994.

As long as we live in this body, we sense and perceive very little of the spiritual, since for us heavenly and spiritual realities drop down into the natural concerns in our outer person, where we lose any sensation or perception of them.

Further, the representative and responsive things in our outer person are of such nature that they do not seem to resemble the things in the inner person to which they are responsive. So they cannot get through to our thinking until we have shed these outer things. Then blessed is the person who is "in correspondence"—that is, whose outer person is completely responsive to the inner.

2995.

Since the people of the earliest church (*A.C.* 1114–1125) habitually saw something spiritual and heavenly in the details of nature (to the point that natural phenomena served them simply as concrete means of thinking about spiritual and heavenly realities), they were able to talk with angels and to be present with them in the Lord's kingdom in the heavens at the same time they were present in His kingdom on earth, the church. For them, natural things were so united with spiritual ones that they were utterly responsive.

However, it was different after that era, when the evil and false began to get control, or when after the golden age the iron age began. Then, since there was no more responsiveness, heaven was closed off, to the point that people scarcely wanted to know that anything spiritual existed. Eventually, they scarcely cared about heaven and hell, or about life after death.

2996.

The most obscure fact in this world (though nothing is more familiar in the other life, even to each individual spirit) is that everything in the human body has a correspondence with something in heaven. This holds true to the point that there is not the smallest particle in the body that does not have something spiritual and heavenly corresponding to it, or—which is the same—that does not have a corresponding heavenly community. For these communities exist according to all the categories and subcategories of spiritual and heavenly realities. Indeed, they exist in a design such that they reflect, taken all together, a single person—this in all detail, both inwardly and outwardly. This is why heaven in its entirety is called the Universal Human (*Maximus Homo*). And this is why it is often stated that a particular community belongs to this particular region of the body, another to another, and so on. The reason is that the Lord is the only person, and heaven portrays Him. The Divine-Good and Divine-True that comes from Him is what makes heaven; and since angels are involved in this, they are said to be "in the Lord."

In contrast, the people who are in hell are outside that Universal Human, and have a correspondence with waste products and disorders.

2997.

Within limits, we can know all this from the fact that our spiritual or inner person (which is our spirit and is called our soul) has a similar correspondence with our natural or outer person. The

40

nature of the correspondence is such that the elements of the inner person are spiritual and heavenly, while the elements of the outer are natural and physical. This we can determine from what has been presented in nn. 2988f. above about facial expressions and bodily actions. A person, that is, as to the inner person, is a little heaven, having been created in the image of the Lord.

2998.

The fact of such correspondence has been made so familiar to me over many years that hardly anything is more familiar; yet people do not know that it exists or believe that they are linked at all to a spiritual world. Yet this is all the linking they have: they could not endure, no part of them could endure for an instant without this link. It is the source of all their being.

I have also been granted knowledge of which heavenly communities correspond with which region of the body, and of their natures—for example, the identity and nature of those that correspond to the region of the heart, the same concerning those that correspond to the region of the lungs, the same concerning the liver, the sense organs such as eyes, ears, and tongue, and other organs. These, by the Lord's divine mercy, will be discussed individually.

2999.

Further, nothing under any circumstances occurs in this created world that does not have a correspondence with things that exist in the spiritual world, and that does not therefore in its own way portray something in the Lord's kingdom. This is the source of the emergence and the continuance of everything.

If people were aware of this situation, they would never ascribe everything to nature, as they tend to.

3000.

This is why each and every thing in the universe portrays the Lord's kingdom, to the point that the universe with its stars, its atmospheres, its three kingdoms, is nothing but a kind of theater that portrays the Lord's heavenly glory. In the animal kingdom, not only does man portray this; so also do particular animals, even the smallest and most insignificant. For example, there are caterpillars that crawl along the ground and feed on herbs. Once their time for mating arrives, they become chrysalids. Soon they are furnished with wings, and are borne aloft thereby from the ground into the air, their heaven. There they enjoy their delight and their freedom, playing together, gathering nourishment from the richness of flowers, laying eggs, and thus providing their future generations. When they are in this heavenly state, they are also in their full beauty. Anyone can see that these events picture the Lord's kingdom.

3001.

From what we have stated and explained in the exegesis of the Word (*A.C.* 1954, 2021, 2536, 2658, 2706, 2886–2889), we can determine that there is only one life, the Lord's, which flows into us and makes us live, makes good and evil people alike live, in fact. Responsive to this life are recipient forms which are brought to life by this divine inflow, in such a manner that they seem to themselves to live independently. This is a correspondence of life with forms recipient of life. The recipients live in keeping with their own natures. People involved in love and charity are in correspondence since they are suitable, and by them the life is received adequately. However, people who are involved in attitudes opposed to love and charity are not in correspondence, because the life itself is inadequately received. They, therefore, have whatever semblance of life suits their nature.

This can be illustrated in many ways. Take, for example, the body's motor and sensory organs. Life flows into them through the soul. Their actions and sensations depend on their own nature. Or take objects into which light is flowing from the sun. Their varieties of color depend on the kinds of recipient forms they are. However, in the spiritual world, all the changes that arise from the inflow of life are spiritual, resulting in corresponding variations in intelligence and wisdom.

3002.

This enables us also to determine how all natural forms, both living and lifeless, are representative of spiritual and heavenly phenomena in the Lord's kingdom. That is, each and every thing in nature is a portrayal, depending on how thoroughly and well it is responsive.

THE UNIVERSAL HUMAN

3213.

In the World of Spirits,* countless and almost constant portrayals occur. They are forms of spiritual and heavenly matters, not unlike the ones that occur in this world. I have been granted knowledge of their origin from association with spirits and angels over a long period of time. They flow into the World of Spirits from heaven, and from the concepts and conversations of angels there. Actually, when angels' concepts and their resulting conversations descend to spirits, they are presented in various pictorial ways. Seeing them, upright spirits can know what the angels are talking about, since there is something angelic within the portrayals that is moving, and is therefore perceived, even as to its quality.

There is no other way angelic concepts and conversations can be presented to spirits, since an angelic concept contains things beyond definition in spirits' concepts. Unless, then, they were given form and presented pictorially, and so offered visually through images, a spirit would hardly understand them at all; for many things are incomprehensible, yet when they are portrayed in (visual) forms, they become comprehensible to spirits in their more general aspects. Remarkably enough, there is not the smallest detail in the things portrayed that does not express something spiritual and heavenly that exists in the angelic community from which the portrayal is flowing down.

3214.

Sometimes portrayals of spiritual and heavenly matters occur in a long series that may last up to several hours, in such a sequential arrangement that one can only marvel. There are communities where this happens, and it has been granted me to spend several months with them. But these portrayals are such that if I were to recount and describe only one in its proper sequence, it would fill many pages. They are thoroughly delightful, for something unexpected is always happening, even while the matter being portrayed is being brought to full completion. And when all the events have been completed, it is

---

* "The World of Spirits" is Swedenborg's name for a spiritual region midway between heaven and hell, and subject to influences from both. It is our present spiritual environment and our first residence after death. Its residents are referred to as "spirits," distinguished from "angels," residents of heaven, and "evil spirits" or "genii," residents of hell.

possible to reflect on them in a single inward view. At this point, too, one can grasp all at once what the details mean. This is also how good spirits are introduced to spiritual and heavenly concepts.

3215.

While the portrayals that are presented to spirits show an incredible variety, still there are many aspects that are like phenomena of this earth and its three kingdoms. To know what these are like, see what we have already said about them in *A.C.* 1521, 1532, 1619–1622, 1623, 1624, 1625, 1807, 1808, 1971, 1974, 1977, 1980, 1981, 2299, 2601, and 2758.

3216.

For a better knowledge of the working of portrayals in the other life—that is, of the ones visible in the World of Spirits—here are some examples.

When there is a conversation among angels about doctrines of charity and faith, there sometimes appears in the lower realm where there is a responsive community of spirits an image of a city or cities, with palaces in it of staggering architectural design, so beautiful that you would say this is the home and the source of the art itself. There are also homes of various styles. The marvelous thing is that in the whole portrayal there is not the smallest point, not the smallest visible detail, that is not portraying something in the angelic concept and conversation. We thus can be assured how innumerably many things the portrayal contains. We can also determine the meaning of the cities seen by prophets in the Word—for example, the Holy City or New Jerusalem, and the cities in the books of the prophets—doctrinal matters of charity and faith (*A.C.* 412, 2450).

3217.

When angels are talking about the ability to discern, then in the world of spirits beneath them or in communities that are responsive there appear horses whose size, shape, color, and stance—even their differing decorative harness—depend on the concepts the angels have of the ability to discern.

There is also a rather deep place a little to the right called "The Home of the Discerning" where horses are constantly seen. This is because the people there are involved in thought about the ability to discern. When angels who are talking about this ability flow into their thoughts, then horses are portrayed. This assures us of the meaning of the horses seen by the prophets and also of horses mentioned in the Word—aspects of discernment (*A.C.* 2760, 2761, 2762).

3218.

When angels are involved in affections and are at the same time talking about them, these matters descend into the lower realm among spirits in kinds of portrayals of animals. When the talk is of good affections, beautiful animals are presented, gentle and useful, the kinds used for sacrifices in symbolic divine worship in the Jewish church, such as lambs, sheep, kids, she-goats, rams, he-goats, male calves, young bulls, and cattle. Then something more appears over the animal, presenting some image of their thought, and upright spirits are granted a perception of it. This assures us of the meaning of the animals in the rituals of the Jewish church and of the same animals mentioned (elsewhere) in the Word—affections (*A.C.* 1823, 2179, 2180).

When however the angels are talking about evil affections, this is portrayed by hideous, fierce, and useless animals, like tigers, bears, wolves, scorpions, snakes, and mice, which also accords with their meaning in the Word.

3219.

When angels are talking together about insights, concepts, and inflow, then there appear in the world of spirits birds that seem to be formed to accord with the topic of their conversation. This is why birds in the Word mean rational matters, or matters of thought (*A.C.* 40, 745, 776, 991).

Some birds once came into my view, one dark and misshapen, and two splendid and lovely. While I was watching them, some spirits assaulted me so violently that they struck up a trembling in my nerves and bones. I thought that now, as several times before, I was being invaded by evil spirits who were trying to destroy me, but it was not like that. Once the trembling and activity of the assaulting spirits subsided, I talked with them and asked what was happening. They told me that they had fallen from a particular angelic community where there had been a discussion of thinking and inflow. They themselves had been of the opinion that matters of thought flowed in from the outside, perhaps through the outward senses, just the way it seems. But the heavenly community where they had been believed they flowed in from within. Since the spirits had a false opinion, they had fallen from that community—not that they were thrown out, for angels never throw anyone out. Rather, since the spirits were involved in falsity, they themselves fell: this was the reason.

This enabled me to know that conversation in heaven about thoughts and inflow is pictured by birds, the conversation of people in the wrong by dark and misshapen birds, and that of people in the right by splendid and lovely birds. I was taught at the same time that all elements of thought flow in from within, and not from the outside even though it seems that way. And I was told that it is against the design for the latter to flow into the prior or the cruder into the purer—the body, then, into the soul.

3220.

When angels are having conversations about matters of intelligence and wisdom and about perceptions and insights, then the inflow into responsive communities of spirits falls into portrayals of the kinds of thing that belong to the vegetable kingdom—of parks, vineyards, woodlands, fields of flowers, and into many charming images that surpass all our imagining. This is why matters of intelligence and wisdom are described in the Word by parks, vineyards, woodlands, and meadows, and why this is the meaning when such things are mentioned.

3221.

Sometimes angelic conversations are pictured by clouds and by the shapes, colors, movements, and shiftings of clouds. Affirmations of truth are pictured by clouds that are bright and rising, denials by clouds that are dense and lowering. Affirmations of falsity are pictured by clouds that are gloomy and black. Agreement and dissent are pictured by clouds coming together and parting in various ways, all this against a deep blue like that of the sky at night.

3222.

Further, loves and their affections are pictured by flames, with a variety beyond description. Truths, on the other hand, are pictured by lights and by countless changes of light. This enables us to determine why flames in the Word are used to mean good elements of love, and lights to mean true elements of faith.

THE UNIVERSAL HUMAN

There are two lights from which we receive light, the light of the world and the light of heaven. The light of the world comes from the sun; the light of heaven comes from the Lord. The world's light is for the natural or outer person, therefore for the matters in that person. Even though it may not seem as though these matters belong to that light, they nevertheless do, for nothing can be grasped by the natural person except by means of the kinds of thing that occur and appear in this subsolar world. This means they must have some trace of form from the world's light and shade. All the concepts of time, all the concepts of space, so significant to the natural person that thinking would be impossible without them, pertain to this light as well. In contrast, heaven's light is for the spiritual or inner person. Our more inward mind, the locus of concepts we call abstract, is in that light. People are unaware of this even though they refer to their discernment as sight and attribute light to it. This is because as long as they are involved in worldly and physical concerns they have perception only of the kinds of thing that are proper to heaven's light. Heaven's light is from the Lord alone: all heaven is in that light.

This light of heaven is vastly more perfect than the world's light. Matters that make a single ray in the world's light make thousands in heaven's light. Within heaven's light dwell intelligence and wisdom. It is the light that flows into the world's light in the outer or natural person and enables that person to perceive objective realities with the senses. If that light did not flow in, we would have no power of observation whatever, for it is the source of the life that dwells in what belongs to this world's light.

Between these lights—or between things in heaven's light and things in the world's light—there is a responsiveness when the outer or natural person is acting as one with the inner or spiritual person, that is, when the former is serving the latter. Then the things that happen in the world's light are portrayals of the kinds of thing that happen in heaven's light.

3224.

It is strange indeed that people still do not know that their intellectual minds are in a particular light that is quite distinct from the world's light. But circumstances are such that to people in the world's light, heaven's light is like darkness, and to people in heaven's

47

light, the world's light is like darkness. People involved in loves of self and the world are therefore in no warmth but that of the world's light. Proportionally, then, they are influenced by things evil and false; and these are the factors that stifle true things that pertain to heaven's light. In contrast, people involved in love for the Lord and love toward the neighbor are in a spiritual warmth that belongs to heaven's light. They are influenced by things good and true that stifle false things. However, with them there is a responsiveness.

As for spirits who are involved in matters only of this world's life, and who are consequently involved in false processes from evil motives, in the other life they do have a certain light from heaven, but it is a deceptive kind of light, like the light that comes from glowing embers or from torches. And this light is quenched at the approach of heaven's light, becoming darkness. People involved in this light are caught in hallucinations, and what they see in their hallucinations they believe to be true—indeed they have no other truth. Their hallucinations are tied to filthy and obscene things that give them the greatest pleasure, so that they think like maniacs or madmen. They do not reason about the reality of false perceptions, but accept them instantly. They do however reason constantly about matters of goodness and truth, winding up in denial. Actually, true and good influences from heaven's light are flowing into the more inward mind, which for them is closed, so that light flows around outside it, becoming varied only by the false things that seem true to them. What is true and good can be recognized only by people whose more inward mind has been opened, with light flowing in from the Lord. To the extent that it has been opened, these things are recognized. This mind is opened only in people who are in innocence, in love for the Lord, and in charity toward the neighbor. It is not however opened in people who are involved in true matters of faith unless they are at the same time involved in what is good as to their lives.

3225.

This then enables us to determine the nature and source of correspondence and the nature and source of representation. Correspondence, in summary, is *between* things of heaven's light and things of the world's light, that is, between phenomena of the inner or spiritual person and phenomena of the outer or natural person. A representation is something that occurs *in* things proper to the world's light (that is, something in the outer or natural person), which is related to phenomena proper to heaven's light (that is, that come from the inner or spiritual person).

3226.

One of the major abilities we have in ourselves without realizing it, which we take with us into the other life when we transfer there after separation from the body, is the ability to perceive the meaning of the portrayals that appear in the other life. Then, too, there is the ability fully to express with the mind's sense in an instant what hours would not suffice for in the body. This is done by concepts drawn from phenomena of heaven's light, aided and so to speak winged by fitting pictorial images of the subject under discussion, so perfect that they are beyond description. Since we come into these abilities after death and there is no need to be taught about them in the other life, we can be assured that we are in them (that they are in us, that is) while we are living in the body, even though we do not realize it.

The reason for this is that there is constant inflow in us through heaven from the Lord. It is an inflow of spiritual and heavenly things that fall into our natural processes and are there presented pictorially. In heaven, among angels, there are no subjects of thought except heavenly and spiritual matters proper to the Lord's kingdom. But in this world, among us, we think of little but the physical and natural matters proper to the kingdom where we are and to the necessities of life that occupy us. Since heaven's inflowing spiritual and heavenly things are presented to us pictorially within our natural concerns, they therefore remain implanted, and we find ourselves in them when we shed physical matters and leave worldly ones behind.

3337.

The statements and explanations above enable us to determine what correspondences and representations are—namely, correspondences exist *between* phenomena of heaven's light and phenomena of this world's light, and things that occur *in* phenomena of this world's light are representations (n. 3225). However, the nature and quality of heaven's light is not recognizable to people in this way, because people are involved in matters of this world's light, and to the extent that they are so involved, things in heaven's light seem like darkness or like nothing. It is this pair of lights that makes all human intelligence as life flows in. Our mental imaging is nothing but forms and likenesses of things we have grasped by physical sight, marvelously

varied and I might say altered. The things that emerge in consequence are intrinsically lifeless, but they are vivified by an inflow of
life from the Lord.

3338.

In addition to these lights there are warmths, which also come
from a dual source—heaven's warmth from its sun, which is the Lord,
and this world's warmth from its sun, which is that bright body so
obvious to our eyes. Heaven's warmth makes itself known to the
inner person through spiritual loves and affections, while this world's
warmth makes itself known to the outer person through natural loves
and affections. The former warmth constitutes the life of the inner
person, while the latter constitutes the life of the outer. For without
love and affection, a human being can have no life whatever. Between
these two warmths also there are correspondences. The warmths
become loves and affections because of the inflow of the Lord's life.
As a result, they seem to us not to be warmths, even though they are.
For unless we had warmth from this source, both for the inner and
for the outer person, we would instantly fall dead. Anyone can see
this from the fact that people do become warm to the extent that they
are kindled with love, and become sluggish as love ebbs away. This
love is the source of the life of one intentionality, while the light
discussed above is the source of the life of our discernment.

3339.

In the other life, these lights and these warmths as well are
perceptible in full reality. Angels live in heaven's light and in the
warmth we have mentioned as well. They get intelligence from the
light and an affection for what is good from the warmth. In fact, the
lights they can see with their outer sight have as their source the
Lord's divine wisdom, and the warmth that they also perceive comes
from the Lord's divine love. For this reason, as spirits and angels are
more involved in intelligence as to what is true and affection for what
is good, they are closer to the Lord.

3340.

The opposite of this light is a darkness, and the opposite of this
warmth is a coldness. Hellish people live in these. They get the
darkness from the false things they are involved in, and the cold from
the evil things. The farther they are from truth, the greater the

darkness, and the farther they are from the good, the greater their cold. When one is allowed to see into the hells where people like this live, one sees a gloomy cloud in which they are living. And when any vapor flows out from it, one perceives ravings breathing from things false, and hatreds from things evil.

Sometimes they are granted illumination as well, but it is a deceptive kind of lighting, and becomes darkness the moment they look at the light of truth. They are also sometimes granted warmth, but it is like the warmth of filthy bathwater, and it turns into cold for them the moment they notice anything of goodness.

A particular individual was sent into that gloomy cloud to learn what things were like for the people there. He was, however, protected by the Lord through angels. He talked with me about it later, saying that there was such a mad turmoil against the good and the true, especially against the Lord, that it stunned him with its irresistibility. For they were breathing nothing but hatred and vengefulness and slaughter, with such violence that they wanted to destroy everyone in the universe. So if this rage were not constantly turned back by the Lord, the whole human race would perish.

3341.

Since representations cannot occur in the other life except by means of discernible differences of light and shade, it is important to realize that all light—specifically all intelligence and wisdom—comes from the Lord, and that all shade—specifically all madness and stupidity—comes from the self-consciousness of people on earth, spirits, and angels. From these two sources flow and derive all the changes that characterize light and shade in the other life.

3342.

Further, everything spirits and angels say is said by means of figures. Using marvelous variations of light and shade, they present what they are thinking; and using shifts that suit their affectional states, they give them persuasiveness. The figures that emerge in their speech are not like the ones we have been discussing. Rather, they are as quick and brief as the concepts of their conversation. It is as though someone would describe something in a long sequence and at the same time display it to view in a picture. For strange as it seems, any spiritual subject at all can be presented pictorially in kinds of images beyond mortal comprehension, which inwardly contain elements of perception of what is true, and still more inwardly elements of perception of what is good. Things like this are within man as well, since we are spirits clothed with bodies. This we can determine from the fact that all spoken words perceived by the ear change, as they rise toward more inward levels, into rather similar concepts of objects of sight, and then change from these into intellectual concepts, resulting in a perception of the meaning of the words. People who reflect properly about these matters can know that there is a spirit within them that is their inner person. They can also know that this will be their style of conversation after separation from the body, since they are involved in it while they are living here; but this involvement is not evident to them because of the darkness, the gloom, that earthly, physical, and worldly concerns impose.

3343.

The speech of angels of the more inward heaven is pictorial in a still more lovely and charming way. But the concepts that are given pictorial form cannot be expressed in words; and if they were expressed to anyone, they would surpass not only understanding, but even belief. Spiritual concerns, which are matters of truth, are conveyed by changes in heavenly light containing affections that shift wondrously in elusive ways. And heavenly concerns, which are matters of goodness, are conveyed through changes in heavenly flame or warmth. In this way, all the affections are stirred.

People do attain this more inward speech after leaving the body, but only people involved in the good on a spiritual level—that is, in the good of faith, or in other words in charity toward their neighbors during their earthly life. For this goodness has this ability within it, even though the people themselves are unaware of it.

3344.

The speech of angels of the still more inward or third heaven is also pictorial, but of such nature that there is no way to grasp any of its concepts; so it cannot be described.

This kind of concept also dwells within people on earth, but in people who are involved in heavenly love (that is, in love for the Lord). And after leaving the body, they come into it as though they had been born in it, even though no concept of it had been perceptible to them while they were living in the body, as we have said.

In brief, through pictorial elements joined to concepts, language virtually comes alive—least of all with people on earth, since they use a language of words; more with angels of the first heaven; still more with angels of the second; and most of all with angels of the third heaven, since they are most nearly in the Lord's life. Anything that comes from the Lord is intrinsically alive.

3345.

This enables us to determine that languages exist in a series of inwardness, yet are so constituted that one emerges from another in sequence and one dwells within another in sequence. We are acquainted with the nature of human language and also with the thought process it comes from, thought processes whose analytic elements are such that there is no way to explore them. The language of good spirits or angels of the first heaven—and the thought it comes from—is still more inward, with still more wondrous and unsearchable things within it. The language of angels of the second heaven—and again the thought it comes from—is more inward still, with still more perfect and unutterable things within it. But the language of angels of the third heaven—and, again, the thought it comes from—is the most inward, with absolutely unutterable things within it. And even though all these languages are so constituted that they seem different and distinctive, they are still one, since one forms another and one dwells in another. But what emerges on a more outward level is figurative of the more inward.

People cannot believe this who do not think beyond worldly and bodily concerns, and who therefore think that their more inward aspects are nothing, when in fact their more inward aspects are everything, and the more outward ones (that is, worldly and bodily concerns), to which they attach supreme importance, are virtually nothing by comparison.

3346.

So that I might know this, and know it with certainty, I have out of the Lord's divine mercy been granted almost constant converse with spirits and angels for a good many years now, talking with spirits or angels of the first heaven in their own language. Sometimes too I have talked with angels of the second heaven in theirs. But the language of angels of the third heaven has appeared to me only as a streaming of light, containing a perception, from its flame, of the good within it.

3347.

I have heard angels talking about human minds, and their thought and consequent speech. They were comparing these processes with the outward human form, which does come into being and exist from countless forms within—from the brains, for example, the medullae, the lungs, the heart, the liver, the pancreas, the loins, the stomach and intestines, among many others including the organs assigned to procreation in both sexes, all these surrounded by countless muscles and ultimately with coverings. They were aware that all of these are built up out of glands and fibers—out of glands and fibers within glands and fibers, even—yielding more minute tubes and forms. So they are built up out of countless elements, which all still come together, each in its own way, to make up an outward form in which none of the inward components is visible. To this form, this outward form, they were comparing human minds and their thoughts and consequent languages. But they were comparing angelic processes to things that lay within, that were relatively indefinable and also incomprehensible. Further, they would compare the ability to think to the organs' ability to act according to the form of their fibers, stating that the ability was not a property of the fibers but of the life within the fibers; just as the ability to think is not a property of the mind, but of the Lord's life flowing into it.

Comparisons like this, when they are made by angels, are at the same time also displayed by means of portrayals through which the more inward forms under discussion are presented both visually and mentally down to the smallest elusive details, and this happens instantaneously. But comparisons using the kinds of spiritual and heavenly phenomena, made by heavenly angels vastly surpass in the beauty of their wisdom comparisons that use natural phenomena.

3348.

Some spirits from another planet were with me for quite a while, and I was telling them about the wisdom of our world. I said that one of the disciplines that gave scholarly repute was a scientific effort to explore aspects of the mind and its thoughts, and that people called it Metaphysics and Logic. However, they had made little progress beyond terms and a few protean rules. They argued about terms, about the meaning of "form," for example, and "substance," and "mind," and "soul." And using these broad, protean rules, they quarreled heatedly about matters of truth.

At this point the spirits perceived that such concerns remove all sense and understanding of the subject when people get tangled in them as terms and think about them by artificial rules. They kept saying that things like this were only little black clouds that blocked intellectual sight and pulled discernment down into the dust. They added that it was not like that for them, but that they had clearer concepts of the subject by knowing nothing about such matters.

I was also granted to see how wise they were. They made a marvelous representation of the human mind as a heavenly form and of its affections as spheres of activity suited to it. They did this so skillfully that the angels were full of praise. They also portrayed how the Lord bends intrinsically unpleasant affections into pleasant ones. Some scholars from our planet were present, but they could not understand a bit of it, even though they had discussed these matters philosophically at great length during their physical life. When the spirits again perceived these scholars' thoughts and how they were simply tangled in terms, tending to quibble about the correctness of details, they called these matters "foaming dregs."

3349.

From what has been presented thus far, we can determine what correspondences are and what representations are. But in addition to the material presented above (nn. 2987–3003, 3213–3227), the reader may refer to the following relevant material elsewhere. Everything in the Word's literal meaning is figurative and indicative of subjects in its inner meaning (*A.C.* 1404, 1408, 1409, 2763). The Word was composed by Moses and the prophets using figurative and indicative elements. To have an inner meaning through which there would be a communication between heaven and earth, it could not have been written in any other style (*A.C.* 2899). The Lord also spoke figuratively, as well because he spoke from the actual Divine (*A.C.* 2900). The source of figurative and indicative elements in the Word and in rituals (*A.C.* 2179). Figurative elements arose from the indicative modes of the ancient church, which in turn arose from the perceptive modes of the earliest church (*A.C.* 920, 1409, 2896, 2897). The earliest people also gained representative elements from dreams (*A.C.* 1977). The ones who collected the perceptive phenomena of the earliest people were "Enoch" (*A.C.* 2896). In heaven there are constant portrayals of the Lord and His kingdom (*A.C.* 1619). The heavens are full of portrayals (*A.C.* 1521, 1532). Angels' concepts are turned into a variety of portrayals in the world of spirits (*A.C.* 1971, 1980, 1981), portrayals through which little children are led into intelligence (*A.C.* 2299). Portrayals in nature come from an inflow of the Lord (*A.C.* 1632, 1881). There are portrayals of the Lord's kingdom in all of nature (*A.C.* 2758). There are things in the outer person that are responsive to the inner, and things that are not (*A.C.* 1563, 1568).

3350.

To make it clear what portrayals are like, I may present one more example. I heard a large number of angels of a more inward heaven, who together or in consort were forming a portrayal. The spirits around me were unable to perceive this except by a certain inflow of a more inward affection. There was a chorus in which many people were thinking the same thing together and said the same thing. Using figures, they were forming a golden crown set with diamonds around the Lord's head. This was accomplished at once by a rapid series of figures like those of thought and speech (described in nn. 3342–3344 above). Marvelously, even though there were very many angels, still they all kept thinking and speaking as one, and so they kept portraying as one. This was because no one wanted to do anything on his own, much less outdo the others or lead the chorus. Anyone who did this would spontaneously leave the group in an instant. Rather, they let themselves be led by each other—all of them, therefore, individually and together, by the Lord. All the good people who come into the other life are led into harmonies like this.

Thereafter, I heard many choruses who presented different things figuratively; and even though there were very many, with many individuals in each chorus, they were still acting as one, and from the form of their different aspects there emerged a unity in which there was a heavenly beauty.

So can the whole heaven, which is made up of millions and millions of people who act as one by being in mutual love, because in this way they let themselves be led by the Lord. Marvelously, the more there are, that is, the more the millions who make up heaven, the more distinctive and perfect is each and every individual. Individuality and perfection also increase as angels are of more inward heavens, for every form of perfection increases as one moves inward.

THE UNIVERSAL HUMAN

3351.

The people who formed the chorus were from the region of the lungs, from the Lord's spiritual kingdom, therefore. They were actually flowing gently into my breathing. But there were separate groups that had to do with voluntary and involuntary breathing.

3472.

We can establish from what has been presented so far—and from things yet to be presented, in the Lord's divine mercy—that each and every element in the literal meaning of the Word is symbolic of spiritual and heavenly matters of the Lord's kingdom in the heavens and is in the highest sense symbolic of the Lord Himself. But since humanity has moved so far from heaven and sunk itself in the lowest level of nature, all the way to earth, it absolutely rejects any statement that there are higher things hidden in the Word than one grasps from the letter. This rejection is stronger when it is stated that it contains things actually divine, which infinitely transcend the discernment of angels. To be sure, Christendom does acknowledge that the Word is divine, but denies at heart if not aloud that it is *that* divine. This is not surprising, since the earthly milieu humanity is involved in nowadays neither grasps nor wants to grasp loftier things.

3473.

Spirits or souls who arrive in the other life are often shown visually that the Word has things like this hidden in its letter. I have often been allowed to be present when this happened, as you can tell from the experiences cited in Part 1, "Sacred Scripture or the Word: there are divine things hidden in it which are visible to good spirits and angels" (nn. 1767–1776 and 1867–1879). In support of the present subject, I may again present the following one.

3474.

A spirit came to me, not long after having left his body, as I could tell from the fact that he did not yet know he was in the other life, still thinking he was living in this world. I perceived that he was devoted to studies that I discussed with him. But then suddenly, to my surprise, he was lifted up on high. I presumed he was one of those people who have high aspirations, since they are commonly borne aloft, or one who had placed heaven on high, since they likewise are

57

often borne aloft to learn that heaven is not on high but within. I soon noticed, however, that he had been carried up to some angelic spirits a little forward on the right side of the first threshold of heaven. Then he talked with me from there, saying that he was seeing loftier things than human minds could ever grasp. While this was happening, I was reading the first chapter of Deuteronomy, about the Jewish people and how some of them were sent to explore the land of Canaan and the things in it. While I was reading this, he said that he was not noticing anything of the literal meaning, but rather elements of a spiritual meaning, and that these were marvelous, beyond his power to describe. This was at the first threshold of a heaven of angelic spirits, which was not within that heaven itself, which in turn was not in an angelic heaven.

Then some spirits who were with me, who had previously doubted that the Word of the Lord was like this, began to repent of their disbelief. In that state of mind, they kept saying that they believed because they had heard him say that he heard and saw and perceived that it was true.

But some other spirits still kept maintaining their disbelief, and kept saying that it was not true, that these were hallucinations. So they too were suddenly borne aloft and talked with me from there. They said that it was anything but hallucination, because they really perceived that it was so, with a perception in fact more exquisite than could ever be granted to any sense in physical life.

Soon still others were raised into the same heaven, among them one man I had known during his physical life. He bore the same witness, saying among other things that he was so stunned that he could not describe the glory of the Word in its inner meaning. And then, speaking with a kind of compassion, he said it was bewildering that people did not know anything about things like this.

Not long after this I saw other spirits raised up into another heaven among angelic spirits; and they talked with me from there. I was reading the third chapter of Deuteronomy then, from beginning to end. They kept saying that they were involved in the inner meaning of the Word only, insisting then that there was not a single jot that did not contain something spiritual and utterly lovely, coherent with everything else, and adding that the names referred to actual things. In this way they too were convinced (for they had not believed it before) that each and every detail of the word was inspired by the Lord. They also wanted to swear to this publicly, but they were not allowed to.

3475.

I have often stated and shown above that the kinds of consecutive images that occur in the Word are presented in the heavens. It is characteristic of these images that spirits and angels see them in a light much clearer than that of noonday on earth. By the nature of these images, angels and spirits perceive in the visible outward form what they mean in an inner way, and in this they perceive things still more internal.

There are actually three heavens. In the first heaven things appear in an outward form, with a perception of what they mean in inner form. In the second heaven, they appear as they are in inner form, with a perception of what they are like in a form still more internal. In the third heaven, there appear within that more internal form things that are most internal. The things visible in the first heaven are the generalities of the things that are visible in the second, and these are the generalities of the things that are visible in the third. So inside the visible images of the first heaven are the visible images of the second, and inside them, those of the third. And since these are set according to levels, you can tell how perfect, how full of wisdom, and at the same time how happy the images of the inmost heaven are. And you can tell how absolutely inexpressible they are, for thousands and thousands of elements are present in one particular generality.

Each and every image involves matters of the Lord's kingdom, and these involve matters proper to the Lord Himself. The people in the first heaven see within their images the kinds of thing that are manifest in the more inward sphere of the kingdom, and within these, things in the still more internal one, seeing in this way images of the Lord, but distantly. People in the second heaven see in their images the kinds of thing that are manifest in the inmost sphere of the kingdom, and within them they see images of the Lord closer to hand. But people in the third heaven see the Lord Himself.

3476.

This enables us to know what the Word is like. The Word was in fact given by the Lord to humanity and to angels as well, so that through it they might be with him. For the Word is a means of making earth one with heaven, and through heaven, one with the Lord. Its literal meaning is what makes a person one with the first heaven. And since there is within the literal meaning an inner meaning that deals with the Lord's kingdom, and within that a highest meaning that is about the Lord, these meanings being sequentially within each other, we can see the nature of oneness with the Lord through the Word.

3477.

We have mentioned that portrayals in the heavens are constant, and do by nature involve the deepest secrets of wisdom. The things visible to humans from the Word's literal meaning are so few by comparison—like the waters of an ocean compared to the waters of a little pond. We can tell what portrayals are like in the heavens from the ones narrated from observation a number of times above, and also from the following ones.

A scene, which I saw, was portrayed for some spirits—the broad way and the narrow way described in the Word—with the broad way leading to hell and the narrow way to heaven. The broad way was so planted with trees and flowers that in outward form it looked lovely and pleasant; but hidden away in them were different kinds of snakes, which they did not see. The narrow way was not landscaped for the eye with trees and flowers in the same way. Rather, it looked depressing and gloomy. In its heaven, there were beautifully dressed angel children in the most charming parks and flower gardens—although they did not see them.

Then they were asked which way they wanted to take. They said, "The broad one"; but suddenly their eyes were opened, and they saw the snakes in the broad way and the angels in the narrow one. Then they were asked again which way they wanted to take. This time they stuck to silence. And as their sight was opened more, they said they wanted to take the narrow way, and as their sight was closed more, they said they wanted to take the broad one.

3478.

Also, there were portrayed for some spirits the tabernacle and the ark. Things like this are often presented visually to people who had taken special delight in the Word while they lived in this world. So this time the scene included the tabernacle and all its furnishings—the courts, the tapestries enclosing them, the inner veil, the golden altar or altar of incense, the table where the bread was, the candlesticks, the mercy-seat with its cherubim. At the same time then, the upright spirits were granted a perception of what the details meant. There were three heavens portrayed by the tabernacle, and the Lord Himself pictured by the covenant within the ark with the mercy-seat on it. As their sight was opened more, they saw within these things matters more heavenly and more divine, things of which they had had no awareness during their physical life. And remarkably, there was not the slightest element of the scene that was not symbolic, right down to the hooks and rings. For one example only, in the bread on the table they perceived, as in a picture or symbol, that food which angels lived on—heavenly and spiritual love—and in the delights they perceived the Lord Himself as the bread or manna from heaven. Beyond this, many details of the form and placement and number of the loaves, of the surrounding gold, of the candlesticks that lighted them, presented images of indescribable subjects. The same held true for everything else. I could tell from this that the rituals or symbols of Judaism contained within themselves all the mysteries of Christianity, and that people to whom the symbols and signs of the Old Testament Word are opened can know and grasp the mysteries of the Lord's church on earth while they are living in this world, and the mysteries within mysteries of the Lord's kingdom in the heavens when they arrive in the other life.

3479.

The Jews who lived before the Lord's advent, like those who lived after it, had no presumption about church rituals except that divine worship was entirely a matter of external things. They were not concerned with what these were picturing or signaling. In fact, they neither knew nor wanted to know that there was an inner side to worship and the Word—that there was therefore a life after death and consequently a heaven. They were in fact wholly sense-oriented and "physical." And since they were involved in outward matters to the exclusion of inner ones, worship as it related to them was quite idolatrous. This is why they were so prone to worship other gods if they were convinced that they could benefit them. A symbolic church was established within this nation because they were of such nature that they would become involved in outward holiness and thus maintain as holy, rituals that pictured the Lord's heavenly kingdom. They could have a holy reverence for Abraham, Isaac, and Jacob, also for

Moses and Aaron, and later for David, who served to picture the Lord. And especially, they could maintain a sense of holiness for the Word, in which each and every detail is symbolic and indicative of divine matters. However, had that nation recognized inner matters to the point of acknowledging them, then they would have profaned them, being therefore in holiness outwardly and in profanation inwardly. This would have meant that there could be absolutely no communication of the symbols with heaven through that nation. This is why more internal things went undetected by them—even the fact that the Lord was within—to save their souls.

This nation has been preserved right to the present day because the Jewish tribes were more of this nature than other tribes. Now as then they maintain the holiness of such rituals as they can observe outside Jerusalem. They maintain a holy reverence for their ancestors, and especially they maintain a sense of holiness for the Old Testament Word. Further, it was foreseen that Christians would virtually cast the Old Testament aside, and would defile their inner reaches with profanation. So the Jewish nation has been preserved in accord with the Lord's words in Matthew 24:34. It would have been different if Christians, besides recognizing inner matters, had lived as internal people. In this case, that nation, like other nations, would in a few centuries have failed.

But the situation of that nation is that their holy attributes, their holy worships, can have no effect on their internal natures, these being impure because of an unclear love of self and of the world and also because of the idolatry of worshiping outward realities apart from inner ones. This means that since they do not have something of heaven in themselves, they cannot bring something of heaven with them into the other life either, except for those few who live in mutual love and therefore do not downgrade others in comparison to themselves.

3480.

I have also been shown how the impurities of that race did not prevent the more internal, or spiritual and heavenly, contents of the Word from being presented in heaven. The impurities were in fact continually removed, as though they were not noticed; evil things were even turned into good, so that the holy external was serving only as a source for presenting the inner contents of the Word to angels with no passive hindrances. So I could see how that people, even with its inner idolatry, could picture the holy, even the Lord Himself, and how therefore the Lord could dwell in the middle of their impurities (Lv 16:16). And I could see how he could have something like a church there; for a church that is only symbolic is a copy of a church and not a real church.

This cannot happen in the same way among Christians because they have recognized the deeper aspects of worship but do not believe them. So they cannot be in outward holiness apart from inward holiness. The exceptions to this are people who are living a life of faith. There is a communication through the good elements within them, as evil and false things are removed. And then, marvelously, every detail of the Word as they read it is visible to angels, even though the people themselves may not be paying attention to what it means. This has been shown to me by a good deal of experience, for the inner level within them, which is not readily perceptible, does serve as a screen.

3481.

I have often engaged in conversation with Jews who, in the other life, are to be found toward the front, in a lower land below the level of the left foot. We have talked about the Word, the land of Canaan, and the Lord. They tended to agree that the Word contained deeply hidden things that were not visible to human beings. They liked the idea that all these hidden things were about the Messiah and His kingdom, too. But when I said that "Messiah" in Hebrew is the same as "Christ" in Greek, they did not want to hear it. Again, I said that the Messiah was most holy and that Jehovah was in Him, that this was the only meaning of "the holy one of Israel" and "The God of Jacob"; and because He was most holy, there could not be anyone in His kingdom except holy people—holy in inward form, not outward—which meant people who were not involved in an unclean love of the world or in self-exaltation over other nations and in hatred among themselves. When I said this, they could not hear it.

Afterward, I said that according to the prophecies, the Messiah's kingdom was to be eternal, and that the people with Him were also to dwell in the land forever. If the kingdom were an earthly one and these people were brought into the land of Canaan, it would be only for the few years that are the years of human life. And further, all the people who died after the expulsion from the land of Canaan would not enjoy this blessing. I said that they could therefore realize that the land of Canaan served to picture and point to a heavenly kingdom, a realization all the clearer now that they knew that they were in the other life and were going to live forever, so they could see that the Messiah had His kingdom there. And if they were granted conversation with angels, they could know that the whole angelic heaven was His kingdom. Further, the new earth, new Jerusalem, and new temple in Ezekiel meant nothing but this kingdom of the Messiah. They could not answer this, except to say that the thought of being brought into the land of Canaan by the Messiah, dying after so few years, and leaving the blessedness they were to have, brought on bitter tears.

3482.

Although the language of the Word seems simple to people, and in places coarse, it is true angelic language, but at its lowest level. When angelic language, which is spiritual, descends into human words, this is the only kind of language it can descend into, since the particular things in this language are pictorial and the particular words are signals. Since early people regularly interacted with spirits and angels, they had no other language. It was full of symbols, and there was spiritual meaning within its details. The books of ancient people were composed in this style, for the effort of their wisdom was to talk and to write in this way. We can also tell them from this how far humanity moved away from heaven in later times. Now no one realizes that there is anything more in the Word than can be seen in the letter, particularly that there is a spiritual meaning within it. Anything referred to as beyond the literal meaning is labeled "mystical," and is rejected on that account alone. This is also why communication with heaven has come to be cut off in our own time, to the point that few people believe that any heaven exists—strangely, fewer of the learned and the scholarly than of the simple.

3483.

Everything that is ever visible in the universe is symbolic of the Lord's kingdom, to the point that nothing whatever occurs in the atmosphere or in space, in the world and its three kingdoms, that is not in its own way symbolic. In fact, each and every thing in nature is a final image. From the divine come heavenly realities whose essence is the good. From the heavenly realities come spiritual ones whose essence is the true. And from these two come natural realities. We can therefore tell how crude, how very earthbound, and how inverted is the human intelligence that credits everything to nature separated from and emptied of any prior inflow or effecting cause. Further, people who think and talk like this seem to themselves to be wiser than others by virtue of crediting everything to nature. Yet angelic intelligence is quite the opposite, consisting of crediting nature with nothing. It rather credits everything to the Lord's divine nature—to life, that is, and not to anything dead.

Scholars know that enduring is constant becoming, yet still it goes against the affection for what is false and therefore against a reputation for learning to say that nature is constantly enduring in the same way it came into being, from the Lord's divine nature. Now since each and every reality does endure (that is, does keep coming into being) from the divine nature, and nothing from that source can help being symbolic of those things through which it has come into being, it follows that the visible universe is nothing but a theater symbolic of the Lord's kingdom, which in turn is a theater symbolic of the Lord Himself.

3484.

I have been taught by an abundance of experience that there is only one life, the Lord's, which flows into us and makes us live— makes good and evil people alike live, in fact. Responsive to this life are forms that are substances, which are brought to life through a constant divine inflow, so that they seem to themselves to live independently. This is a correspondence of organs with life; but the recipient organs live in keeping with their own natures. People involved in love and charity are in correspondence, and life itself is received adequately by them. People however who are involved in things opposed to love and charity are not in correspondence, because life itself is not received adequately by them. So their natures depend on the kind of life that becomes present in them.

We can illustrate this by forms of nature. Sunlight flows into them: depending on the kinds of recipient forms they are, there are alterations in that light. In the spiritual world, these alterations are spiritual. So in that world, the natures of the recipient forms determine the kind of intelligence and wisdom they have. This is why good spirits and angels look like absolute forms of charity, while evil and hellish spirits look like forms of hatred.

EMANUEL SWEDENBORG

3485.

    The portrayals that happen in the other life are appearances, but living ones, because they come from the light of life. The light of life is divine wisdom, which comes from the Lord alone. So all the things that emerge from that light are real, unlike the things that emerge from this world's light. Consequently, people in the other life often say that what they are seeing there is real, and what people on this earth are seeing is relatively unreal, because otherworld phenomena are alive and therefore directly affect their life. This world's phenomena are not alive, and do not affect people's life directly—only as and to the extent that phenomena of this world's light are united fitly and responsively to phenomena of heaven's light within them. This enables us to determine what representations correspondences are.

The Universal Human

PART 2

THE CORRESPONDENCE OF ALL THE INNER AND OUTER HUMAN ORGANS AND MEMBERS WITH THE UNIVERSAL HUMAN, WHICH IS HEAVEN

CHAPTER 1
The Universal Human Form

3624.

I am now allowed to report and describe some remarkable things, which to my knowledge have never been recognized by anyone or even crossed anyone's mind—namely that heaven in its entirety is so formed that it is responsive to the Lord, to the divine–human, and that man is so formed that in every detail he is responsive to heaven and through heaven to the Lord. This is an immense mystery that must now be unveiled, and will occupy us in subsequent pages.

3625.

This is why we have sometimes said above in dealing with heaven and angelic communities that they belonged to a particular region of the body—to the region of the head, for example, or of the chest or of the abdomen, or to the region of some member or organ within them. The reason is the responsiveness just mentioned.

3626.

The existence of this kind of responsiveness is very well known in the other life, not just to angels, but to spirits as well, even evil ones. As a result, angels know the most obscure things within people, the most obscure thing in the world and all its nature. Quite often, I have been able to determine this from the fact that when I talked about some human part, they knew not only the whole structure, dynamics, and use of that part, but countless other things, more than we are capable of investigating or understanding. They knew these in their design and in their sequence, as a result of their sense of the heavenly design they were following, to which the design of that part was responding. So being involved in the fundamentals, they consequently knew their corollaries.

3627.

It is a general rule that nothing can come into being and endure from itself, but only from something else—that is, through something else. It is also a general rule that nothing can be held in a form except by or through something else, as we can conclude from everything in nature. It is recognized that the human body is held together in its form from the outside by some active or living force; otherwise, it would instantly collapse. Anything that is not connected to something prior, and through prior things to a first, does perish instantly. What follows will enable us to see that the Universal Human—or the inflow therefrom—is that "prior thing" through which the human being in all particulars is connected with the First—that is, with the Lord.

3628.

I have been taught about these matters through an abundance of experience. I have been taught, for example, that it is not only elements of the human mind—of its thought and affection—that correspond to spiritual and heavenly realities, but that it is also in a general sense the whole person, and in a detailed sense everything within the person. This holds true to the point that there is not the smallest part or the smallest bit of a part that does not correspond. Then, too, I have been taught that this is the source of human genesis and continuance. And I have also been taught that if it were not for this kind of correspondence of the human with heaven, and through heaven with the Lord (that is, with its prior, and through the prior to the First), he would not last even a moment, but would dissolve into nothingness.

As we have just stated, there are always two forces that are holding any entity together in its integrity and in its form, namely a force acting from the outside and a force acting from the inside, with the thing that is being held together in the middle. This is true of the human being in even the smallest parts. It is acknowledged that the atmospheres are what hold the whole body together from the outside, by their constant pressure or weight, and also that the air-atmosphere does the same for the lungs through its inflow. It does the same for its own organ, the ear, with its inner forms built for the modifications of the air. The ether-atmosphere does the same for more inward connections, since it flows freely in through all the pores and holds the inner organs of the whole body together by an almost identical pressure of mass—by an active force, therefore. And the same atmosphere does the same thing for its own organ, the eye, with its inner forms built in for the etheric modifications. Unless there were corresponding inner forces that were reacting to these outer forces, holding the intermediate forms together and keeping them in balance, they would not last even a moment. We can see from this that there must at all costs be two forces if anything is to come into being and last. The forces that flow in and act from within are from heaven, and come through heaven from the Lord; and they have life within them.

This is wholly obvious in the organ of hearing. Unless there were more inward modifications of the life, to which the modifications of the air corresponded, hearing would not happen. We can also see it in the organ of sight. Unless there were an inner light, a light of life, to which the outer light of the sun corresponded, there would be no way for sight to happen.

The same holds true for all the other organs and members in the human body. There are outside forces acting that are forces of nature and are not intrinsically alive; and there are inside forces acting that are intrinsically alive. These hold every entity together and enable it to live, depending on the form granted it for the sake of its use.

3629.

Not many people can believe that this is true, the reason being that they do not know what the spiritual is and what the natural is, let alone how they are to be distinguished. Nor do they know what correspondence is or what inflow is, or that when the spiritual flows into the body's organic forms, it sets up the kinds of life process that we observe. Nor do they know that without this kind of inflow and responsiveness, not the smallest particle of the body would be able to possess life and be moved. As to how this happens, I have been taught by live experience that not only does heaven flow in, in a specific way; I have been taught which and what kinds of community flow into this or that organ of the body and into this or that member. I have also been taught that it is not just one community that flows into a given organ or member but many, and that there are many individuals in each community. For the more there are, the better and stronger is the responsiveness, since perfection and strength come from a harmonious gathering of many constituents, which act as one in a heavenly form. So the impulse that reflects in specific instances is more perfect and stronger depending on the abundance of constituents.

3630.

As a result, I have been able to determine that the particular viscera and members, or motor and sensory organs, are responsive to communities in heaven exactly as though they were distinct heavens, and that from them (that is, through them) heavenly and spiritual forces flow into people. They flow into forms that are both sufficient and suitable, and in this way set up the results that people observe. But to human beings, these results seem to be entirely matters of nature—that is, in a completely different form and in another guise, so different that there is no way to recognize that they are coming from a spiritual source.

3631.

Once I was shown with utter realism which communities make up the province of the face and flow into the muscles of its forehead, cheeks, chin, and neck. I was shown what they are like, how they flow in and act, and how they communicate with each other. To present this vividly, they were allowed to make an image of a face in various modes by flowing in. In the same way, I learned which and what kinds of communities flow into the lips, the tongue, the eyes, and the ears. I was also allowed to talk with them, and in this way I was thoroughly informed.

I was also able to conclude from this that everyone who enters heaven is an organ or member of the Universal Human, and that heaven is never closed. Rather, the more the people, the stronger the impulse, the stronger the force, the stronger the action. I could also conclude that the Lord's heaven is vast, so vast that it exceeds all belief. The inhabitants of this planet are few indeed in comparison, almost like a lake compared with an ocean.

3632.

The divine (and therefore heavenly) design reaches its boundaries for people only in their bodies—in their motions, actions, facial expressions, speech, and outward sensations, that is, and in the pleasures that belong to these functions. These are the outmost elements of the design and the outmost elements of inflow, both of which then come to a close. But the deeper things that are flowing in are not what they seem outwardly to be. Rather, they have a different face, a different expression, a different sensation, and a different pleasure. Correspondences, as well as representations (which we have been discussing), teach what they are like.

We can determine that they are different from actions, which flow from intentionality, and from words, which flow from thinking. Physical actions are not the same in intent, and verbal expressions are not the same in thought. We can also see from this that acts in the realm of nature flow from spiritual causes, since elements of intent and thought are spiritual. We can also see that the latter are imaged correspondentially in the former, but variously.

3633.

   All spirits and angels look like people to themselves, with normal faces and bodies, organs and limbs. This is because their inmost being tends toward this form. In the same way, the most rudimentary form of an individual, which comes from the parents' soul, strives to form a complete person in the ovum and in the womb, even though this rudimentary form is not in the form of a body but in another most perfect form known only to the Lord. Since everyone's inmost being has the same tendency and striving toward this kind of form, all spirits and angels look like people to themselves.

   Further, heaven as a whole is of such nature that each individual is like a center of all. In consequence, an image of heaven is reflected in each individual and makes that individual like itself—that is, a person. The nature of the inclusive whole in fact determines the nature of the part of the whole, since the parts must be like their whole to belong to it.

3634.

   A person who is in correspondence—in love to the Lord and charity toward the neighbor, and thereby in faith—is in heaven as to spirit and in the world as to body. Also, by thus acting as one with angels, this person is also an image of heaven; and since the inflow of everything or of the inclusive whole is as stated into the details or parts, this individual is also a minimal heaven, in human form. It is from the good and the true that people are human, and can be distinguished from dumb animals.

3635.

   There are two things in the human body that are the wellsprings of all motion, of all action and sensation of the outer body, the body alone. These are the heart and the lungs. These answer to the Universal Human or heaven of the Lord in a particular fashion, by virtue of the fact that heavenly angels there make one kingdom and spiritual angels a second one, the Lord's kingdom being heavenly and spiritual. The heavenly kingdom consists of people who are involved in love to the Lord, the spiritual kingdom of people who are involved in charity toward the neighbor (nn. 2088, 2669, 2715, 2718, 3235, 3246). The heart, and its kingdom in the human being, answers to heavenly matters; the lungs, and their kingdom, answer to spiritual matters. Further, these so flow into elements of the heart and the lungs that these latter actually come into being and are maintained by this inflow. But, by the Lord's divine mercy, we need to deal specifically with the correspondence of heart and lungs in the Universal Human.

3636.

The most universal principle is that the Lord is heaven's sun, and is the source of all light in the other life. To angels and spirits (or to people in the other life) nothing whatever of the world's light is visible—the world's light, which comes from the sun, is nothing but profound darkness to angels. From heaven's sun or the Lord there comes not only light, but warmth as well, but the light is spiritual and the warmth is spiritual. To the eyes of spiritual beings, the light looks like light, but because of its source it contains intelligence and wisdom. And by the senses of spiritual beings the warmth is perceived as warmth, but because of its source, there is love within it. So too love is called spiritual warmth and causes the warmth of human life; and intelligence is called spiritual light and causes the light of human life. From this universal correspondence flow the rest. For each and every reality goes back to the good, which is a matter of love, and the true, which is a matter of intelligence.

3637.

Relative to humanity, the Universal Human is the Lord's whole heaven. But in the highest sense, the Universal Human is the Lord alone: heaven actually comes from Him and everything there corresponds to Him.

Since the human race has by a life of evil and consequent false convictions become completely reversed, and since the lower elements of people were beginning to control the higher, the natural to control the spiritual, to such an extent that Jehovah or the Lord could no longer flow in through the Universal Human or heaven and restore things to the design, it was therefore necessary for the Lord to come into the world, clothe Himself in human nature, and make that nature divine, thereby restoring the design so that the whole heaven was grounded in Him as the only person and was responsive to that sun itself. This happened once the people who were involved in evil and therefore in what is false were cast out beneath the fact—that is, outside the Universal Human. As a result, people who are in heaven are said to be in the Lord, for the Lord is all of heaven. It is in the Lord that every individual there is assigned a place and a function.

3638.

    This is why all the communities in the other life, no matter how many there are, have their fixed locations relative to the Lord, who appears to the whole heaven like a sun. And what is remarkable—scarcely credible because it is impossible to grasp: the communities there keep their places relative to each individual no matter where that individual is or turns or travels. For example, communities seen to one's right are always to one's right, even though one may change orientation as to face or body. This is something I have very often been granted to observe by turning my body.

    We can see from this that heaven's form is of such nature that it is constantly grounded in the Universal Human relative to the Lord. We can also see that all angels are not only with the Lord but in the Lord—or, in other words, that the Lord is with them and in them. Otherwise, this would not happen.

3639.

    Consequently, all locations there are arranged relative to the human body, in accord with regions of the body—that is, right, left, front, back, whatever the specific situation. For example, they are arranged by planes, relating to the plane of the head, say, or of its parts, like the forehead, temples, eyes, or ears. Or they may be related to the plane of the body, specifically to the plane of the shoulders, the chest, the abdomen, the loins, the knees, the feet, the soles, or even above the head and below the soles of the feet, at any angle. Or they may be related to the back, from the occiput downward. It can be recognized from locations just which communities are present and what regions of human organs and members they belong to; it never fails. But one can tell more from their affectional nature and bent.

3640.

    The hells—and there are many of them—also have fixed locations, so that one can tell by location alone which hells are present and what their quality is; these locations are arranged in the same way. They are all beneath the person, distributed in levels below the soles of the feet. Some of them do also appear here and there above the head and elsewhere. However, it is not that they have locations there, since that is a convincing semblance that makes a deceptive imitation of location.

3641.

Everyone, those in heaven and those in hell alike, looks upright, head up and feet down, but intrinsically, and to angels' sight, they are variously oriented. Specifically, people in heaven have their heads toward the Lord, who is the sun there and who serves as the common center, the source of all direction and location. But hellish people are to angels' sight head down and feet up, oppositely oriented, or also slanted. What is above to heavenly people is actually below to hellish people, and what is above to hellish people is below to heavenly ones.

So we can begin to see in some measure how heaven can make one with hell, in a manner of speaking, or how the two together can have a single ground of location and direction.

3642.

One morning I was in the company of angelic spirits, who were busy thinking and speaking as one in customary fashion. This activity was also penetrating toward hell, where it was so maintained that (the hellish people) seemed to be acting as one with the angelic spirits. What was happening, though, was that the good and true in the angels was by a marvelous inversion being turned into something evil and false in the hellish people. This happened step by step as the activity flowed downward, where hell was acting as one through its false convictions and evil cravings. Even though the hells are outside the Universal Human, they are still brought into a kind of unity in this manner, and are thereby kept in a design that determines their patterns of association. In this way, the Lord from His divine nature also rules the hells.

3643.

I have noticed that people in heaven are in a serene aura of light, like the light of morning or noon, even tending toward evening. Similarly, they are in a warmth like the warmth of spring, summer, and fall. In contrast, people in hell are in a dense, cloudy, dark atmosphere, and in the cold. I have noticed that there is a general balance between them. To the extent that angels are involved in love, charity, and consequent faith, they are in an aura of light and the warmth of spring. And to the extent that hellish people are involved in hatred and thereby in what is false, they are in darkness and cold. Light in the other life, as already noted, contains intelligence, warmth contains love, darkness, insanity, and cold hatred.

3644.

Everyone in every land on earth has a place either in the Universal Human, that is, in heaven, or outside in hell, as to soul, or what is the same, as to the spirit, which is to live after the death of the body. People do not know this while they are living in the world, but still the spirit is there and is governed from there. People are in heaven in accord with the good of love and consequent truth of faith, and in hell according to the evil of hatred and consequent falsity.

3645.

The Lord's whole kingdom is a kingdom of ends and uses. I have been granted open perception of this divine sphere, the sphere of ends and uses, perception then of things beyond conveying. Everything flows out from that sphere: everything is governed through it. To the extent that affections, thoughts, and actions have within them the end of benefiting others from the heart, the person, spirit, or angel is in the Universal Human—that is, in heaven. But to the extent that a person or spirit has at heart the end of harming others, that person or spirit is outside the Universal Human—that is, in hell.

3646.

As to inflows and correspondences, dumb animals are situated similarly to humans in that they are subject to an inflow from the spiritual world and an impinging flow from the natural world, being held together and living by means of these. But the actual functioning is arranged differently, depending on the forms of their souls and the resulting forms of their bodies. This works like our world's light, which flows with one intensity and manner into different earthly objects, and yet acts differently in the different forms. In some it produces lovely colors, in others unattractive ones. So when spiritual light flows into the souls of dumb animals, it is received quite differently and therefore affects them quite differently than it does human souls. These latter are actually on a higher level and in a more perfect state, and can by nature look upward, toward heaven and toward the Lord. So the Lord can join them to Himself and give them eternal life. But dumb animals by nature can look only downward, only toward earthly things, and can be joined only to them; so they perish along with their bodies. It is the ends that show what kind of life a human has and what kind an animal has. The human can have spiritual and heavenly ends, can see them, recognize them, believe them, and be moved by them; but animals can have only natural ends. So a human can be in the divine sphere of ends and uses that is in heaven and constitutes heaven, while animals can be only in the sphere of ends and uses on earth. Ends are nothing but loves, since what is loved is held as an end.

The reason many people do not know how to differentiate between their own life and animal life is that they are similarly involved in outward matters, being concerned at heart only with earthly, physical, and worldly issues. Being like this, they also believe that they are like beasts as to life and that they too will be dissipated. For they neither care nor know what spiritual and heavenly matters are. This is the source of the madness of our century, likening ourselves to beasts and seeing no inner difference. But people who give credence to heavenly and spiritual realities, or who allow spiritual light to flow in and work, see exactly the opposite, how much higher the human is than dumb animals. But we must deal with the life of dumb animals separately, by the Lord's divine mercy.

3647.

I have also been shown what this is like. I had been granted to see some people who entered the other life who during their physical lives had focused solely on earthly matters and had held nothing else as ends, and had not been led into the good and the true by any insights. They were nautical and rustic types. They seemed, as far as I could perceive, to have so little life that I thought they could not share eternal life like other spirits. They were like machines, barely animate. But the angels maintained an intense care for them, and through the faculty these people like others possessed, the angels instilled a life of the good and true. So more and more they were led through from an animal-like life into human life.

THE UNIVERSAL HUMAN

3648.

There is also an inflow from the Lord through heaven into the members of the vegetable kingdom, such as trees of all kinds and their ability to be fruitful, and plants of all kinds and their ability to multiply. Unless something spiritual from the Lord were constantly acting within, into their elementary forms, which exist in seeds, they would never sprout and grow in such a marvelous sequence. But their forms by nature cannot receive anything of life.

It is from this inflow that they have in them an image of the eternal and infinite. This we can see in their ceaseless effort to propagate their own genus and species, and in this way to live to eternity, so to speak, and also to fill the universe. This is inherent in every single seed.

But people have credited all these miraculous things to nature, and have not given credence to any inflow from a spiritual world because they denied that world at heart. Yet they should have known that nothing can exist except through the means by which it came into being, that is, that being is a ceaseless becoming, or in other words that production is a constant creation. It may be seen in n. 3483 that all nature is therefore a theater portraying the Lord's kingdom. But these matters too, and their correspondence with the Universal Human, must by the Lord's divine mercy be discussed elsewhere.

The heavenly kingdom is like a single person because all its details correspond to the Lord alone, to His divine-human in fact, who alone is Person (nn. 49, 288, 565, 1894). Heaven is called the Universal Human by virtue of its correspondence to, reflection of, and likeness to Him. From the Lord's divine nature come all heavenly realities (which pertain to the good) and all spiritual realities (which pertain to the true) in heaven. All angels there are forms, or substances formed according to their acceptance of divine elements that come from the Lord. The divine elements they receive are what are called heavenly and spiritual things, together with divine life, and a consequent divine light occurs and is modified within them as recipients. This is why the material forms and substances for humans are of the same nature but on a lower level, being denser and more compacted. We can see clearly that they too are forms recipient of heavenly and spiritual realities from quite visible indications. There is thought, for example, which flows into the organic forms of the tongue and produces speech. There are affections of the spirit *(animi)*, which present themselves to sight in the face. There is intentionality, which through muscular forms determines actions, and so on. The intent and thinking that produce these events are spiritual and heavenly, but the forms or substances that receive them and set them in action are material. It follows that the latter are formed wholly to receive the former. We can see from this that material things come from spiritual ones, and that apart from the spiritual, they could not occur.

3742.

As to there being a single life, from the Lord alone, and as to angels, spirits, and mortals being only recipients of life, this has been made known to me by such manifold experience that there is not the slightest doubt left. Heaven itself is involved in a perception that this is true, even to the point that angels openly perceive the inflow, including how it is happening and the amount and quality they are receiving. When they are in a more fully receptive state, they are in their proper peace and happiness: otherwise they are in a state of restlessness and some anxiety. Nevertheless, the Lord's life is made their own in such a way that they feel as though they were living independently even though they know that they are not. The "appropriation" of the Lord's life comes from His love and mercy toward the whole human race, specifically His will to give Himself and what is His to each individual, and His actual giving to the extent that an individual accepts—that is, to the extent that one is as a likeness and image of Him, involved in a life of goodness and a life of truth. Since this kind of divine effort from the Lord is constant, His life is appropriated, as stated.

3743.

However, if people are not involved in a love for the Lord and in charity toward the neighbor (therefore not in a life of goodness and truth), they cannot recognize that there is a single life flowing in, let alone that that life comes from the Lord. Rather, all such people feel insulted and are actually repelled when someone says that they are not living in their own right *(a se)*. Self-love is what does this. And strange as it seems, even though they are shown by first-hand experience in the other life that they are not living in their own right, and cannot help admitting that this is true, they still afterward maintain the same opinion. They think that if they were living from some other source, not from themselves, all the joy of their life would be destroyed, not realizing that the truth is precisely the opposite. This is why evil people make evil their own, because they do not believe that evil things come from hell; and it is why nothing good can be made their own, because they believe that the good comes from themselves and not from the Lord.

Nevertheless, evil and even hellish people are forms that receive life from the Lord, but they are forms that by nature either reject or stifle or corrupt whatever is good and true. So the good and true things that come from the Lord's life become evil and false within them. It is like sunlight, which in spite of its singleness and purity, is changed as it passes through or flows into (particular) forms, giving rise to some lovely and pleasing colors, and to some ugly and unpleasant ones.

3744.

This, then, enables us to determine what heaven is like, and why it is called the Universal Human. That is, the variant forms there of the life of goodness and truth are countless, and are arranged according to people's acceptance of life from the Lord. They are in precisely the relationship that applies to the organs, members, and viscera in the human body, all of which are forms in constant variety, receptive of life from their soul—or, better, through their soul from the Lord. Yet even though they exhibit such a variety, taken together they constitute a single person.

3745.

We can determine the extent and nature of this variety from the variety within the human body. It is recognized that no one organ or member is like another—that the organ of sight, for example, is not like the organ of hearing, or the organ of smell, or the organ of taste, or the organ of touch, which last is distributed through the whole body. This is true also of the members, such as arms, hands, loins, feet, and soles. It is true also of the soft organs (viscera) that lie hidden within, like the ones in the head—the cerebrum, the cerebellum, the medulla oblongata, and the medulla spinalis, with all the minute organs and tissues and ducts and fibers they are made of. It is true of those organs within the body below the head, like the heart, the lungs, the stomach, the liver, the pancreas, the spleen, the intestines, the mesentery, and the kidneys, and the organs assigned to procreation in either sex. It is recognized that each and every one of these differs from all the others in form and function—differs so as to be quite unlike. The same holds true of the forms within these forms, which also exhibit such a variety that there is not a single form nor even a single particle that is exactly like another—that is so like, that is, that it could be substituted in another place without some change, even though it might be very slight.

These correspond, each and every one, to the heavens. But they do so in such a way that the physical and material parts of the human body are spiritual and heavenly in the heavens. And they correspond in such a way that the physical realities come into being and are maintained in being from the spiritual.

3746.

Broadly, all the various forms may be assigned to matters of the head, of the chest, of the abdominal area, and of the organs of procreation. They may also be assigned to things more inward and things more outward in each area.

3747.

I have several times talked with spirits about the learned of our times—how they are unable to do more than divide man into an internal and an external, and even this is not based on any reflection on more inward elements of thought and affection in themselves, but rather on the Lord's Word. They still do not know what the inner person is. Further, many of them doubt that the inner person exists, and even deny it, because they are not living the life of the inner person but of the outer. Many of them, too, are gravely misled by the fact that brute animals seem to resemble humans as to organs, viscera, senses, appetites, and feelings. I have said also that learned people know less about such matters than do simple folk, and yet they seem to themselves to know a great deal more. They actually argue about the interaction between the soul and the body and even about the nature of the soul, while simple folk know that the soul is the inner person, and is the spirit that will go on living after physical death— that it is then the real person who is within a body. I have also said that the learned more than the simple come to resemble dumb animals, credit nature with everything, and credit the divine with virtually nothing. They do not pause to think that human beings, unlike dumb animals, can think about heaven and God and can thereby be lifted above themselves, that they can therefore be united with the Lord through love and so after death must of necessity live to eternity. Above all, they do not realize that absolutely everything in a human being depends, through heaven, on the Lord, and that heaven is the Universal Human to which absolutely everything in a human being corresponds, as do also the details of nature. If by chance they were to hear or read these principles, they would be so paradoxical to them that, lacking the support of experience, they would do the same if they were to hear that the three levels of life in a person are like the three levels of life in the heavens (that is, three heavens) and that people correspond to the three heavens, so as to be in image actually miniature heavens when they are involved in lives of goodness and truth, being images of the Lord by virtue of those lives.

On these levels of life, I have been taught that the most remote level of life is the one called the outer or natural person, by reason of which the human bears a resemblance to animals in cravings and projections *(phantasias)*. Then I have been taught that there is a second level called the inner or rational person, by virtue of which the human is higher than animals, since it is a means to thinking and intending what is good and true and controlling the natural person by restraining and even rejecting its cravings and consequent projections. The inner person controls the outer especially by reflecting inwardly on heaven and God, which brute animals are utterly incapable of doing. I have also been taught that there is a third level of life, utterly unknown to humanity, and that this is, notwithstanding, the level through which the Lord flows into the rational mind, giving it the ability of human thinking, giving it conscience, and giving it a perception of what is good and true and a raising up by the Lord toward Himself. But these facts are far removed from the concepts of the learned of our times, who only argue whether (the soul) exists, and meanwhile cannot know what it is, or even that it does exist.

3748.

There was one spirit who had been well known in learned circles while he lived on earth, a man with a subtle bent for confirming false perceptions, and quite dense as regarded things good and true. He tended to think (as he had before, on earth) that he knew everything, for people like that believe they are the wisest of all, that nothing escapes them; and their nature in the other life is the same as it was during their physical life. In fact, everything that is part of an individual's life—part, that is, of his love and affection—follows with him and dwells in him like a soul in a body, because he has formed his soul as to quality out of these materials.

This man who was by then a spirit came to me and talked with me. Since he was the kind of person just described, I asked him who was more intelligent, someone who knew a great many false things or someone who knew a little of the truth. He answered, "Someone who knows a little of the truth," because he thought that the false things he knew were true, and that this made him wise. Then he wanted to reason about the Universal Human and the inflow therefrom into the details of the human being. But since he did not understand anything about the subject, I kept asking him how he understood the fact that thought, which is spiritual, moves the whole face and determines its expression, that it also moves all the organs of speech quite distinctly according to a spiritual perception of one's thought, and that intention moves the muscles of the whole body, with all their thousands of widely distributed fibers, into a single action, when in each case something spiritual is doing the moving and something physical is being moved. However, he did not know what to answer.

I went on to talk about energy *(conatus)*, asking him whether he knew that energy produced acts and motions, that there must be energy within act and motion for them to occur and persist. He said he was not aware of this. So I asked him how he intended to reason when he did not even know the basics, and said that in this case the reasoning would be like scattered dust with no coherence. False principles would scatter it so completely that eventually he would not know anything and therefore would not believe anything.

3749.

There was a spirit who came to me unexpectedly and flowed into my head (spirits can be recognized by the parts of the body they flow into). I was wondering who he was and where he was from, but after he had been silent for a little while, some angels who were with me were saying that he had been selected from some spirits who were with a particular scholar now living on earth. He—the scholar—had gained an exceptional reputation for learning. Then there was granted through the mediation of that spirit a communication with the scholar's thought. I kept asking the spirit what concept the scholar had of the Universal Human and its inflow, and the consequent correspondence: he kept saying that he had none. Then I asked what concept he had of heaven. He said he did not have any except some slanderous ones, such as that the people there beat on musical instruments and in a kind of country style produced a sort of sound. Yet this man was highly esteemed, and people thought he knew what inflow was, what the soul was, and how it interacted with the body. People might even have thought that he knew more than others about heaven.

We can determine from this the kind of people who are teaching others nowadays—they use nothing but obstacles to what is good and true of faith, even though they put up a very different front.

3750.

I have also been shown vividly the kind of concept of heaven people have who are believed to have a special communication with heaven and therefore a special inflow. Some spirits who appeared above my head were people who on earth had wanted to be worshiped as gods. In them, love of self had been raised to the highest level of power and therefore to the highest level of unrestrained fancy. At the same time, they are cunning, under the guise of innocence and of love for the Lord. They seem to be high above the head as a result of an illusion of height, but they are actually under the feet, in hell. One of them was coming down to me: others said that he had been a high ranking clergyman on earth. He talked with me very mildly, first about Peter and his keys (which he thought he possessed). But when he was asked about the power of letting anyone he wanted into heaven, he had such a crude idea of heaven that he pictured it like a door that gave access. He said that he opened it freely to the poor, but that the rich were assessed and that what they offered was holy. I asked whether he believed that the people he admitted stayed there, and he answered that he did not know—if they didn't, then they left. He was told that he could not know the more inward nature of these people, whether they were worthy. They might be thieves destined for hell. He replied that this was no concern of his—if they were not worthy, then they could be expelled.

But he was informed what Peter's keys mean—namely a faith of love and charity, and since only the Lord gives such faith, it is the Lord alone who admits people to heaven. Peter does not appear to anyone; he is a simple spirit who has no more power than anyone else.

His only notion of the Lord was that He was to be worshiped to the extent that He granted this kind of power; but if He did not grant it, I could see that he thought the Lord should no longer be worshiped. Further, when I talked with him about the inner person, he had a foul concept of it.

I was shown vividly what a freedom, fullness, and pleasure of breathing he had had while he was sitting in solemn conclave on high, believing he was speaking from the Holy Spirit. He was assigned to the same state he had enjoyed there (for in the other life people can readily be assigned to any state of life they have had in the world since all the states of their lives remain after death) and the kind of breathing he then enjoyed was communicated to me. It was free, pleasant, gentle, steady, deep, filling the chest. But when he was contradicted, then there was something in his abdomen, an extension of his breathing, that seemed to be writhing and creeping. While he thought his pronouncements were divine, he perceived this from a kind of breathing that was quieter and, so to speak, agreeing.

I was then shown by whom such clergymen are controlled at these times, namely by a group of seductive women above the head, who have taken on a nature and life of insinuating themselves into the affections, of controlling a person's spirit, making him subservient to themselves, and finally of subverting him wholly to their purpose, using holiness and innocence as means. They are afraid of themselves and act cautiously, but given the chance they plunge into ruthless cruelty on their own behalf.

CHAPTER 2
The Heart and Lungs

3883.

We have already stated what the Universal Human is, and what correspondence with it is. The Universal Human is the entire heaven, which as a whole is a likeness and image of the Lord. Correspondence is between the Lord's divine and the heavenly and spiritual realities of heaven, and between the heavenly and spiritual realities there and the natural phenomena that are found in this world, primarily those in human beings. So it is a correspondence of the Lord's divine through heaven or the Universal Human with the human being and with the details of the human, even to the point that the human comes into being (that is, exists) as a result of it.

THE UNIVERSAL HUMAN

Since it is utterly unknown in this world that correspondence is between heaven or the Universal Human and the details within the human being, and that this is the source of humanity's coming into being and existence—so that the things that need to be said will seem like paradoxes, beyond belief—for this reason I am allowed to relate some things that are matters of experience and thereby, for me, of confirmed faith.

One time, when a more inward heaven was opened to me and I was talking with some angels there, I was allowed to witness the following. It should be realized that even though I was there, I was still not outside myself but in my body. Heaven is in fact within people wherever they may be; so when it pleases the Lord, an individual can be in heaven without being led out of his body.

As a result of this opening, I was allowed to perceive the most general workings of heaven as plainly as what I perceive by any other sense.

There were four workings that I perceived then. The first was into the cerebrum at the left temple, and was the general working related to organs of reason. The left part of the brain does in fact correspond to rational or discriminatory processes, while the right corresponds to affections or matters of purposing.

I perceived a second general working into the breathing of the lungs, which was gently leading my own breathing, but from within, so that I did not need to control my breath, or breathe, through any intent of my own. At that time the actual breathing of heaven was plainly perceptible to me. It is internal and therefore imperceptible to man, but it flows by a marvelous correspondence into human breathing, which is external or physical. Anyone cut off from this inflow would instantly fall dead.

The third working I perceived was into the systole and diastole of the heart, which were then gentler for me than under other circumstances. The beats were regular, about three to each breath, and yet by nature they came to a close in the respiratory and thereby governed the respiratory process. I was enabled to witness, in a way, how the rhythms of the heart insinuate themselves into the rhythms of the lungs at the close of each breath. The rhythms of the pulse were so evident that I could count them: they were distinct and gentle.

The fourth general working was into the loins. This I was also allowed to perceive, but dimly.

I could see from this that heaven or the Universal Human has a heartbeat and breathing. I could also see that the heartbeat of heaven or the Universal Human has a correspondence with the heart and with its systolic and dyastolic motions, and that the breathing of heaven or the Universal Human has a correspondence with the lungs and their breathing. But I could also see that both are beyond human observation, since they are imperceptible because they are internal.

3885.

Again, once when I was being led out of concepts that stem from the physical senses, a heavenly light appeared to me. This light itself led me further out of these concepts, since a spiritual life is inherent in heaven's light (cf. nn. 1524, 2776, 3167, 3195, 3339, 3636, 3642).

While I was in this light, physical and worldly things seemed to be below me—I was still noticing them, but as though they were rather remote from me, and did not belong to me. I then seemed to myself to be in heaven as to my head but not as to my body.

In this state, I was also enabled to observe the general breathing of heaven and what its quality was. It was more inward, effortless, spontaneous, and corresponded to mine in a ratio of about three to one. I was enabled to observe heaven's reciprocal heartbeats in the same way.

Then I was told by angels that this is the source of the heartbeat and breathing of each and every creature on earth. The reason the physical movements are not synchronous is that the heartbeat and the breathing of the lungs that occur in heaven descend into a kind of continuum and thereby into an energy; and the nature of that energy is such that it stimulates these motions in different ways depending on the state of each individual.

3886.

However, it needs to be realized that the variants of pulse and respiration in the heavens are manifold, as many as there are communities. They are in fact distributed according to their states of thought and affection, which in turn follow from states of faith and love. But the general pulse and the general respiration is as described above.

Again, I was once granted to observe the heartbeat of some people from the province of the occiput, attending separately to the pulses of the heavenly people there and the pulses of the spiritual people there. The pulses of the heavenly people were quiet and soft, while those of the spiritual ones were strong and vibrant. The ratio between the rhythm of the heavenly to that of the spiritual was about 5:2. The pulse of the heavenly people actually flowed into the pulse of the spiritual ones, moved out by this route, and crossed over into the world of nature.

It is also remarkable that the conversation of heavenly angels is not audible to spiritual angels, but is perceived in the guise of their heartbeat. This is because the conversation of heavenly angels is unintelligible to spiritual angels, since it occurs by means of affections, which are matters of love, while the conversation of spiritual angels occurs through intellectual concepts (see nn. 1647, 1759, 2157, 3343). The former belong to the province of the heart, the latter to that of the lungs.

3887.

In heaven or the Universal Human there are two kingdoms: one is called heavenly and the other spiritual. The heavenly kingdom is made up of angels who are called heavenly, and are the people who are involved in love for the Lord and thereby in all wisdom; for they especially are in a state of peace and innocence. They look to others like children because a state of peace and innocence presents this appearance. Everything they see seems to be alive, for whatever comes directly from the Lord is alive. This is the heavenly kingdom.

The other kingdom is called spiritual. In it dwell people who had lived in charity toward the neighbor, finding the joy of their lives in the ability to do good to others without recompense. Their recompense was the freedom to do good to others. The more this is their intent and longing, the more intelligence and happiness they find, for in the other life, everything is gifted with intelligence and wisdom according to the use he serves from purposeful affection. This is the spiritual kingdom.

The inhabitants of the Lord's heavenly kingdom all belong to the province of the heart; and the inhabitants of the spiritual kingdom all belong to the province of the lungs.

The inflow from the heavenly kingdom into the spiritual is arranged like that of the heart into the lungs—like the inflow of cardiac functions into pulmonary functions, then. The heart, that is, dominates through the entire body, in every detail, by means of the blood vessels, and the lungs also, in every detail, by means of respiration. So everywhere in the body there is a kind of inflow of the heart into the lungs, but differently depending on the forms in a given place, and their states. This is the source of all sensation, as well as all action, proper to the body.

This can be demonstrated in fetuses and newborn infants. These are incapable of physical sensation until their lungs are opened, and the inflow of the one into the other is thus established. It is much the same in the spiritual world, but with the difference that things there are not physical and natural but heavenly and spiritual, matters of the good of love and the good of faith. So for people in the spiritual world, the heartbeat depends on the state of their love, and the activity of breathing on the state of their faith. The inflow of the one into the other enables them to be spiritually active.

These matters cannot help but seem paradoxical to people in this world, because their only concept of the good of love and the truth of faith is that they are abstractions of some sort, powerless to accomplish anything. Yet the truth is quite the contrary: they are the source of all perception and sensation, all strength and activity, even in people on earth.

3888.

These two kingdoms are established in man by means of the two kingdoms that are within him—that is, the kingdom of intent and the kingdom of discernment. These two constitute the human mind, the actual human being, in fact. It is intent to which the heartbeat is responsive, and discernment to which the breathing is responsive. This is also why there are in the human body two kingdoms, of the heart and of the lungs. One who understands this can also understand the nature of the inflow of the good of love into the truth of faith and vice versa, and therefore the nature of human regeneration.

But people who are involved in strictly physical concepts—that is, in intent of evil and discernment of the false—cannot grasp these matters. In fact, they can think about spiritual and heavenly things only in sensory and physical terms. This means they can think only from darkness about things that are matters of heavenly light or the truth of faith, only from cold about things that are matters of heavenly flame or the good of love. Each of these, the darkness and the cold, so smothers heavenly and spiritual matters that they seem to them like nothing.

THE UNIVERSAL HUMAN

3889.

In order to learn not just the fact that there is a correspondence of heavenly things (matters of love) with heart motions and of spiritual things (matters of faith from love) with lung motions, but to learn also how this happens, I was allowed on one extraordinary occasion to be for some time among angels who presented this vividly.

By a marvelous flowing into circles, quite beyond the power of words to describe, they formed a likeness of a heart and a likeness of lungs, with all their inner and outer fibers. They were then following the flow of heaven freely, since heaven strives toward this kind of form because of the inflow of love from the Lord. In that way they presented the details within the heart and then a oneness between heart and lungs, which they also pictured by a marriage of the good and the true.

I could also see from this that the heart corresponds to what is heavenly, which is a matter of goodness, and the lungs to what is spiritual, which is a matter of truth. And I could see that the union of the two in material form is like that of heart and lungs. I was told that it is like this in the whole body—in the details of its members, organs, and viscera—with the things there that are connected with the heart and those that are connected with the lungs. In fact, anywhere the two are not active, each in its proper turn, there can be no motion of life on any voluntary basis and no feeling of life on any cognitive basis.

3890.

We have already stated several times that heaven or the Universal Human is divided into countless communities, broadly speaking as many as there are organs and viscera in the body, and that any given community belongs to one of these (cf. n. 3745 above). We have also stated that even though there are countless different communities, they still act as one, as all the parts of the body act as one despite their variety. The communities in heaven that belong to the province of the heart are heavenly communities and are in the center or in the inmost regions, while the communities in heaven that belong to the province of the lungs are spiritual, and are round about in the more outward regions. The inflow from the Lord comes through the heavenly ones into the spiritual ones, or through the center into the circumference—that is, through inmost things into more outward

91

things. This is because the Lord flows in through love or mercy—therefore through everything heavenly in His kingdom. And through love or mercy, He flows into the good of faith, therefore into everything spiritual in His kingdom. This He does with inexpressible variety; but the variety arises not from the inflow but from the way it is received.

3891.

 As to the fact that it is not just heaven that breathes as a single person, but also the particular communities together, and even all the angels and spirits, this has been made certain to me by many first-hand experiences, to the point that there is no doubt left me. Indeed, spirits are surprised if anyone is doubtful about this.

 However, few people have any concept of angels and spirits except as something insubstantial—as being only thought processes without substance, by no means people who enjoy the sense of sight, the sense of hearing, and the sense of touch. So they are even less capable of conceiving that angels and spirits have breathing and therefore a life like that of people on earth but more inward, like the life of a spirit compared to the life of a mortal. Because of this ignorance, I am allowed to cite some further experiences.

 I was once told in advance, before I went to bed, that there were many spirits plotting against me, to destroy my spirit *(animus)* by suffocation. However, I gave no heed to their threats because I was protected by the Lord. So I slept safely. But when I woke up in the middle of the night, I felt clearly that I was not breathing on my own, but from heaven. The breathing was not actually mine, but I was breathing.

 Beyond this, I have on countless occasions been allowed to sense the breathing or respiration of spirits and also of angels, and by this means to sense that they were breathing in me, and that my breathing was nevertheless real and distinct from theirs. But no one can feel this unless his more inward reaches have been opened, and a communication with heaven has thereby been afforded.

3892.

 I have been told by the earliest people, who were heavenly people and involved more than anyone else in a love for the Lord, that they did not have an outward breathing, like their descendants, but an inward one; and they breathed with the angels in whose

92

company they were, because they were involved in a heavenly love. I have also been told that the state of their breathing was in precise accord with the state of their love and consequent faith (on this topic see nn. 608, 805, 1118, 1119, 1120).

3893.

There were some choirs of angels who were rejoicing in the Lord together out of a heartfelt happiness. Sometimes the rejoicing sounded as though it were part of a soft song. Actually angels and spirits have resonant voices in each other's hearing, and are just as audible to each other as one person is to another on earth. But beside the sweetness and harmony of heavenly speech, human song has nothing to compare. I perceived from the variety of the sound that there were many choirs. I was informed by some angels who were with me that they belonged to the province of the lungs and their functions. They actually had their song because this is a proper function of the lungs. I was granted to know this by experience as well. They were allowed to flow into my breathing, which became so soft and gentle, and so inward as well, that I scarcely sensed my own breathing. I was also informed that the angels assigned to involuntary breathing are not the same ones assigned to voluntary breathing. I was told that the ones assigned to involuntary breathing become present when a person sleeps, because the moment someone goes to sleep, his voluntary breathing stops and his involuntary breathing starts.

3894.

Since the breathing of angels and spirits, as stated above at n. 3892, is in complete accord with their states of love and consequent faith, one community does not breathe in the same way as another. Further, evil people, who are involved in a love of self and the world, cannot be in the company of good ones. Rather, as they approach them, they seem to themselves to be unable to breathe, almost to suffocate. As a result, they fall half dead like rocks all the way into hell, where they regain the ability to breathe that they hold in common with the people there. This enables us to conclude that people who are involved in what is evil and false cannot be in the Universal Human or heaven, when their breathing actually begins to stop as they draw near. They also then begin to lose all their attentiveness and thought and also all their energy to do evil and to convince of falsity. And with this energy dies all their vital activity and motion, so that they have no recourse but to dive down from there headlong.

3894.

Because of this, when even upright people arrive in the other life, they are first returned to the kind of life they had in the world (n. 2119)—into the loves and pleasures of that life, then. So not until they have been prepared can they be in the company of angels, even as to breathing. For this reason, when they are being prepared, they are first led into the angelic life through harmonies in breathing, and then at the same time they come into more inward perceptions and into a heavenly freedom. This happens in community with many, or in choirs, where one person breathes like another when he perceives like another and acts similarly from freedom. How this happens I have also been shown at firsthand.

3895.

In the other life, one characteristic of a persuasiveness to what is evil and false—even a persuasiveness to the truth when the person is involved in an evil life—is that it virtually suffocates other people, including upright spirits before they have been led into heavenly breathing. So people who are involved in persuasiveness are removed by the Lord and kept in hell. There they cannot hurt each other because the persuasivess of one person is so like that of another that their breathing agrees.

Some individuals who had this kind of persuasiveness came to me to suffocate my spirit *(animus)* and did indeed inflict a measure of suffocation; but I was set free by the Lord. Then a child was sent by the Lord, at whose presence they were so tormented that they could scarcely breathe. They were kept in this state until they were reduced to pleading, and in this way they were driven down into hell.

It is characteristic of a persuasiveness to truth when a person is involved in a life of evil that it convinces him that the truth is true not for good purpose but for evil purpose—specifically, as a means of gaining prestige, renown, and wealth. The worst people of all can have this kind of persuasiveness, even an apparent zeal so strong that they consign to hell everyone who does not have the truth, even though they may be involved in good (on this persuasiveness, see nn. 2689, 3865). When people like this first arrive in the other life, they believe they are angels; but they cannot come close to any angelic community without being virtually suffocated by their own persuasiveness. These are the people the Lord was talking about in Matthew: "Many will say to me in that day, 'Lord, Lord have we not prophesied through your name, and driven out demons through your name, and done many fine deeds in your name?' But then I will confess to them, 'I do not know you. Depart from me, you who work iniquity.'"

CHAPTER 3
The Cerebrum and the Cerebellum

4039.

Having just discussed the correspondence of the heart and lungs with the Universal Human or heaven, we should now discuss the correspondence of the cerebrum and the cerebellum, and of the medullae that are connected with them. But before dealing with the correspondence, we need to present some information about the general form of the cerebrum, its source, and what it pictures.

4040.

When the cerebrum is uncovered from the skull and the membranes that surround it, one sees marvelous convolutions and curves, in which are placed the substances called "cortical." From these, the fibers extend that constitute the medulla of the cerebrum. These fibers continue on from the medulla through the nerves into the body, and there perform their functions according to the will and choice of the cerebrum.

All these connections are in precise accord with the heavenly form. This kind of form is actually stamped on the heavens by the Lord, and consequently this kind of form is stamped on the inner elements of the human, especially on its cerebrum and cerebellum.

4041.

Heaven's form is awesome, and utterly surpasses all human understanding. It in fact is far loftier than any concepts of form that anyone can possibly grasp even by analysis of earthly matters. All the heavenly communities are arranged according to this form. And marvelous as it is, there is an orbiting according to the forms, which angels and spirits do not feel. It is like the earth's daily rotation on its axis and its annual orbit of the sun, which its inhabitants do not notice.

I have been shown what the heavenly form is like in a lower sphere. It is like the form of the convolutions we see in the human cerebrum. I was allowed to see this rotation or these orbits graphically. This lasted for several days. I could see from this that the brain is formed in accord with the form of heaven's rotation. But deeper regions of the brain, which are not visible to the eye, are in accord with the forms of more inward heavens, which are wholly beyond comprehension. I was also told by angels that this enables us to see that man was created in accord with the forms of these heavens, and that in this way an image of heaven was stamped on him, so that man is a tiny heaven in miniature. I was also told that this is the source of his correspondence with the heavens.

4042.

This is why it is only through humanity that there is a descending from the heavens into the world and an ascending from the world into the heavens. It is the cerebrum and its inner reaches through which the descending and ascending occur. There we find the basic essentials, the first and final ends, from which flows and derives each and every thing in the body. There too we find the source of thoughts, which are proper to discernment, and of affections, which are proper to intent.

4043.

The reason the more inward forms (which are also more universal) are, as we have said, beyond comprehension is that the use of the word *forms* connotes a concept of space and of time. Yet in the inner reaches where heaven is, nothing is perceived by means of space and time because these are proper to the realm of nature. Perception occurs rather by means of states and their differences and changes. However, since the differences and changes cannot be grasped by people on earth apart from concepts of form—as we have said, apart from matters of space and time, even though things like this do not exist in the heavens—we can conclude how incomprehensible these things are, and how inexpressible. All the human words we must use to express and to comprehend these matters are inadequate to explain them because the words involve natural phenomena. In the heavens, subjects like this are presented by using variations of heavenly light and heavenly flame, which come from the Lord. This is done so well and so fully that thousands upon thousands of perceptions can scarcely fit into anything perceptible to people on earth.

However, heavenly realities are pictured in the world of spirits by forms to which the forms we see in this world do bear some resemblance.

4044.

"Representations" are simply images of spiritual things in natural ones, and when the former are properly represented in the latter, then they "correspond." However, if someone does not know what the spiritual is, only the natural, he may think that such representations and consequent correspondences cannot occur. He may in fact say to himself, "How can something spiritual act into something material?" But if he is willing to reflect on what is going on inside himself at every moment, he can gain some concept of these matters. Let him observe, that is, how his intent can act into the muscles of his body and give rise to substantive actions. Let him also observe how his thinking can act into his organs of speech, moving his lungs, trachea, throat, tongue, and lips, and giving rise to speech. Then let him observe how his affections can act into his face and present their images there, so that often someone else can tell what he is thinking and intending. These phenomena afford some concept of representations and correspondences.

Now, since these things are observable in human beings, and since there is nothing that can endure on its own, only from something else, and from something behind that, and ultimately from a First, all by the linking of correspondences—since this is the case, anyone gifted with more than average judgment can conclude that there is a correspondence between humanity and heaven and, further, between heaven and the Lord, who is the First.

4045.

Correspondence being of this nature, and heaven being divided into many smaller heavens, these into still smaller ones, and being divided throughout into communities, there are heavens that reflect the cerebrum and the cerebellum in general. Further, within those heavens there are heavens that reflect the parts or members within the brains—the dura mater for example, and the soft or pia mater, the sinuses, and the bodies and hollows in them: the corpus callosum, the corpora striata, smaller glands, ventricles, infundibulum, and so on. The nature of the heavens that reflect one or another of these facts has been disclosed to me, as will be shown below.

4046.

A number of spirits appeared in the middle distance above my head, acting in a general way by means of my heartbeat, but it was a kind of alternating wave motion, up and down, with a kind of cold breath on my forehead. I could determine from this that they were of an intermediate kind, belonging to the province of both the heart and the lungs, and also that they were not particularly internal spirits.

Later, these same spirits presented a flaming light, coarse but still luminous, that first appeared under the left side of my chin, then under my left eye, then above the eye. It was dim, but still flaming, not bright, which enabled me to know their quality. For lights signal affections and also levels of intelligence.

Later, when I put my hand to the left side of my skull or head, I felt a pulse under my palm, with the same kind of up-and-down wave motion. I knew from this clue that they belonged to the cerebrum. When I asked who they were, they were unwilling to talk. I was told by some others that they did not talk readily. When they were eventually impelled to speak, they said that this would disclose their quality. I perceived that they were some of the spirits who make up the province of the dura mater, which is the general covering of the cerebrum or cerebellum. Then their quality was disclosed, for it was possible to tell this from talking with them.

When they lived on earth, they were people who gave no thought to spiritual and heavenly matters, who did not discuss them, because by nature they did not believe that anything existed beyond the realm of nature. This was because they were unable to penetrate beyond nature, though they would not admit it. Still, like other people, they worshiped the divine, set aside time for prayers, and were good citizens.

Later there were others who also flowed into my pulse, but with a horizontal wave motion rather than a vertical one. Then there were still others who did not flow alternately, but more continuously, and others as well by whom my pulse was impelled to skip from one location to another. They said that they reflected the lamella outside the dura mater, and that they were of the sort who thought about spiritual and heavenly matters only on the basis of things like the objects of the outer senses, with no other means of grasping deeper subjects. They sounded to me as though they were feminine.

If people reason about matters of heaven or spiritual matters of faith and love on the basis of outer, sensory criteria, especially worldly and earthly ones, then the more they unite and confuse them, the farther outward they move, even to the outer skin of the head, which they portray. Still, they are within the Universal Human, even though they are its very borders, if they lived a life of good. In fact, every individual who is involved in a life of good out of an affection of charity is saved.

4047.

Some other spirits also appeared above my head, whose general action flowing in above my head was fluid, crossing from front to back. Others also appeared whose inflowing action was from each temple toward the center of the cerebrum. I perceived that these were spirits who belonged to the province of the pia mater, which is the other covering and more closely clothes the cerebrum and the cerebellum, communicating with them by strands extending from it.

I was allowed to know what they were like from their speech, since they did talk with me. They were the same as they had been in the world, not placing much reliance on their own thinking and thereby disciplining themselves to think about holy matters within certain fixed limits, but relying on the faith of others and not troubling whether something was true. I was also shown that this was their nature, through the inflow of their perception into the Lord's Prayer when I read it; for the nature of all spirits and angels without exception can be known from the Lord's Prayer, specifically by the inflow of their thoughts and affections into the contents of the prayer. In this way, too, I perceived that they were of this kind, especially that they could serve angels as means. There are in fact intermediate spirits between the heavens, through whom communication takes place. Their concepts are actually not closed, but unlocked, so they let themselves be guided and readily admit and accept inflow. They were particularly temperate and peace-loving and they said they were in heaven.

4048.

There was a particular spirit near my head who talked with me. I perceived from the tone that he was in a state of tranquillity, as though of a kind of peaceful sleep. He asked me this and that, but with a care that no watchman could surpass. I perceived that more internal angels were speaking through him, and that he was in a state to perceive and relay. I asked about this state and told him that he was exhibiting this kind of state. He answered that he spoke nothing but what was good and true, and that he noticed if it were not. If anything else were to flow in, he would not let it in or convey it. He described his state as peaceful, and I was also allowed to perceive him through the communication. I was told that this kind of spirit reflects the sinus or larger blood vessel in the cerebrum. They resemble the ones who reflect the longitudinal sinus between the two hemispheres of the cerebrum; and there they are in a calm state no matter how disturbed the cerebrum may be on either side.

4049.

There were some spirits above my head, slightly in front, who talked with me. They talked pleasantly, and flowed in quite gently. They differed from the others in their constant longing and desire to enter heaven. I was told that this is the nature of the spirits who reflect the ventricles or larger hollows of the cerebrum, and belong to that province. The reason was also given that it is the nature of the better kind of lymph, which is in this area, to go back into the cerebrum, which gives it this kind of impulse. The cerebrum is heaven, the impulse is the longing and desire: that is what correspondences are like.

4050.

A particular face appeared to me first, above a blue window, and the face soon took itself into itself. Then I saw some little stars around the region of the left eye, then some more little stars, reddish with a white sparkle. Afterward I saw a wall, but not a complete one. It was a wall only on the left side; at the end it was like a star-studded sky. Since I saw this in a place where there were evil people, I thought it was something foul that was being cast up for me to see. But shortly the wall and the sky disappeared, and a well appeared with a kind of white cloud or vapor coming out of it. It also seemed as though something were being drawn out of the well.

I asked what this meant and pictured. I was told that it was a representation of the infundibulum in the cerebrum, above which was the cerebrum meant by the sky. What I then saw was that vessel meant by the well and called the infundibulum; and the cloud or vapor coming from it was the lymph that passed through it and was drawn from it. This lymph is of two kinds, one mixed with animal spirits and included among the useful lymphs, and the other mixed with puslike substances and included among the excretory lymphs.

Then I was shown what the spirits are like who belong to this province, but only those of the worst sort. I also saw them. They run hither and yon, busy themselves with whatever they see; they pay attention to details and announce what they hear to others. They tend to be suspicious; they are impatient, restless—in imitation of that lymph which is inside and goes back and forth. Their reasoning processes are the fluids there that portray them. These, however, are of the intermediate kind.

The ones that reflect the excretory lymphs are spirits who bring spiritual truths down to earthly ones and there pollute them. For example, when they hear anything about marriage love they associate it with wanton behavior and adultery, thereby dragging principles of marriage love down to this level, and they do the same with other subjects. They appeared in front, at some distance, toward the right. But the good ones are like the ones described just above (n. 4049).

4051.

There are communities that reflect the region in the cerebrum called the isthmus, and communities also that reflect the fibrous nodes in the cerebrum that look like glands, and have fibers going out for various functions. These fibers act as one in their beginnings, the small glands, but in different ways at their termini.

I was shown one community to which these kinds of features responded, and would note the following. The spirits came in front of me and addressed me, saying that they were people. I was given to answer to them that they were not people equipped with bodies, but were spirits. So they were still people, since everything spiritual strives toward what is human, even toward a form like that of a person equipped with a body. The spirit is actually the inner person. Further, since people are people by virtue of their intelligence and wisdom, and not by virtue of their shape, good spirits and especially angels are people more than are people in physical bodies, because they are more in the light of wisdom.

After I had given this answer, they said that there were many of them in their community, no two alike. But since it seemed to me impossible that there be a community of unlike people in the other life, I talked with them about this. Eventually I was taught that even though they were unlike, they were together as to their goal, which was the same for them all. They went on to say that it was characteristic of them that each one behaved differently from the others and also talked differently, and yet their intentions and thoughts were similar. They also illustrated this with an example. When one member of the community talked about an angel as the smallest aspect of heaven, another said an angel was the greatest aspect, and a third that an angel was neither the smallest nor the greatest. So they talked with a great deal of diversity because their thinking was united. For they were thinking that whoever wants to be smallest is greatest, and that he is therefore greatest in a relative sense, and yet neither smallest nor greatest because they are not thinking about eminence. The same holds true in other areas. So they are together in principles, but behave differently in the most outward things.

They attached themselves to my ear, and said that they were good spirits and that this was their usual style of speaking. I was told that no one knows where they come from, and they are wanderers among the communities.

4052.

Further, it is characteristic of the correspondence of the cerebrum with the Universal Human that spirits who are involved in principles of what is good reflect those parts of the cerebrum that are its fundamentals, and are called glands or cortical substances. In contrast, people who are involved in principles of what is true reflect those parts of the cerebrum that derive from these fundamentals and are called fibers. But there is still this distinction: the spirits who correspond to the right part of the cerebrum are the ones involved in the intent of good and derivatively in the intent of what is true; while the ones who correspond to the left part of the cerebrum are the ones involved in discernment of what is good and true and derivatively in an affection for these things. This is because the people in heaven who are on the Lord's right are the ones who are involved in what is good on the basis of intention, while the ones on the Lord's left are involved in what is good on the basis of discernment. The former are the ones called heavenly, the latter the ones called spiritual.

THE UNIVERSAL HUMAN

4053.

No one until now has recognized that correspondences like this exist, and I know that people will wonder when they hear. This is because they have not known what the inner person is in the spiritual world and the outer in the natural, or that it is the inner person that is alive within the outer, flows into it, and governs it. They could still, on the basis of these facts and those presented in n. 4044 above, know that inflow and correspondence do exist.

The truth of this is most familiar in the other life, as is the fact that the natural is nothing but a picture of the spiritual from which it comes into being and endures. So too is the fact that the natural portrays the spiritual in the manner in which it is responsive to it.

4054.

The cerebrum, like heaven, is in a sphere of goals that are uses. Everything that flows in from the Lord is in fact a goal that looks toward the salvation of the human race. This is the goal that rules in heaven and that consequently rules in the cerebrum as well. The cerebrum, where the human mind dwells, looks toward goals in the body—specifically, that the body serve the soul and that the soul be happy to eternity.

But there are communities that have no useful goals, only to be with friends of both sexes and to have a good time. So their inhabitants are completely self-indulgent and care about nothing but sex. Whether at home or in public, they seek the same goal. There are more communities of spirits like this nowadays than anyone would believe.

The moment they impinge, their sphere is activated, and they smother the affections in other people for what is true and good. Once these have been smothered, then the people are caught up in a delight in these spirits' friendship. These are blockages in the cerebrum, and they bring about forms of stupidity in it.

Communities of spirits like this have been with me, and I have perceived their presence by a lassitude, sloth, and loss of affections. I have talked with them several times. They are annoying and vicious even though on earth they had seemed good, pleasant, witty, and clever in public life. For they are skilled in civility and ingratiation, especially in the area of friendship. They neither know nor want to know what a friend to the good is or what friendship to the good is.

Their lasting lot is a sad one. At the end, they live in squalor, and in such stupidity that there is, as far as anyone can tell, scarcely anything human left to them. For the goal makes the person—like purpose, like person—especially the kind of human nature an individual will have after death.

4218.

In the preceding pages, some of the things I have been granted to see and perceive in the world of spirits and the heavens of angels have been related, followed by material on the Universal Human and correspondence. We continue now on the subject of Universal Human, the purpose being a fuller knowledge of the nature of man—the reality of the link with heaven, not only as to affections and thoughts, but also as to organic forms, both outer and inner. Without that link, humanity would not last for a moment.

4219.

To know in general terms what the Universal Human is like, we must maintain that the whole heaven is the Universal Human because it corresponds to the Lord's divine-human. The only real person is the Lord, and the amount that angels or spirits or people on earth have from the Lord determines how human they are. Let no one believe that a person is a person by virtue of having a human face and a human body, a human brain, human viscera and members. These we have in common with dumb animals, so these are what die and become a corpse. A person is a person by virtue of the ability to think and intend like a person, thus to accept things that are divine, or that are the Lord's. This is how humanity is distinguished from beasts and wild animals. Further, the quality a person takes on in the other life is the quality of the things that have been made part of him by his acceptance of them during physical life.

4220.

People who have accepted divine things, which are the Lord's, during their physical life (that is, who have accepted His love toward the whole human race, and specifically charity toward the neighbor, and have accepted a mutual love for the Lord) are given intelligence and wisdom in the other life, and an indescribable happiness; for they become angels, which means they truly become people.

But as for people who have not accepted divine things, which are the Lord's during their physical life (that is, who have not accepted a love for the human race, let alone a mutual love for the Lord, but have loved themselves exclusively, to the point of self-worship, and whose goals have therefore been selfish and worldly), after undergoing brief courses of living in the other life, they are deprived of all their intelligence, become extremely stupid, and live in the spiritual world with the people who are hellish and stupid.

4221.

To learn this I have been allowed to talk with people who had lived like that, even with one I had known during his physical life. While he lived on earth, whatever good he did for a neighbor was done in his own interest—for his own prestige and profit, to be precise. He looked down on other people and even had a hatred of them. He did acknowledge God verbally, but not at heart.

When I was allowed to talk with him, an almost physical sphere was drifting out of him. His speech was not like spirits' speech but like that of people still living on earth. For the speech of spirits differ from human speech in being full of concepts, or having a spiritual content, so alive that it cannot be expressed, while human speech is not like that.

This kind of sphere was drifting out of him, and was perceptible in everything he said. He was to be found there among the worthless, and I was told that people like this gradually become so coarse and stupid in their thoughts and affections that no one on earth is more stupid than they. They have a place under the buttocks, where their hell is. Another individual from the same area had also appeared to me earlier, not in the guise of a spirit, but in the guise of a coarsely physical man, with so little of the life of intelligence that is properly human that you would call him the very image of stupidity. I could see from this the nature of people who have no involvement in love toward the neighbor or society in general, let alone toward the Lord's kingdom, but are involved only in self-love, focusing on themselves in everything, actually worshiping themselves like gods and wanting to be revered by others. This is their effort in everything they do.

4222.

On this correspondence of the Universal Human with the parts of the human body, it is a correspondence with each and every part— with its organs, members, and viscera. It is so complete that there is no organ or member in the body, no part in any organ or member, not even a tiny part of a part, with which there is no correspondence.

It is recognized that every organ and every member in the body is made up of parts and of parts of parts. Take the brain, for example. In general, this consists of the cerebrum, the cerebellum, the medulla oblongata, and the spinal medulla, this last being a continuation or a kind of appendix. Yet the cerebrum itself consists of many members that are its parts, namely the membranes called the dura mater and the pia mater, the corpus callosum, the corpora striata, the ventricles and hollows, the lesser glands, and the septa. It consists generally of gray matter and medullary matter, with sinuses, blood vessels, and ganglia.

The same is true of the body's sensory and motor organs and the viscera, as is sufficiently familiar from anatomical studies.

All of these, in general and in specific, correspond very precisely to the Universal Human, and in the same measure, so to speak, to the heavens. In fact, the Lord's heaven is similarly divided into smaller heavens, these into still smaller ones, and these into the smallest. Ultimately it is divided into angels, each of whom is a miniature heaven corresponding to the greatest one. These heavens are quite distinct from each other, each belonging to its own general part, and the general heavens to the most general or the whole, which is the Universal Human.

4223.

It is indeed characteristic of correspondence that the particular heavens mentioned correspond to the actual organic forms of the human body, which is why we say that certain communities or certain angels belong to the province of the brain or the province of the heart or to the province of the lungs or to the province of the eye, and so on. However, they correspond primarily to the functions of those viscera or organs.

It is the same as it is with the organs or viscera themselves—the functions make one with their organic forms. In fact, a function is inconceivable apart from forms—that is, substances, which are actually the subsidiary means. For example, sight is inconceivable apart from the eye, and breathing apart from the lungs. The eye is the organic form that is the basis and means of sight, and the lungs are the organic form that is the basis and means of breathing, and the same holds true elsewhere.

THE UNIVERSAL HUMAN

So it is the function to which heavenly communities primarily correspond, and since it is the functions, it is also the organic forms to which they correspond. For form and function are inalienable, inseparable, to the point that it scarcely matters whether you speak of the function or of the organic form through which and from which the function occurs. This is why correspondence is with organs, members, and viscera—because it is with their functions. So when a function is called forth, its organ is stimulated.

The same holds for anything a person does. When someone wants to do something or other in some manner or other, and thinks about it, then the organs move in accord. They move, that is, according to the direction of the function or use. It is the use that controls the forms.

We can also see from this that uses existed before the organic forms of the body, and that the uses produced the forms and fitted them to themselves, not vice versa. But once the forms have been produced, the organs adapted, then uses emanate from them; and then it seems as though the forms or organs were prior to the uses. Yet this is not the case. Use flows in from the Lord, which happens through heaven according to the design and form in which heaven has been structured by the Lord—according to correspondences, that is. Humanity comes into being in this way; humanity is maintained in being in this way. We can also see from this why the human being corresponds to the heavens in each and every detail.

4224.

The organic forms are not just the ones visible to the eye or discernible through microscopes. There are also still purer organic forms that cannot in any way be discerned by the naked eye or by the technically assisted eye. These are more inward forms, like the forms that are proper to inner sight and thus to discernment. They are unfathomable, and yet they are forms—that is, substances. No sight, even mental, can occur except from some such form.

This too is recognized in the learned world, that apart from some substance as subject, there is no mode or modification or attribute that actively presents itself. The purer or more inward forms, the unfathomable ones, are the foundations of the inner senses and produce the more inward affections. With these forms the more inward heavens correspond, because they correspond with their senses and with the affections of their senses.

But since so many things have been disclosed to me about these forms and their correspondence, I cannot explain them clearly without going into considerable detail. So in the following pages, by the Lord's divine mercy, I may continue the discussion of the correspondence of man with the Universal Human begun above. The goal is that people may know, not from logic or from hypothesis but from actual experience, what the situation is in this regard and in regard to their inner person called the soul—ultimately then in regard to their union with heaven and through heaven with the Lord. So they may know what makes people human and how they differ from animals, and eventually how people themselves cut themselves off from this union and unite themselves with hell.

4225.

At the outset, we need to say who are within the Universal Human and who are outside. All people who are involved in a love for the Lord and in charity toward the neighbor, and who do the neighbor good, from the heart, responding to the neighbor's welfare, and who have a conscience as to what is just and fair—all these are within the Universal Human. They are in fact in the Lord, specifically in heaven.

In contrast, all people who are involved in love of self and love of the world and thereby in cravings, who do what is good solely because of the laws, their own prestige, worldly wealth and consequent renown, who are therefore inwardly ruthless, caught in hatred and vindictiveness against their neighbor for the sake of themselves and the world, who delight in his misfortunes when he does not favor them—all these are outside the Universal Human, and are actually in hell. These do not correspond to any organs or members within the body, but to various extraneous flaws and diseases, which too we will by the Lord's divine mercy discuss below.

If people are outside the Universal Human—that is, outside heaven—they cannot enter it, since their lives are opposed to it. In fact, if they do by some means gain entrance (which sometimes happens with people who learned to imitate angels of light during their physical life), once they arrive, these people who are pretending to be angels of light can stay only a few moments. They are allowed access in order that their quality may be known, but they are admitted only to the first entryway, to people who are still simple and not fully instructed. They can stay only a few moments because a life is presei.t there of love for the Lord and charity toward the neighbor. And because nothing there corresponds to their life, they are barely able to breathe (for the fact that spirits and angels also breathe, cf. nn. 3884–3893). So they begin to choke, since breathing depends on freedom of life. Remarkably enough, eventually they can barely move: they become like women in labor, seized inwardly by contractions and pains. So they hurl themselves, out headlong, all the way to hell, where they do have breathing and freedom of movement. This is why life in the Word is pictured by movement.

But the people who are within the Universal Human have a freedom of breathing when they are involved in the good of their love. Yet they are all different as regards the quality and amount of the good, which is why there are so many heavens, called "mansions" in the Word (Jn 14:2). Each individual is in his own heaven when involved in his own life, and has an inflow from the whole heaven. Each person there is a center of the inflows of all and is therefore in the most perfect balance. This depends on the incredible form of heaven, which comes from the Lord alone; so it happens in all variety.

4226.

Once there were complaints from some recently arrived spirits who had been inwardly evil while they lived in the world, but had striven for an outward appearance of goodness by doing things for others, with themselves and the world in mind. They complained that they were not being let into heaven. The only notion of heaven they actually had was one of admission out of grace.

At one point, they were told that no one is denied heaven, and that they could be let in if they wished. Some of them were allowed to enter heavenly communities nearest the entrance; but when they arrived, because of the opposition and repulsion of life, they felt the breath stoppage, constriction, and virtually hellish torment we have mentioned. They hurled themselves out, claiming that for them, heaven was hell, and that they had never believed heaven was like that.

4227.

There are many people, of both sexes, who during their physical lives characteristically tried whenever they could to gain power over other people's spirits by craft and subterfuge, with the goal of dominating them. They sought their victims especially among the influential and wealthy in order to be the sole rulers under their names. They worked secretly, and removed others, especially honest people, by various means, though not by outright defamation because they did stand up for honesty. Rather, they used other means—subverting their plans, referring to them as simplistic or even evil, blaming them for things that might go wrong, and other similar devices.

People who were like that during their physical life are the same in the other life, for everyone's life follows with him. This I have ascertained by firsthand experience of people like this while they were with me, because they were still behaving the same way, but even more skillfully and adroitly. For spirits act more subtly than earthly people, because they have been freed from connections with the body and from bonds with the cruder modes of sensation. They were so subtle that sometimes I did not perceive that their purpose or goal was one of dominance; and when they were talking to each other, they were careful that I did not hear, and perceive this. But I was told by others who did hear them that their plans were unspeakable, that they were working out how to reach their goal by the use of magical skills, with the aid, that is, of the devilish mob. They regarded the murder of honest people as trifling. They claimed that they wanted to rule under the Lord's aegis, but they trivialized Him, regarding Him only as another mortal, offered worship as happens in other nations where mortals have been deified and worshiped, leftovers from antiquity. They did not dare to speak out against Him because they had been born in that worship and they would harm their reputations.

I can say this much about them, that they lay seige to the thoughts and intent of similar folk and insinuate themselves into their affections and purpose, so that if it were not for the Lord's mercy, one could never know that such spirits were present, that he was in the company of spirits of this sort.

These spirits correspond to impurities in that purer blood in people which is called the blood of the life-spirit. There is no pattern to the way these impurities enter, and they spread in all directions. They are like poisons that bring on coldness and numbness in the nerves and fibers, leading to the outbreak of the most critical and fatal diseases.

When they are acting in consort, their hallmark is that they go on all fours, so to speak, and sneak into the back part of the head, under the cerebellum on the left. The spirits that work underneath the occiput do in fact work more secretively than others, and the ones who work at the back crave dominion.

They argued with me about the Lord, and said it was strange that He did not hear their prayers when they prayed, and so did not help suppliants. But I was given to reply that they cannot be heard because the kinds of things they have as goals are contrary to the salvation of the human race and because they pray for themselves against others. When they pray like this, heaven is closed. In fact, the inhabitants of heaven pay attention only to the purposes of the people praying. They really did not want to admit this, but they still could find no answer to it.

There were some men of this sort, in company with some women. They said that they could gain better advice from women, because they were quicker and more skillful at perceiving such matters. They enjoyed especially the company of the women who were prostitutes.

People like this devote themselves excessively to secret arts and magic in the other life, for there are many magical arts in the other life that are utterly unknown in this world. It is in their nature that the moment such people arrive in the other life, they devote themselves to them and learn to bewitch the people around them, especially the people they want to rule under. They do not shrink from unspeakable practices.

I will speak elsewhere about their hell, what it is like, and where they are when they are not in the world of spirits. We can determine from this that everyone's life stays with him after death.

CHAPTER 4
The Senses

Section 1.   *The Senses in General*

4318.

The pinnacle of angels' intelligence is to know and perceive that all life comes from the Lord and that heaven in its entirety corresponds to this divine-human, with the consequence that all angels, spirits, and people correspond to heaven. Then it is to know and perceive how they correspond. On this basis they know and perceive countless things that are in the heavens and also things that are in this world. For the things that occur in this world and its realm of nature are causes and effects deriving from the heavens as their origins. In fact, the whole realm of nature is a theater where the Lord's kingdom is portrayed.

4319.

An abundance of experience has shown me that neither people nor spirits nor even angels think or speak or act on their own, but rather from others. Nor are these others independent—they depend on still others, and so on. So each and every one depends on the first source of life, namely the Lord, no matter how independent they may seem.

This has often been demonstrated to spirits who during their physical life had confirmed a belief that they were complete in and of themselves, or that they thought and spoke and acted on their own, from their own souls, in which life seemed to be inherent. I have also been shown by firsthand experiences (kinds that happen in the other life but cannot happen in this world) that evil people think and intend and act from hell, and good people from heaven, that is, through heaven from the Lord. Still their evil or good deeds alike seem to come from themselves.

Christians know this on the basis of doctrinal information drawn from the Word, namely that evil deeds come from the devil and good deeds from the Lord, but there are few who believe it. And since they do not believe it, they make their own the evil things they are thinking and intending and doing. But the good things are not made their own, for if people believe they themselves are the source of good things they lay claim to them, take credit for them, and so place merit in them. They do also know, from doctrinal information within the church, that no one can do anything good on his own, to the point that anything that stems from self or the self-image (*proprio*) is evil, no matter how good it seems. But this too few people believe, even though it is true.

There were some people who had convinced themselves of the notion that they lived independently, especially that what they thought and intended and did came from themselves. When they were shown that the actual situation was precisely as described by doctrine, they stated that they did not believe it. However, they were told that knowing is not believing. Believing is internal, and can only happen within an affection for what is good and true. So it can only happen to people who are involved in the good of charity toward the neighbor. Since these spirits were evil, they maintained that now they believed because they saw. But they were explored by means of an experience common in the other life, being examined by angels.

When they were examined, it seemed as though the tops of their heads were removed, and that their brains were covered with hair and full of darkness. I could see from this what people are like inwardly whose faith is based only on information, not on truth, and I could see that knowing is not believing. If people do know and believe, their heads look human, their brains seem neat, snow-white, and bright, since heavenly light is being received by them.

But if people only know, and think that they therefore believe, because they are living in evil, the heavenly light is not being received by them. So they are not receiving the intelligence and wisdom inherent in that light. So when they approach angelic communities, which means approaching heavenly light, it is turned into darkness for them. This is why their brains seem to be full of darkness.

4320.

The reason the life that comes from the Lord alone seems to every individual to be within himself stems from the Lord's love or mercy toward the whole human race. He wants us all to make what is His our own, and to give us all happiness to eternity. It is recognized that love gives over its own to others. It actually establishes itself in the other and makes itself present there. What about divine love, then?

As for even evil people receiving the life that comes from the Lord, this is like objects in the world all of which get light and therefore their colors from the sun, but according to their own forms. Objects that stifle and corrupt the light look dingy and dirty. They are actually getting their dingy and dirty colors from the sunlight. This is like light or life from the Lord in evil people. But this life is not life: it is, as people say, spiritual death.

4321.

Even though these matters seem paradoxical and unbelievable to people, they still should not be rejected because experience itself demands it. If everything were denied whose cause was unknown, this would mean the denial of countless things that occur in the realm of nature, of whose causes we know scarcely the thousandth part. There are so many major mysteries in nature that what we know is practically nothing compared to what we do not know. What then about the mysteries that occur in that sphere which is above nature—in the spiritual world?

Take, for example, the fact that there is a single life only, and that all creatures live from it, no two in the same way. Take the fact that even evil people, even the hells, are living from the same life. Take the fact that the inflowing life acts variously, depending on the way it is received. Take the fact that heaven is so structured by the Lord that it reflects a person, and is therefore called the Universal Human so that the very details of the earthly human correspond to it. Take the fact that without the inflow into their inner specifics, people could not survive for a moment. Take the fact that all the inhabitants of the Universal Human have a fixed location according to their quality and according to the state of the good and the true they are in. Take the fact that location there is not location but state, so that invariably people on the left appear on the left, people on the right appear on the right, people in front appear in front, people in back appear in back, at the level of the head, chest, back, loins, feet, above the head or beneath the soles of the feet, straight out or at an angle, nearer or farther—they are where they are, no matter what direction a spirit may turn. Take the fact that the Lord as the sun invariably appears on the right, at a middle elevation there, a little above the level of the right eye, and that everything there is oriented toward the Lord as the sun, as the center, so to the only source of emergence and survival. And because everyone there appears in the Lord's sight in a constant location that depends on his state as to what is good and true, the specifics therefore appear in similar fashion. This is because the Lord's life—the Lord, in fact—dwells within everyone in heaven. And there are countless other mysteries besides.

4322.

Who nowadays does not believe that people are produced from sperm and egg in accord with natural law, and that inherent in the sperm from first creation is the power of reproducing itself in such forms, first within the egg, then within the womb, and later outside—and that it is no longer the divine that accomplishes this?

The reason for this belief is that no one knows that there is any inflow from heaven (that is, through heaven from the Lord); and this is because they do not want to know that there is a heaven. In fact, the learned in their meetings openly discuss whether hell exists and therefore whether heaven exists. And since they are doubtful about heaven, they cannot accept as a principle the idea that there is an inflow through heaven from the Lord. Yet this inflow produces everything in earth's three kingdoms, especially those in the animal kingdom, and specifically those in humanity, and keeps them in their forms according to their use.

Because of this doubt, then, they are also unable to know that there is a correspondence between heaven and humanity, let alone that the nature of this correspondence entails that the details of humanity, even the smallest, come into being from it. They also endure from it, since enduring is a constant coming into being. So maintenance in connection and in form is a constant creation.

4323.

In the chapters preceding, I have started to show that there is a detailed correspondence of human beings with heaven, and to do this from firsthand experience drawn from heaven and the world of spirits. The goal is that people know where they come from and what keeps them in existence, and that there is a constant inflow into them from this source. After that, again on the basis of experience, I must show that people reject the inflow from heaven (that is, through heaven from the Lord) and receive an inflow from hell; but that they are still kept in correspondence with heaven by the Lord, so that if they so choose, they can be led from hell to heaven, and through heaven to the Lord.

4324.

The correspondence of the heart and lungs and of the brain with the Universal Human have been discussed in previous chapters. At this point, following my outline, we need to deal with the correspondence of the outer human sensory organs, specifically the organ of sight or eye, the organ of hearing or ear, and the organs of smell, taste, and touch. But first, let us deal with sensation in general.

4325.

Sensation in general, or generalized sensation, can be distinguished into voluntary and involuntary. Voluntary sensation is proper to the cerebrum, while involuntary sensation is proper to the cerebellum. These two general kinds of sensation are united in the human being, but they are still distinguishable. The fibers that proceed from the cerebrum are the basis of the voluntary senses in general, and the fibers that come from the cerebellum are the basis of the involuntary senses in general. These two kinds of fiber unite in the two appendices called the medulla oblongata and medulla spinalis. They pass through these into the body and shape its members and viscera and organs.

The outside parts of the body, like the muscles and the skin, including also the sensory organs, receive for the most part fibers from the cerebrum. They are the source of a person's sensation and intentional motion. The parts that are surrounded or closed in within, called the viscera of the body, receive fibers from the cerebellum. People do not have sensation from this source, nor is this under the control of their intentionality.

This enables us to determine to some extent what sensation in general is, or general voluntary sensation and general involuntary sensation.

Further, we need to realize that there must be a general entity if there is to be anything specific, that there is no way for the specific to come into being or to endure apart from the general, and particularly that it endures within the general. We need also to realize that every specific is basically in accord with the quality and with the state of its general. This holds true for human sensation and also therefore for motion.

4326.

I heard a muttering rumble that rolled down from above, over the back of my head, and lasted around its whole area. I wondered who these people were. I was told that they were the ones related to general involuntary sensation, and I was also told that they were perfectly capable of perceiving people's thoughts but unwilling to present or express them—like the cerebellum, which perceives everything the cerebrum does, but does not make it known.

When their perceptible operation in the whole occipital province stopped, I was shown how far their operation extended. Its first boundary was the whole face; then it drew back toward the left side of the face and finally toward the left ear. This indicated what the operation of general involuntary sensation was like in primal times for the people of our planet, and how it has changed.

The inflow from the cerebellum slips into the face primarily, which is confirmed by the fact that the spirit (*animus*) is written on the face, and affections are visible in the face. This latter usually happens unintentionally, with fear, awe, shame, various kinds of happiness and sadness, and other emotions that observers recognize in the face, so that they know from the face what affections and what changes of someone's spirit and mind are occurring. This happens from the cerebellum and its fibers when there is no pretense within.

I was shown in this way that in primal times, or among the earliest people, this general sense controlled the entire face, that in succeeding times it gradually came to control only the left side, and that then even later it moved itself out of the face. So nowadays scarcely any general involuntary sensation is left in the face. The right side of the face, including the right eye, is responsive to the affection for what is good, while the left is responsive to the affection for what is true. The area around the ear responds to obedience only, apart from any affection.

Actually, among the earliest people (whose era was called the golden age because being in a unique state of wholeness and in a love for the Lord and consequently in mutual love, they lived like angels), the whole involuntary content of the cerebellum was open to view in their faces. In those days they had absolutely no knowledge of how to present anything by facial expression except as heaven flowed into their involuntary impulses, and from there into their intent.

But for the subsequent early people (whose era was called the silver age because they were in a state of truth and consequently in charity toward the neighbor), the involuntary content of the cerebellum was not open to view in the right side of the face but only in the left.

Then, among their descendants (whose time was called the iron age because they were not involved in an affection for truth but acted in obedience to truth), involuntary phenomena were no longer open to view in the face, but found reception only in the area around the left ear. I have been taught that the fibers of the cerebellum changed their outreach into the face in this way, and fibers from the cerebrum were transferred into their place and thereafter controlled what had depended on the cerebellum. This resulted from the effort to make the facial expression conform to the will of self-conscious intent that comes from the cerebrum.

The truth of this is not visible to people on earth, but it is clearly apparent to angels as a result of the inflow of heaven, and as a result of correspondence.

4327.

General involuntary sensation is like this nowadays in people who are involved in what is good and true of faith. But for people who are involved in evil and consequently in what is false, there is no longer any general involuntary sensation that is evident—neither in the face nor in the speech nor in actions. There is rather a voluntary control that pretends to be involuntary, or, as they say, "natural," which these people have built up by regular use or habit from childhood.

I have been shown the nature of this sensation of theirs by means of an inflow that was silent and cold, into the whole face, the right side and the left side alike. From there it focused itself toward the eyes, and from the left eye it spread itself into the face.

This meant that the fibers of the cerebrum forced themselves upon and were controlling the fibers of the cerebellum, and that as a result, something counterfeit, imitative, deceptive, and crafty was ruling within and was sincere and good in outward appearance. Its focusing toward the left eye and spreading from there to the face as well meant that these people have evil as their goal and use their cognitive side to gain their good. The left eye does mean the cognitive.

These people are the ones who for the most part make up general involuntary sensation nowadays; in ancient times they were the most heavenly of all, but nowadays they are the most villainous, especially the ones from Christendom. They are abundant, and appear under the back of the head at the rear, where I have very often seen and perceived them. For the people who relate to this sense nowadays are ones who are crafty. They devise evil plots against their neighbor and wear a friendly expression, as friendly as can be, in fact, with actions to match. They talk pleasantly, as though they were gifted with exceptional charity. And yet they are the bitterest enemies, not only of whatever person they are dealing with, but of the whole human race as well. Their thoughts have been communicated to me. They were unspeakable and disgusting, full of cruelty and butchery.

4328.

I have also been shown the general circumstance of the voluntary and the cognitive functions. The earliest people, who constituted the Lord's heavenly church (who have been described in nn. 1114–1123), had a voluntary capacity that contained good and a cognitive capacity that contained truth from that good. For them, these two had made one.

In contrast, the subsequent early people who formed the Lord's spiritual church had a wholly corrupted voluntary capacity, but an intact cognitive one in which the Lord, by a process of regeneration, was forming a new voluntary capacity and through it a new cognitive capacity as well (nn. 863, 875, 895, 927, 928, 1023, 1043, 1044, 1555, 2256).

I was shown the nature of the good of the heavenly church by means of a column descending from heaven, azure in color. On its left side it was shining, like the flamy shining of sunlight. By this their first state was portrayed. The azure color pictured their good voluntary capacity, and the flamy shining their cognitive capacity.

Later, the azure of the column changed into a dull flamy color, picturing their second state and the fact that their two lives—intent and discernment—were still acting as one, but more dimly in regard to the good from intent. Azure indicates what is good, and a flamy shining indicates what is true from the good.

Later still, the column became completely black, and around the column there was a shining that was shifting with a kind of glittering effect, and displayed various colors. This pointed to the state of the spiritual church. The black column indicated the cognitive capacity in which there was a new voluntary capacity from the Lord. The cognitive is actually pictured in heaven by a shining.

4329.

Some spirits came to me at a moderate elevation. Judging by the noise, it sounded as though there were many of them. From the concepts of their thought and speech that flowed down to me, I ascertained that they seemed to lack any clear concepts, but to have a general notion of many things. Consequently I was thinking that they would not be able to perceive anything that was clear, only fuzzy and therefore dim generalities. I was actually of the opinion that there was no other kind of generality. I could observe clearly from the things that were flowing from them into my thinking that their thought was general—that is, that it involved many things at the same time.

However, they were granted a mediating spirit through whom they talked with me, since the only way this kind of generality can fit into speech is through other people. While I was talking with them through this intermediary, I voiced my opinion that generalities could not present a clear concept of anything, only one so dim as to be virtually no concept at all.

However, after a quarter of an hour, they showed me that they did have a clear concept of generalization and of many details within the generalities. They showed me this especially by the fact that they observed the shifts and changes of my thoughts and affections so precisely and clearly, including the details, that no other spirit could have done better. I conclude from this that a fuzzy general concept—the kind characteristic of people who do very little thinking and are therefore fuzzy about everything—is one thing; but that a clear general concept is quite another thing—the kind characteristic of people who are well informed in the true and good elements that are latent in a generality in their proper pattern and sequence, so patterned that they can see them clearly from the generality.

These are the people who in the other life make up *general voluntary sensation.* Also, by the insights into what is good and true, they have acquired an ability of seeing into things from the standpoint of their generality, thereby reflecting on things all together, quite fully, and immediately investigating whether they are true. They do see things a little dimly because they see their contents from the standpoint of generality, but because things are clearly patterned within the generality, the things themselves are still in brightness.

This general voluntary sensation occurs only in wise people. I ascertained that these spirits were wise, for they were seeing within me all the details that made up my decisions, from which they drew conclusions about the more inward aspects of my thoughts and affections so skillfully that I began to be afraid to think anything more. For they were discovering things that I did not know were in me, and yet from the conclusions they drew from them, I could not avoid acknowledging them.

As a result of this I perceived in myself a hesitance in talking with them, and when I noticed the hesitance, there appeared something that seemed hairy, and something there that was speaking silently. I was told that this was indicative of a general physical sensation that corresponded to them.

The next day I talked with them again and experienced again the fact that they had a clear general perception, not a fuzzy one, and that as there were changes in the generalities and in the state of the generalities, there were corresponding changes in the specifics and their state, because these latter reflected the former in their arrangement and sequence.

I was told that even more perfect kinds of general voluntary sensation occur in the more inward sphere of heaven, and that when angels are involved in a general or all-inclusive concept, they are at the same time involved in the details, which are distinguishably arranged within the all-inclusive concept by the Lord. I was also told that things general and all-inclusive are nothing unless there are specifics and details within them, constituting them and giving them their name, and that their import depends on how much they contain. I was also told that one could see from this that without the minute details that it contains and that constitute it, the Lord's all-inclusive providence would be nothing whatever, and that it is senseless to maintain the existence of something all-inclusive in the divine and then take the specifics away from it.

4330.

Since the three heavens together make up the Universal Human, and since all the members, viscera, and organs of the body correspond to it in keeping with their functions and uses, as already stated, it is not just the outer parts, those open to view, that correspond, but also the inner ones that are not open to view. So this applies to matters of the outer person and matters of the inner person.

The communities of spirits and angels to which the parts of the outer person correspond are mainly from this planet, but the ones to which the parts of the inner person correspond are mainly from elsewhere. In the heavens, these communities act as one, the way the inner and outer person do in someone who has been regenerated.

But nowadays not many people arrive in the other life from this planet whose outer person does act as one with their inner. In fact, many of them are sense-oriented, even to the point that few of them believe anything except that the outward aspect of people is all there is to them. So they believe that when this passes away, as happnes when someone dies, there is scarcely anything left that is alive. How then could they believe that it is the inner that is alive within the outer, so that when the latter passes away, the former really comes to life?

I was shown by firsthand experience how these people are opposed to the inner person. There was a large number of spirits from this planet who had been like this during their lives in the world. Some spirits came into their view who related to the inner sensory person, and suddenly the first group began to attack them, almost the way irrational people attack rational ones. They were talking and calculating constantly on the basis of sensory deceptions and illusions and groundless hypotheses, believing nothing unless it could be confirmed by data from the outer senses. And, in addition, they heaped insults on the inner person.

But people related to the inner sensory person did not care about all this. They were amazed not only at these people's insanity, but also at their stupidity. And remarkably enough, when the outer sensory people approached the inner sensory ones and almost entered the sphere of their thoughts, the outer sensory people began to have trouble breathing (spirits and angels, like people on earth, do breathe, but their breathing is relatively internal—nn. 3884, 3885f., 3893). Thus they began to suffocate, so they drew back; and the farther they got from the inner sensory people, since then they breathed more easily, the more tranquil and quiet they became toward each other. Then again, the closer they came the more disturbance and restlessness there was.

This was because when sense-oriented people are involved in their illusions, fantasies, and hypotheses, and in the falsities that follow from them, they have a tranquillity. And conversely, as things like this are taken away from them (which happens when the inner person flows in with the light of the truth), then they have a restlessness. There are actually spheres of thoughts and affections in the other life, and they are reciprocally communicated in proportion to presence and accessibility (nn. 1048, 1053, 1512, 1695, 2401, 2489).

This contest lasted for several hours; and in this way I was shown how opposed people from this planet nowadays are to the inner person, and that outward sensation is virtually all there is to them.

Section 2.   The Eye and Light

4403.

I have been enabled to discover and know the quality of spirits and what province of the body they belonged to, by their location and placement relative to me, and also by the level they were on and their distance from me on that level. Normally, the ones I have seen nearby have been representations of whole communities. Communities do in fact send spirits from themselves to others; through them they perceive thoughts and affections, and in this way they communicate. But we must, by the Lord's divine mercy, discuss these so-called representatives or emissary spirits specifically.

I have observed the following things about them. The ones that appear above the head and near at hand are ones who teach and who are easily teachable. The ones below the back of the head are ones who act quietly and carefully. The ones near at hand behind are similar but not identical. The ones near the loins are ones involved in marriage love. The ones near the torso or chest are ones involved in charity. The ones near the feet are ones who are nature-oriented with those near the soles being the coarser of this sort. But the ones near the face are of various kinds depending on correspondence with the sensory organs there. For example, the ones near the nose are the ones who are skilled in perceptiveness, the ones near the ears are the ones who are obedient, and the ones near the eyes are the ones who are discerning and wise, and so on.

4404.

The five outer senses—touch, taste, smell, hearing, and sight—have specific correspondences with inner senses; but these correspondences are virtually unknown nowadays because hardly anyone knows that any correspondences exist, let alone that there are correspondences of spiritual realities with natural ones or of elements of the inner person with elements of the outer, which is the same thing.

On the correspondence of the senses, the sense of touch corresponds in general to affection for what is good; the sense of taste to affection for knowing, the sense of smell to affection for perceiving, the sense of hearing to affection for learning, and to obedience, and the sense of sight to affection for discerning and being wise.

4405.

The reason the sense of sight corresponds to affection for discerning and being wise is that physical sight answers precisely to spiritual sight and therefore to discernment.

There are in fact two lights, one proper to this world, from the sun, and one proper to heaven, from the Lord. There is no discernment within this world's light, but there is discernment within heaven's light. So to the extent that matters of this world's light are illumined in someone by matters of heaven's light, that person is discerning and wise. It depends, that is, on how completely they correspond.

4406.

Since eyesight corresponds to discernment, we also speak of discernment as having sight and call it intellectual sight. Matters that an individual perceives are referred to as objects of that sight, and again in everyday speech we speak of people seeing when they understand. Further, we predicate light and enlightenment of discernment—brightness, then, and on the other hand shade, shadow, and therefore darkness.

These and similar idioms have come into the usage of human speech because they correspond. The human spirit is actually in heaven's light, and the human body in the world's light. It is the spirit that is alive in the body, and it is also the spirit that thinks. Consequently many things that are more inward descend into specific words in this way.

4407.

The eye is the noblest organ of the face, and communicates more directly with discernment than do the other human sensory organs. Further, it is affected by a more subtle atmosphere than the ear is, so sight penetrates to the inner sensory function in the brain by a shorter and more inward path than does speech perceived by the ear. This is also why some animals, lacking discernment as they do, have two "auxiliary brains" within the compass of their eyes. Their discerning function actually depends on their sight.

The human being, however, is not like this, but is furnished with a full-scale brain, so that human discernment does not depend on sight, but sight on discernment.

We can see clearly that sight depends on discernment from the fact that people's natural affections duplicate themselves representatively in the face. But the deeper affections, the thoughtful ones, appear in the eyes, in a certain flame of life, and in a consequent radiation of light that sparkles in response to the affection that envelops the thought.

Further, people do recognize and notice this even when they have not been taught any information about it. The reason is that their spirits are in the company of spirits and angels in the other life who know this from a clear perception. On every individual being in the company of spirits and angels as to his spirit, see nn. 1277, 2379, 3644, 3645.

4408.

It is obvious to people who reflect on it that the correspondence of eyesight is with discernment-sight. The objects of this world, all of which derive something from sunlight, enter through the eye and come to rest in the memory. Here they obviously have something like a visual form, since things recalled from the memory are seen within. This is the source of human imaging, whose ideas philosophers have called "material ideas." When these ideas appear on a still more inward level, they are the basis of thinking, which also has a kind of visual form, but a purer one. The ideas of this process are called "nonmaterial ideas," or "intellectual ideas."

It is marvelously clear that the more inward light is the one that has life in it, that has especially the discernment and wisdom that enlighten inner sight and intersect the things that have entered through outward sight. It is equally clear that this more inward light works within the limits of the arrangement of the objects that are present as a result of the world's light.

Things that come in through hearing are also changed into forms like visual ones inside, forms derived from the world's light.

4409.

Since eyesight does correspond to discernment-sight, it also corresponds to things that are true, for everything proper to discernment has to do with what is true. It has also to do with what is good, its purpose being not simply to know what is good but to be moved by it. Further, everything proper to outward sight has to do with what is true and good, since it has to do with the proper proportions of objects, with their various forms of beauty and of consequent charm. The perceptive person can see that absolutely everything in the natural realm has to do with what is true and good, and can thereby know that the entire natural realm is a theater portraying the Lord's kingdom.

4410.

It has been made clear to me by an abundance of experience that the sight of the left eye corresponds to things true, which are proper to discernment, and that the right eye corresponds to affections for what is true, which are also proper to discernment. So I have been shown that the left eye corresponds to true elements of faith and the right eye to good elements of faith.

The reason for this kind of correspondence is that the light that comes from the Lord contains warmth as well as light. The light itself is the true that emanates from the Lord, and the warmth is the good. It is because of this and because of the inflow into the two hemispheres of the brain that the correspondence is as it is. For people involved in what is good are on the Lord's right, and people involved in what is true are on His left.

4411.

Every single thing in the eye has its correspondence in the heavens—the three humors, for example, aqueous, vitreous, and crystalline, and not only the humors but the sheaths as well—every single part. The more inward parts of the eye have more beautiful and delightful correspondences, but variously in the particular heavens.

When the light that emanates from the Lord flows into the inmost or third heaven, it is there received as that something good which is called charity. When it flows into the intermediate or second heaven (indirectly and directly) it is received as that something true that comes from charity. But when that something true flows into the furthest or first heaven (indirectly and directly), it is received in a substantial form. It looks sometimes like a park, sometimes like a city with palaces in it. So correspondences follow down all the way to angels' outward sight. In similar fashion, in that final form, the eye, of people on earth, this inflow is presented in material form. This happens by means of sight, whose objects are parts of the visible world. If people are involved in love and charity and therefore in faith, they have their more inward realms in this kind of state, since they are responsive to the three heavens, and are miniature heavens.

4412.

There was a man I had known during his physical life, though I had not known about his spirit (*animum*) and deeper affections. He talked with me several times in the other life, but briefly and from quite far away.

He showed himself in a general way by charming visual effects, since he had the ability to present things that brought delight—all kinds of colors, for example, and lovely colored forms. He could bring in children beautifully adorned, like angels, and a great many other things that were charming and cheering.

He worked by a smooth, soft inflow, into the sheath of the left eye. By means like this, he slipped into other people's affections, with a view to making their lives pleasant and cheerful.

I was told by angels that this is characteristic of people who belong to the sheaths of the eye, and that they have a communication with the parklike heavens where things good and true are portrayed in substantial form (cf. n. 4411 above).

4413.

I have been enabled to know by firsthand experience that heaven's light contains discernment and wisdom, and that what appears to angels' eyes as light is the discernment of truth and the wisdom of goodness from the Lord.

I was raised into a light that was sparkling like the light that rays out from diamonds. While I was being held in this light, I seemed to be led out of physical concepts and into spiritual concepts, into things therefore that involved the discernment of what is true and good. The thought-concepts that had their source in the world's light then seemed to be remote from me and almost as though they did not belong to me, although they were still vaguely present.

This enabled me to recognize that to the extent that a person enters this light, he enters discernment. This is why the more intelligent angels are, the greater and more brilliant is the light they are in.

4414.

There are as many different kinds of light in heaven as there are angelic communities that make up heaven—as many even as there are angels in each community. This is because heaven is arranged according to all the different forms of the good and the true, according then to all the states of discernment and wisdom, and therefore according to the forms of reception of the light that comes from the Lord. This is why there is not exactly the same light in any two places anywhere in the entire heaven; rather it varies according to the proportions of flaminess and brilliance and according to levels of intensity. For discernment and wisdom are nothing but the most significant modification of the heavenly light that comes from the Lord.

4415.

Recently arrived souls or novice spirits, that is, ones who are arriving in the other life a few days after physical death, are absolutely amazed to discover that there is light in the other life. They have in fact brought their ignorance with them, their opinion that the only sources of light are the sun and physical flame. They are even more unaware that there is a light that shines on discernment, for they have not noticed this during their physical lives. And they are even less aware that this light affords the ability to think, and by flowing into forms derived from the world's light, provides the basis for all the cognitive functions. If these people had been involved in what is good, so that they are teachable, they are taken up into heavenly communities and led from one community to another, so that they may perceive by firsthand experience that there is light in the other life, more intense than ever occurs in the world, and so that they may perceive at the same time that they have discernment to the extent that they are in the light there.

Some people who have been taken up into spheres of heavenly light have talked with me from there. They swear that they never would have believed it, and that the world's light is darkness by comparison. They also looked from there through my eyes into the world's light, and perceived it only as a dark cloud, and they said sympathetically that this is the kind of light humanity is in.

We can also conclude, from what has been said, why angels are called "angels of light" in the Word; and we can conclude that the Lord is the light and therefore the life of mankind (Jn 1:1–9, 8:12).

4416.

Spirits in the other life appear as they are because of the light they are in, because the light in which they see does correspond to the light from which they perceive, as we have stated. If people have known truths and have confirmed in themselves but still lived lives of evil, they appear in a snow-white but cold light, like winter light. But at the approach of people who are in heaven's light, their light is utterly obscured and becomes a dense darkness. Further, when they move away from heaven's light, there follows a yellowish light, like the light from sulphur, in which they look like ghosts and their truths look like hallucinations. For their truths were matters of secondhand faith, which by nature is such that they believed because they could get prestige and wealth and renown out of it. It was all the same to them what the truth was, as long as people accepted it.

In contrast, people who are involved in evil and consequently in things false appear in a light like the light of burning charcoal. This light becomes completely black next to heaven's light. Still, the lights by which they see vary, depending on the evil and false things they are involved in.

I could see from this why there is no way for people who have led a life of evil to have a wholehearted belief in divine truths. They are actually involved in that smoky light, and when heavenly light shines down into it, it becomes darkness for them, so that they can neither see with their eyes nor see with their minds. In addition, they are in pain at such times, and some of them fall down as though they had fainted. This is why there is no way evil people can accept what is true: only good people can.

People who have lived evil lives cannot believe that they are in this kind of light because they cannot see the light their spirits are in. They can only see the light their eyesight and therefore their natural minds are in. However, if they were to see the light of their spirit and experience its quality, if the light of the good and the true were to flow into it from heaven, they would know clearly how far they are from accepting things proper to the light—that is, things proper to faith—and how much further they are from accepting things proper to charity. They would know, then, how far they are from heaven.

4417.

I was having a talk with some spirits about life, and we were discussing the fact that no one has any trace of life from self, but rather from the Lord, even though people seem to be living from themselves (cf, n. 4320). Then we began to talk about what life is, specifically that it is discerning and intending, and that since all discerning has to do with what is true and all intending with what is good (n. 4409), life is discernment of the true and intent of the good.

But some debating spirits were talking. There are spirits who must be called debaters because they debate about the truth of everything; they are especially in the dark about all truth. They were claiming, as I was about to say, that even people with no discernment of truth and no intent of goodness are alive; in fact they believe that they are more alive than anyone else. But I was given to answer them that the life of evil people may indeed look like life, but that in fact it is the life that is called spiritual death. This they could know from the fact that if life from the Lord is discerning what is true and intending what is good, then discerning what is false and intending what is evil cannot be life because evil and false things are opposites to life itself.

In order for them to be convinced, they were shown the quality of their own life. When it was visible, it looked like the light of burning charcoal, with something smoky mixed in. While they were in this light, they could not help thinking that the life of their thinking and the life of their intent was the one and only life. This opinion was all the more inevitable because the light of discernment of truth, which is proper to life itself, could not appear to them at all. In fact, the moment they entered that light, their own lighting became so dark that they could see absolutely nothing and could therefore perceive nothing as well.

I was also shown the quality of their state of life then. This was done by the removal of the delight they had in what is false, which is accomplished in the other life by a separation from the spirits they are in community with. Once this was done, they seemed to have sallow faces, so corpselike that you could call them images of death.

We will discuss the life of animals separately, though, by the Lord's divine mercy.

4418.

The people who are in the hells are said to be in darkness, but they are said to be in darkness because they are involved in things false. In fact, just as light corresponds to things true, darkness corresponds to things false. They are actually in a light like the light of burning charcoal or yellow sulphur, as already stated.

This latter light is the one meant by darkness, for the light, and equally the resultant sight, determines their discernment, because they correspond. It is called darkness because these lights become darkness next to heavenly light.

4419.

There was a spirit with me who had been very well informed while he lived in the world and therefore believed he was wiser than anyone else. From this belief he developed the evil trait that wherever he was, he wanted to control everything. He was sent to me by a particular community to serve as their representative or agent for communication (cf. n. 4403) and also to get rid of him—he was an awkward companion because he wanted to control them by his own discernment.

While he was with me, I was allowed to talk with him about self-derived discernment—how it is so prized in Christendom that people think it is the source of all discernment, and that none comes from God. People believe this in spite of the fact that when they are talking from the doctrinal tenets of their faith, they say that everything good and true comes from heaven and therefore from the divine, especially all discernment, since this is a matter of what is true and good.

However, when the spirit did not want to pay attention to this, I said that it would help if he moved further away because the sphere of his discernment was being aggressive. But since he was convinced that he was more discerning than other people, he did not want to.

Then he was shown the quality of self-derived discernment and the quality of discernment from the divine. This was done by means of lights. Matters like this are in fact marvelously presented to view in the other life by the use of changes of light. Self-derived discernment was demonstrated by a light that looked like a will-o'-the-wisp with a dark cloud around it, which spread itself noticeably a little distance from its center (*a foco*). In addition, he was shown that it was instantly extinguished when it was looked at by a particular angelic community, just like a will-o'-the-wisp in the face of daytime sunlight.

Then he was shown the quality of discernment from the divine. Again this was done by means of light. This one was more clear and radiant than the noonday sun, stretching out as far as could be, limiting itself like sunlight in the universe. He was told that discernment and wisdom come in from all sides within the sphere of light, giving rise to the perception of what is true and good by an almost unlimited insight, though this depended on the quality of the good and the true.

4420.

We can determine from this that things proper to the world's light in people on earth correspond to things proper to heaven's light. This means that the outer person's sight, the sight of the eye, corresponds to the inner person's sight, the sight of discernment. We can also conclude that the quality of discernment is visible in the other life through lights.

4523.

Anyone familiar with air and sound can realize that the ear is precisely designed for the nature of their changes, that the ear, then, in its physical and material aspects, is wholly responsive to those changes. And anyone who has gathered information about the ether and light knows that the eye, in its physical and material aspects, is designed responsive to their changes. This holds true even to the point that if there is anything mysterious hidden in the nature of air and sound, it is inscribed in the organism of the ear; and anything mysterious in the nature of ether and light is inscribed in the organism of the eye.

As a result, someone skilled in both anatomy and physics can know through research that not only the sensory organs but also the motor organs and all the viscera, in their physical and natural aspects, are responsive to things in the natural world. The whole body then is an organ put together out of the most mysterious things that exist in the natural world, put together according to its hidden active forces and its marvelous modes of flowing. This is why the ancients called man a miniature world or microcosm.

Knowing this enables us to know that if anything exists in the world and its realm of nature, it does not come forth from itself but from something prior to itself, and that this prior something cannot come forth from itself but from something prior to itself, all the way to a First, from which subsequent entities emerge in sequence. And since they come forth from this source, they continue in existence from this source, for continued existence is constant coming into being.

It follows from this that absolutely everything, right down to the most remote forms of nature, not only has come into being from the First but also continues in existence from the First. Unless it did in fact constantly come into being, and unless the connection from the First and therefore with the First were constant, it would instantly collapse and cease to be.

4524.

Now since absolutely everything in the world and its natural realm does come and constantly continues to come into being (that is, does continue in being) from things prior, it follows that everything comes into being and continues in being from a world that is higher

THE UNIVERSAL HUMAN

than the natural realm, the world that is called spiritual. Since in order to continue in being or constantly come into being there must be a constant connection with that world, it follows that that world is the source of the purer and more inward realities that are within nature, and therefore within human beings. It also follows that those purer or more inward realities are forms that by nature can receive an inflow. Further, since there cannot be more than one single fountain of life (as in the realm of nature there is only one single fountain of light and warmth), we conclude that all life comes from the Lord, who is "the First" of life. And in view of this, we also conclude that absolutely everything in the spiritual world corresponds to Him—especially everything in the human being, since this is, in the smallest reproduction, a miniature spiritual world. Because of this, the spiritual person is also an image of the Lord.

4525.

We can see from this that especially in human beings the correspondence of everything is a correspondence with the spiritual world, and that without that correspondence nothing could continue to exist, even for a moment. For without that correspondence, there would be no continuity from the essential reality of life (that is, from the Lord). There would thus be a discontinuity, and anything unconnected disintegrates into nothing.

The reason the correspondence with the human being is more direct and therefore tighter is that people were created to attach life from the Lord to themselves, which yields the power to be raised above the natural world by the Lord in thoughts and affections. This in turn yields the power to think about God and to be influenced by the Divine, and in this way to be united to Him, unlike earth's other living creatures. And people who can be united to the Divine in this way do not die when their physical aspects, which are proper to this world, are taken away, since their more inward reaches continue to be united.

4526.

Continuing the discussion of the correspondence of eyesight begun above, we need to be aware that its correspondence is with elements of discernment, for discernment is inner sight, and this inner sight is in a light that is higher than the world's light. The reason people can acquire discernment by means of things seen in the world's light is that the higher light, the light of heaven, flows into the objects that come from the world's light and makes them appear in representative or correspondential modes.

The light that is higher than the world's light is actually the one that emanates from the Lord, who gives light to heaven in its entirety. The very discernment and wisdom that come from the Lord appear as light there. This light is what makes human discernment or human inner sight. When it flows through discernment into the objects that are coming from the world's light, it makes them appear in representative or correspondential modes—in the mode of discernment, that is.

Further, since the eyesight that occurs in the natural world corresponds to the discernment-sight that is in the spiritual world, it corresponds to true elements of faith, these being proper to genuine discernment. True elements do actually make up the whole of human discernment, for all of thinking revolves around whether something is so or not—that is, whether it is true or not true. On the correspondence of eyesight with true and good elements of faith, see n. 4410 above.

4527.

I talked with some people a few days after their decease, and since they were so newly arrived, they were in a light that to them differed only slightly from the world's light. Since the light did look like this to them, they were doubtful that light was coming to them from any new source. So they were taken up into the beginning of heaven where the light is still more brilliant; and they talked with me from there. They kept saying that they had never seen such light, and this happened long after sunset. At that point, they were amazed that spirits had eyes that they saw with, though they had during their physical lives believed that the life of a spirit was nothing but thought, even thought quite apart from any (thinking) subject. This was because they were incapable of thinking about any thinking subject because they could not see it. And as a result of this, they could not avoid perceiving that thought, being nothing but thought, would vanish away with the body it dwelt in, rather like an aura or a fire, if it were not miraculously held together and maintained by the Lord. They also saw how easily scholars fall into error about life after death, and that scholars particularly do not believe unless they see.

So they were amazed then that they possessed not only thought but even sight, and the other senses as well. They were even more amazed that they looked exactly like people to each other—they saw and heard each other, they talked with each other, they had tactile sense of their members, and this with finer sensitivity than during their physical lives. As a result, they were speechless at the fact that while people are living in the world, they are utterly unaware of this. And they felt a pity for the human race, for its knowing nothing about such matters because it believed nothing, especially the people who were in more light than others—the ones within the church, who possessed the Word.

Some of them believed only that people became like specters after death, supporting this notion with ghosts they had heard about. But the only conclusions they drew from this was that there was something alive in some crude fashion that was breathed out from physical life at first, but that it went back into the body again and was thereby snuffed out.

Then some believed that they would be revived only at the time of the last judgment, and that then they would be revived with that body which had disintegrated into dust. Then it would be gathered together and they would rise up again, complete with flesh and bone. And since they had been waiting in vain for that last judgment or end of the world for so many centuries, they had slipped into the error of believing that they never would be revived. They did this without thinking of what they had learned from the Word and from saying that when people die their souls are in the Lord's hands, with the blessed or the wretched depending on the lives they had made habitual; nor were they thinking about what the Lord said about the rich man and Lazarus.

They were, however, informed that individual's "last judgment" happens at death. Then people do appear to themselves to be equipped with bodies just as they were in the world and to enjoy every sensory ability they had there, though the senses now are purer and more finely sensitive because there are no physical obstructions, and because matters of the world's light are not casting their shadows on matters of heaven's light. They were told that they were in purified bodies, so to speak, and that no one there could carry around a flesh-and-bone body like the ones in the world because that would be surrounding themselves again in earthly dust.

I talked about this with some of them on the very day their bodies were being buried, and through my eyes they saw their bodies, their coffins, and their interments. They said that they cast them off—they had served them for useful activities in the world where they had been, and now they were living in bodies that served them for useful activities in the world in which they now were. They wanted me to say all this to their friends who were in mourning, but I was given to answer that if I did, their friends would treat it as absurd. For anything they themselves could not see with their own eyes, they believed to be nothing, and relegated to the realm of visions that are illusions. There was actually no way to lead them to believe that spirits see each other with their eyes just the way people see each other with theirs, and that people cannot see spirits except with the eyes of their own spirits. They see spirits, then, when the Lord opens their inner sight, as He did to the prophets, who saw spirits and angels and many things in heaven. There is room to doubt whether the people who are living nowadays would have believed these things if they had been living in those times.

4528.

The eye—or, more precisely, its sight—corresponds primarily to communities in the other life that are in parklike regions, which appear above, in front, and a little to the right. This is where vivid visual images are presented of gardens with so many genera and species of tree and flower that all the kinds in the whole earth are few in comparison. In each object there, there is something of discernment and wisdom that shines forth, so that you would say you were in gardens of discernment and wisdom at the same time. These are things that affect the people there from within and thus delight not only the eye but at the same time the discerning mind as well.

These parks are found in the first heaven, in its very threshold and toward the inner regions of that heaven; and they are representative of things that come down from a higher heaven where angels of the higher heaven are talking perceptively with each other about true elements of faith. The speech of angels there takes place by means of spiritual and heavenly concepts that to them are the forms of words. It extends by sequences of representations so beautiful and charming that there is no way to express them. It is these beautiful and charming facets of their conversation that are portrayed as gardens in the lower heaven.

This latter heaven is divided into a number of heavens, to which correspond the specifics in the interiors of the eye. There is the heaven where parklike gardens are. There is a heaven where the atmospheres are multicolored, where the whole aura is aglow as if with gold, silver, pearls, jewels, the finest flowers, and countless other things. There is a rainbow heaven with the loveliest rainbows, large and small, shaded with the most brilliant colors. These specific forms arise through the light that comes from the Lord, which has discernment and wisdom in it. From that source there is something of the discernment of what is true and the wisdom of what is good in the particular objects there, something that is presented figuratively in this way.

If people have not had any concept of heaven or of the light there, they can scarcely be led to believe that things like this exist there. So people who bring their disbelief with them into the other life, provided they have lived in the truth and goodness of faith, are carried into these phenomena by angels; and when they see them, they are speechless. On parks, atmospheres, and rainbows, see the material from experience in nn. 1619–1626, 2296, and 3220, and on the constant occurrence of portrayals in the heavens, see nn. 1807, 1808, 1971, 1980, 1981, 2299, 2763, 3213, 3216–3218, 3222, 3350, 3475, and 3485.

4529.

One man who had been celebrated and widely known in the learned world for his skill in the field of botany heard in the other life, after his death, that there too flowers and trees were presented to view. He was speechless at this. And since this had been the delight of his life, he was on fire with a longing to find out whether this was true.

So after being taken up into a park area, he saw the loveliest groves and the most charming flowers over a vast area. Since this brought him into the full intensity of the delight of his affection, he was allowed to roam through a field and not only to look at particular things there but also to pick them, hold them up to his eye, and thoroughly examine them to see whether they were what they seemed to be.

He talked with me from there and said that he never would have believed it, and that if he had heard things like this in the world, he would have classed them paradoxes. He went on to say that he had observed an overwhelming abundance of flowering plants there that have never been seen in the world. They could scarcely be grasped by any earthly perception, and particular ones glowed with an incomprehensible radiance because they came from heaven's light. He was not yet able to grasp the fact that the glow had a spiritual source, namely, the presence in particular forms of some element of the discernment and wisdom proper to what is good and true, which gave them their glow.

He also said that earthly people would never believe this because there weren't many that believed any heaven or hell existed; the ones that did believe only knew that there was joy in heaven; and a few of them knew that there were things there that "eye hath not seen, nor ear heard, nor could the mind conceive." This was the case in spite of the fact that they knew from the Word that the prophets saw awesome things, like many seen by John and described in the book of Revelation. Yet these were only samples of the things that happen constantly in heaven and that are seen when someone's inner sight is opened.

But these matters are relatively minor. The people these phenomena come from, who are in real discernment and wisdom, are in such a state of happiness that they would class what we have just described as rather insignificant to them. Some of the ones who spoke to me while they were in the parks and said that these things surpassed every level of happiness were for this reason taken up a bit more to the right into a heaven that gleamed even more brilliantly. Eventually they were raised to the heaven where they perceived the blessedness of discernment and wisdom that lay within such things. Then while they were there, they talked with me again. They said that what they had seen before was relatively trivial.

Finally, they were taken up to a heaven where the sense of well-being flowed from such a deep affection that they could scarcely stand it. For this sense of well-being penetrated to the medullary substances, which were virtually unraveled by it, so that they were beginning to slip into a loss of consciousness in the presence of holiness (*in sanctum deliquiium*).

4530.

There are also colors that people observe in the other life that so surpass in brilliance and splendor the luster of colors in this world that there is scarcely any comparison. These come from the shifting of light and shade there. And because there is a discernment and wisdom from the Lord there that looks like light to the eyes of angels and spirits and at the same time enlightens their discernment within, the colors there are essentially changes or, so to speak, alterations of discernment and wisdom.

I have seen the colors there so many times that I can barely count them—not just the colors that adorn the flowers and light up the atmospheres and give the rainbows their variety, but also colors that are presented distinctly in other forms. Their brilliance comes from the truth that is proper to discernment and their splendor from the goodness that is proper to wisdom, with the specific colors resulting from the brightness and dimness of these sources. So they result from light and shade the way hues do in the world.

This is why the colors that are mentioned in the Word pictured things characteristic of discernment and wisdom—the colors of the precious stones on Aaron's breastplate, for example, and of his holy vestments, the colors of the courts of the tabernacle where the ark was, and the colors of the stones of the foundation of the new Jerusalem described by John in the Book of Revelation, among others. However, what they picture specifically will by the Lord's divine mercy be presented in the course of exegesis.

In general, the more glory the colors there have and the more they are on the white side, the more they come from the truth that is proper to discernment. The more splendor they have and the more they are on the reddish side, the more they come from the goodness that is proper to wisdom. The phenomena that come from this source also belong to the provinces of the eyes.

4531.

Since discernment and wisdom from the Lord is what looks like light in heaven, angels are called angels of light. By the same token, folly and madness from people's self-image (*a proprio*) is what rules in hell, so the people there are referred to as coming from darkness.

There is not actually darkness in hell, but there is a very dim lighting like the light from burning charcoal, in which people do see each other. Otherwise they could not live. This lighting of theirs has its source in the light of heaven, which changes into this form when it descends into their senselessness—that is, into their false notions and their cravings. The Lord is everywhere present with His light, even in the hells: otherwise they would have no power to think and therefore to talk. But light occurs in keeping with its acceptance.

This lighting is what is called in the Word "the shadow of death" and is compared to darkness. It does also turn into darkness for the people there when they approach heaven's light; and when they are in their darkness, they are in a senselessness and a stupidity.

We can therefore conclude that as light corresponds to what is true, darkness corresponds to what is false, and that people who are involved in false things are said to be in blindness.

4532.

There are people who believe that they discern what is true and what is good on their own and therefore rely on no one but themselves. So they think they are wiser than anyone else when, quite the contrary, they are in ignorance of what is true and what is good. In the other life, these people—especially the ones who do not want to discern what is true and good, and are involved in false things as a result—are sometimes sent into a state of darkness. While they are in this state, they talk inanely, since they are in stupidity. I have been told that there are many people of this sort, including people who believed they were firmly placed in the greatest light and seemed so to others as well.

4533.

Among the marvels that happen in the other life is this, that when angels examine evil spirits, these latter look completely different from the way they look to each other.

When evil spirits and genii are together and are in their own deceptive light (like the light of burning charcoal, as already stated), then they look to each other to be in human form; in keeping with their own illusions, they are not unlovely. But when these same people are examined by angels of heaven, that light is instantly dissipated, and they appear with utterly different faces, each in keeping with his own nature. Some are swarthy and black like devils; some have faces as sallow as corpses; some are almost faceless, with something hairy instead; some are like lattices of teeth; and some are like skeletons. Astonishingly too, some are like monsters, crafty as serpents, vicious as vipers. There are other different appearances. But the moment the angels move their gaze away from them, they appear in the form they had before, in their own light.

Angels examine the evil ones as often as they notice that they are working their way up out of the hells into the world of spirits and threatening others with evil. In this way they are discovered and sent back. The reason there is such an effectiveness inherent in angelic sight is that there is a correspondence between discernment-sight and eyesight. As a result, there is an inherent acuity in their sight that leads to the dissipation of hellish lighting so that people appear in their own proper form and nature.

Section 3. Odor and the Nose

4622.

There are homes of different kinds for the blessed in the other life, built with such skill that they are virtually *in* the art of architecture, or directly from it. On the homes of the blessed, see the material from experience in nn. 1119 and 1626–1630). These are apparent not only to angels' sight, but to their touch as well. In fact, everything in the other life is suited to the senses of spirits and angels, so that there are things there that by nature are incompatible with the kind of physical sensation people on earth have, but are compatible with the kind of sensation people in the other life have.

I know that this is unbelievable to many people, but this is because nothing is believed that cannot be seen by physical eyes and touched by hands of flesh. This is why people nowadays, whose deeper reaches are closed off, know nothing about the things that occur in the spiritual world or heaven. Of course, they say on the basis of the Word that there is a heaven and that the angels there are in joy and glory, but beyond this they know nothing. They would like to know how things are, but when they are told, they still do not believe any of it, because at heart they deny that anything of this nature exists. When they would like to know, it is simply because they are temporarily caught up in a doctrinal curiosity, not because they are in a delight that stems from faith. People who are not in faith are at heart negative as well.

But people who do believe do gain some ideas of heaven and its joy and glory from various sources, each from the kinds of thing proper to his own discernment and wisdom, and simple folk from sensitivities that are proper to the body.

Still, most people do not grasp the fact that spirits and angels are equipped with senses far more delicately sensitive than people in the world have—sight, hearing, smell, something like taste, and touch, and especially with their affectional delights. If they only believed that their deeper essence was a spirit and that their bodies and physical senses and members were suited only to useful activities in this world, while their spirits and their senses and organs are suited to useful activities in the other life, then on their own, almost involuntarily, they would come into concepts of the state of their spirits after death. They would then in fact be thinking to themselves that their spirit was the actual person that was thinking, longing, desiring, and being moved. And they would consequently think that all the sensory functioning observable in the body was proper to their spirit, and belonged to the body only by inflow. Afterward they would find ample confirmation of all this; and ultimately they would find more pleasure in matters of their spirit than in matters of their body.

The actual fact is that it is not the body that sees, hears, smells, and feels: it is the spirit. So when the spirit is drawn out of the body, it is then in possession of the senses it had while it was in a body—far more delicately sensitive ones, in fact. Actually, since physical things are relatively crude, they dull the senses, all the more because they submerge them in earthly and worldly matters.

I can testify to the fact that spirits have far more sensitive sight than people in bodies do. The same holds true for hearing and, remarkably enough, the sense of smell and especially the sense of touch. They see each other, hear each other, and touch each other.

If people do believe in a life after death, they may reach this conclusion from the fact that no life can occur without sensation and that the quality of the life depends on the quality of the sensation. Particularly, there is the fact that discernment is nothing but a delicate sensing of more inward matters, and higher discernment a sensing of spiritual things. This is also why matters of discernment and its perception are said to belong to an inner sense.

As for the sensory ability people have immediately after death, it is like this. As soon as people die and their physical components become cold, they are awakened into life, and into a state then that includes all the senses. So at that point, they scarcely realize that they are not still in their bodies. In fact, the senses they possess lead them to believe this.

But when they notice that they have more delicate senses, and especially when they start to talk with other spirits, then they realize that they are in the other life and that the death of their bodies was a continuation of the life of their spirits.

I talked with two people I had known, on the very day they were being buried. One of them saw his coffin and bier through my eyes, and since he had access to all the senses he had had in the world, he was talking with me about the funeral services while I was following the procession. He also talked about his body, saying they could get rid of it because he himself was alive.

It must be realized, though, that people who are in the other life can see nothing whatever in this world through the eyes of anyone on earth. The reason they could see through mine was that I was in spirit with them and in body with people in this world (see also n. 1880). It must also be realized that I was not seeing the people I talked with in the other life with my physical eyes but with the eyes of my spirit. Still this was just as clear as my physical sight and sometimes even clearer. For by the Lord's divine mercy, the things proper to my spirit have been opened.

But I know that what has been said thus far will not be believed by people who are immersed in physical, earthly, and worldly matters, at least by those of them who regard these things as goals. These actually grasp nothing but what is scattered by death. I also know that it will not be believed by people who have done a great deal of thinking and research about the soul and have not at the same time understood that the soul is a person's spirit and that the spirit is the actual person that is alive within the body. The only notion of the soul these people can grasp is that it has something to do with thought or flame or ether, and that it acts only into the organic forms of the body and not into purer forms that belong to the spirit within the body. They therefore believe that it is a sort of thing that is destroyed along with the body. This ignorance is especially characteristic of people who have convinced themselves of these notions with insights inflated by a persuasion of their exceptional wisdom.

4623.

It must however be realized that the sensory life of spirits is of two kinds, real and not real. They differ from each other in that everything that appears to the people who are in heaven is real, while everything that appears to the people who are in hell is not real. Actually, whatever comes from the divine, that is, from the Lord, is real, because it is coming from the essential reality of things (*ab ipso Esse rerum*) and from intrinsic life. But whatever comes from a spirit's self-image is not real, because it is not coming from the reality of things and is not coming from intrinsic life. People who are involved in an affection for what is good and true are in the Lord's life, so they are in real life. For the Lord is present in what is good and true by means of affection. But people who by affection are involved in what is evil and false are in a life of their self-image. So they are in a nonreal life, since the Lord is not present in what is evil and false.

The real can be distinguished from the nonreal by the fact that the quality of the real actually is what it seems to be and the quality of the nonreal is not in fact what it seems to be. The people who are in hell have senses just as convincing as anyone else's, and have no awareness that things are not really and actually the way they sense them. Still, when they are examined by angels, then these same things seem like illusions and disappear; and the people themselves look like monsters rather than people.

I have been allowed to talk with them about this, and some of them said that they believed things were real because they saw and touched them, adding that their senses could not lie. But I was given to answer that they were nevertheless not real, and that this was because they themselves were involved in things contrary or opposed to the divine—in evil and false things—no matter how real they seemed to them. Further, to the extent that they were involved in cravings for evil and false persuasions, they themselves were nothing but illusions as far as their thoughts were concerned, and seeing real things as not real and nonreal things as real. Further, were they not gifted with this mode of sensation, by the Lord's divine mercy, they would have no sensory life. By the same token, they would have no life at all, since sensation constitutes all of life. To cite all my experience on this subject would fill pages and pages.

So let people be careful when they enter the other life. Evil spirits know how to present different kinds of illusions to newcomers from the world. And if they cannot deceive them, they still try by the same means to persuade them that nothing is real, but that everything is abstract (*idealia*), even the things in heaven.

4624.

But let us turn to the correspondence of the sense of smell, and consequently the nose, with the Universal Human. To this region belong people who possess a general perception, so that they might even be called "perceptions." The sense of smell corresponds to them and, by the same token, so does its organ. This is why smelling, scenting, keen-scented, and the nose are predicated in common speech of people who are perceptive. The deeper aspects of the words of human speech derive a great deal from correspondence with the Universal Human, because people are in the company of spirits as to the spirit, and with people on earth as to the body.

4625.

There are however many communities of which the entire heaven or Universal Human is composed, and they are more or less inclusive. The more universal ones are the ones to which whole members or organs or viscera correspond; the less universal ones are the correspondents of parts of them and of parts of those parts.

Each community is an image of the whole, since any completely harmonious entity is made up of a number of images of itself. The more inclusive communities, which are images of the universal, have within them specific communities that correspond in the same way. I have from time to time talked with members of communities where I had been sent, who belonged to the province of the lungs, heart, face, tongue, ear, or eye, and with members of the province of the nose. From these last, I have been enabled to know their quality, learning that they are perceptions. They do in fact perceive in a general way whatever in the community has touched them, but unlike the members of the province of the eye, they do not perceive it in a specific way. These latter discriminate and examine matters of perception. I have also been allowed to observe that their perceptive function varies according to general changes in the state of the community they are in.

4626.

When a spirit approaches, even though that spirit may be far away and in obscurity, still its presence is perceived whenever the Lord grants it. It is perceived from a certain spiritual sphere, and from this sphere the quality of the spirit's life can be recognized, as can the quality of its affection and the quality of its faith. The angelic spirits who are in possession of a more delicate perception can learn countless things about a spirit's life and faith from this. This has been demonstrated to me many times.

When the Lord pleases, these spheres are also changed into odors. The actual odor is clearly sensed. The reason the spheres are changed into odors is that an odor corresponds to a perception; and since perception virtually is spiritual odor, an odor flows down from perception. But the reader may refer to material from experience already cited—on spheres in nn. 1048, 1053, 1316, 1504–1519, 1695, 2401, 2489, and 4464; on perception in nn. 483, 495, 503, 521, 536, 1383, 1384, 1388, 1391, 1397, 1398, 1504, and 1640; and on odors from perception in nn. 1514, 1517–1519, 1631, and 3577.

4627.

The people who relate to the more inward parts of the nose are in a more perfect state, as to perception, than the ones discussed above who relate to its more outward parts. I have leave to relate the following information about the former.

I saw something like a bathing pool with long seats or benches, and a warmth was radiating from it. A woman appeared there who soon disappeared into a blackish cloud. I also heard children saying that they did not want to be there. Afterward I noticed some angelic bands that had been sent to me to turn aside an effort caused by particular evil spirits. Then suddenly, above my forehead, there appeared larger and smaller openings through which a lovely golden light was shining, and in the brilliance within I saw some things in a snow-white light. Then the openings appeared again in a different arrangement, with the things that lay behind showing through. There were other openings behind, through which the brilliance did not pass in the same way. Finally, I saw a light growing brighter.

I was told that these were the dwellings of the people who made up the province of the inner parts of the nose—they were of the female sex—and that the acuity of the perception of the women there was pictured in the world of spirits by openings like these. Spiritual phenomena in heaven are actually pictured in natural ones (more precisely, in phenomena like natural ones) in the world of spirits.

Afterward, I was allowed to talk with them, and they said that they could see through these representative openings precisely what was happening below them, and that the openings seemed to turn toward the communities they were intent on observing. Since they were turned toward me at that point, they said that they could watch all the concepts of my thinking and also those of people around me. In addition, they claimed that they not only watched my concepts, they also saw them pictured for themselves in various ways. For example, matters of affection for goodness were pictured by appropriate little flames, and matters of truth by variations of light. They added that they saw particular angelic communities with me and saw their thoughts pictured by things of different hues—by purple things as in tapestries and also on a dimmer level by rainbows. They said that they perceived in consequence that these angelic communities were from the province of the eye.

Then I saw some other spirits, who were cast down from there and scattered hither and yon. In this regard, the women said that they were the kind who sneaked in with a view to observing something and seeing what was going on below, but with the goal of taking over. This casting down was observed whenever the angelic bands were approaching.

I talked with these latter also. As to the ones who had been cast down, they said that they related to nasal mucus and that they were dull and stupid, and also without conscience. So they were entirely lacking in more inward perception. The woman I saw (as mentioned above) was a sign of these infiltrations. I was also allowed to talk with them, and they were amazed that anyone had a conscience. They were absolutely ignorant of what conscience is. And when I told them that it is a more inward awareness of what is good and true, and that behavior contrary to it brings an anxiety, they did not understand. This is the nature of people who correspond to the mucus that clogs up the nose, and is therefore expelled.

Then I was shown the brilliance in which the people live who relate to the inner parts of the nose. It was a brilliance beautifully chased with veins of golden flame and silver light. Affections for what is good were pictured in it by the veins of golden flame, and affections for what is true by the veins of silver light.

I was also shown that they have spaces that open out on the side, through which they see something like a sky, with stars against a deep blue. I was also told that there is such a light in their councils that noontime on earth cannot compare. And I was told in addition that they have a warmth like that of springtime and summer on earth. There are also children among them, but children of several years old, and that they do not like being there when the infiltrators—the muci—approach.

Countless such images appear in the other life, but these were representative of perceptions, to which correspond matters of the sense of smell of the inner parts of the nose.

4628.

Continuing with the odors that spheres of perception turn into, these are sensed just as clearly as odors on earth, but they do not get through to the sense of anyone whose more inward reaches are closed because they flow in by an inner path but not by an outer one.

There are two sources of these odors—perception of what is good and perception of what is evil. The ones that come from perception of what is good are exceedingly pleasant, smelling rather like the scents of flower gardens and like other scents—so delightful, and so varied as to be beyond description. The people in heaven are in spheres of odors like these.

But the odors that come from perception of what is evil are repulsive, foul and rank like stagnant water, excrement, carrion, smelling horrible like mice or house lice. The people in hell are in spheres of stenches like these. Strange as it seems, the people in them do not sense their foulness; in fact they find these stenches delightful, and when they are in them they are in the sphere of their pleasures and delights. However, when a hell is opened and a breath from it reaches good spirits, they are gripped both with horror and with anxiety, like people in this world who chance into a sphere of stenches of this sort.

4629.

To cite all the experience I have had about spheres of perception changed into odors would mean writing by the ream (*membranam exarare*, lit., "plough up the parchment"). The reader may refer to what has already been noted in nn. 1514, 1517–1519, 1631, and 3577), to which I may add just the following.

Once I perceived a general kind of thinking of a large number of spirits about the Lord's being born a human, and I noted that it consisted of nothing but libels. For what spirits are thinking, both generally and specifically, is openly perceived by others. The odor of this sphere was perceived like that of stagnant water and water polluted by decaying sewage.

4630.

Someone inconspicuous was near my head. I was aware that he was there because of a smell like that of abcessed teeth. And afterward I noticed a smell like that of burnt horn or bone. Then a huge crowd of the same sort of people came, rising up from below not far from my back, like a cloud. Since they were so inconspicuous, I presumed that they were subtle ones, but evil. I was told, though, that they are inconspicuous where the sphere is spiritual, but obvious where the sphere is natural. For if people are so bound to the realm of nature that they do not think about spiritual matters at all or believe that heaven and hell exist, and if they are nevertheless subtle in their business dealings, then they are like this, and are called inconspicuous natural people. Sometimes their presence is made known to others by the smell mentioned above.

4631.

Two or three times, an odor of carrion has drifted to me, and when I tried to find out whom it was coming from, there were signs that it was coming from a hell where infamous thieves and assassins lived, and people who perpetrated crimes of a serious nature. Sometimes too the odor of excrement has reached me, and when I asked where it came from, I was told that it came from a hell where adulterers lived. And when the odor of excrement was mixed with that of carrion, I was told that it was coming from a hell where there lived adulterers who were also cruel, and so on.

4632.

Once when I was thinking about the way the soul rules in the body and the inflow of intent into actions, I noticed that the people in a hell of excrement (which was opened for a short while then) were thinking only about the soul's control of the buttocks and of the inflow of intent into the expulsion of excrement. I could see from this what kind of perception they had, and consequently what a loathsome sphere. Much the same thing happened when I was thinking about marriage love. Then the people in a hell where adulterers live dwelt on nothing but dissolute thoughts like thoughts of adultery and filth. And when I was thinking about sincerity, then people who were involved in guile were thinking about nothing but crime by deceit.

4633.

From the material presented about perceptions and odors, we can see that everyone's life and by the same token everyone's affection is clearly open to view in the other life. So anyone who thinks that people there will not know what he was like and what kind of life he has in consequence, anyone who expects to be able to conceal his spirit the way we can in the world, is much mistaken. In the other life, people can see not only what others know about themselves; they can also see what others do not know about themselves. This means those things that by constant practice they have submerged in their life's pleasures, for these then disappear, beyond the reach of sight and reflection. The actual goals of people's thought and speech and action, which have become concealed for the same reason, are perceived in heaven with the greatest clarity. Heaven is actually in the sphere and perception of goals.

Section 4.   Hearing and the Ear

4652.

If we want to know the nature of the correspondence between soul and body, or between the matters of the spirit, which is within a person, and the body, which is outside, we can clearly determine it from the correspondence, inflow, and communication of thought and affection, which are proper to the spirit, with speech and hearing, which are proper to the body. The thinking of someone who is talking is nothing but the speech of the spirit, and the awareness of speech is nothing but the hearing of the spirit. True, when someone is talking, his thought does not seem like speech to him because it unites itself with his physical speech and dwells within it. Also, the awareness when someone is hearing does not seem to be anything but the hearing in the ear. This is why many unreflective people know only that all sensation is in the organs of the body, so that when those organs deteriorate by reason of death, no further sensation remains. Yet it is then that the person, that is, the spirit, enters its truest sensory life.

I have been able to determine clearly that the spirit is what speaks and what hears, from conversations with spirits. Their speech, as communicated to my spirit, descended into my more inward speech, and from there into the corresponding organs. In those organs, it resolved into an impulse (*conatum*), which I sometimes clearly perceived. As a result of this process, their speech was audible to me with just as much resonance as human speech has. When spirits have on occasion talked with me while I was in a group of people, since their speech was so resonantly audible, some of the spirits thought that they were being heard by the people present as well. But I answered that this was not the case because their speech flowed into my ear by an inner path, while human speech flowed in by an outer path.

We can see from this how a spirit talked with prophets—not as mortal with mortal, but as spirit with mortal—in such instances as Zechariah 1:9, 13, 19; 2:3; 4:1, 4, 5; 5:10; 6:4, and elsewhere.

But I know that this is beyond the grasp of people who do not believe that people are spirits, and that bodies serve them for useful activities in the world. People who have convinced themselves of this do not even want to hear about correspondence; and if they do hear, being in a negative state, they reject it. They are even distressed that anything is being taken away from the body.

4653.

The spirits who correspond to hearing or make up the province of the ear are people characterized by simple obedience, people who do not debate whether something is true but rather believe that it is because other people say so. So they can be called "forms of obedience" (lit., "obediences"). The reason they are like this is that hearing relates to speech as something passive to its active, like the person who hears a speaker and agrees. So in everyday speech, "to be listening to someone" is to be obedient and to "hear someone's word" is to obey. The more inward aspects of human speech actually have their source in large measure in correspondence, because the human spirit is among spirits who are in the other life, and that is where the human spirit thinks. This is something people are utterly unaware of, and people preoccupied with physical concerns do not want to know.

There are many different kinds of spirits who correspond to the ear, that is, to its functions and abilities. These are the ones who relate to its particular organic parts—to the outer ear, the membrane called the eardrum, the more inward membranes called the fenestrae, the hammer, stirrup, anvil, cylinders, cochlea, and who relate to still more inward parts, even including those nearer the spirit but clothed with substance and those that are even within the spirit, and finally those most closely united to element of inner sight. They can be distinguished from these last elements by the fact that they are not so discriminating, but are like passive allies to them.

4654.

There were some spirits with me who were flowing very forcefully into my thinking when it was occupied with matters involving providence, especially when I was thinking that things I was looking and hoping for were not happening. I was told by angels that these were spirits who had been upset when during their physical lives they had prayed for something and not gotten it, and who had entertained second thoughts about providence on this account. Nevertheless, when they were out of this state they behaved with piety in keeping with whatever other people told them. So they were in simple obedience. I was told that people like this belong to the outer ear or the earlobes. That is also where they appeared when they talked with me.

4655.

In addition, I have often noticed spirits right around my ear, and also apparently within it. The reason they seemed to be within it is that this is the nature of the appearance. It is state that makes appearance in the other life. These were all simple and obedient people.

4656.

There was a spirit who was talking with me near my left earlobe, toward the back of it where the elevator muscles of the earlobe are. He told me that he had been sent to me to say that he did not reflect on what other people were saying, he only took it in with his ears. When he talked, he virtually belched his words; and he told me also that that was the way he talked. I could tell from this that there was no deeper content dwelling within his speech, so there was not much life in it, which was the reason for that kind of belching. I was told that people like this, who give little heed to the meaning of things, belong to the cartilaginous and bony part of the outer ear.

4657.

There are spirits who have talked with me occasionally but by muttering, very near the left ear as though they wanted to talk inside the ear so that no one would hear them. But I was given to tell them that this was not appropriate in the other life, since it was clear that they had been gossips and were therefore now saturated with a gossipy nature; also that many of them were the kind that observed other people's failings and faults and told their friends when no one was listening, or whispered to them when there were people around. I said that they looked at and interpreted everything in a bad light, and thought they were better than other people, and that for this reason there was no way they could be admitted into the company of good spirits, who by nature do not conceal their thoughts.

I was told that, contrary to what one might expect, this kind of speech is more loudly audible in the other life than open speech is.

4658.

To the more inward parts of the ear belong people who have a view of the more inward hearing, obey what its spirits say there, and relay its sayings accurately. I have also been shown what they are like.

I was aware of something loud penetrating from within, near my left side, all the way to my left ear. I noticed that there were spirits who were trying to force their way out in this manner, but I could not tell what kind they were. But when they did get out, they talked with me, saying that they were logicians and metaphysicians and that they had buried their thinking in these matters with no end in view but gaining a reputation for learning and attaining prestige and wealth as a result. They were complaining that they led wretched lives now because they had absorbed these things with no useful purpose, and had therefore not perfected their rational capacity with them. Their speech was slow and barely audible (*mute sonans*).

While this was going on, two spirits talked to each other above my head. When I asked who they were, I was told that one of them was most renowned in the world of letters, and I was given to believe that it was Aristotle. There was no mention of who the other one was.

Then the first one was returned to the state he had been in while he lived in the world (anyone can readily be returned to the state of life he had in the world because everyone has his whole state of life with him). Surprisingly, he attached himself to my right ear and talked there, hoarsely but still intelligibly.

From the meaning of what he said, I was aware that he was of a wholly different genius than the scholastics who sprang up immediately after him. That is, he ruled out of his thinking what he had written and the philosophy he had promoted in this way. For example, the terms he had found and imposed on matters of thought were an outward system for describing more inward things. Further, he was stirred up to this kind of enterprise by the delight of his affection and desire for knowing things that had to do with thinking, and he faithfully obeyed what his spirit said. This was why he attached himself to my right ear.

This was not the way his followers worked, who are called the scholastics. They do not proceed from thinking to terms but from terms to thinking—the opposite way, that is. And many of them do not even proceed to thinking, but cling strictly to terms, using them only to confirm what they wish and to force the guise of truth upon things that are false, in keeping with their craving to convince others. So for them, philosophy is a means to madness rather than a means to wisdom, and they therefore have darkness instead of light.

Then I talked with him about the science of analysis. I was given to say that children said more in half an hour in the realm of philosophy, analysis, and logic than he could describe in volumes, because every facet of human thinking and consequent speech is an analytic element whose laws come from the spiritual world. Anyone who wants to think artificially on the basis of terms is rather like a dancer who wants to learn to dance by knowing about the motor fibers and muscles. If his attention were fastened on these matters while he was dancing, he could barely move a foot. Yet without this knowledge, the same person moves all the motor fibers that are spread over his whole body, and uses his lungs, diaphragm, sides, arms, neck, and so on, all of which volumes could not describe. I said that it was like this for people who wanted to think from terms. He agreed with this, and said that if they were taught the path they would travel the wrong way on it. He added that if anyone wanted to be fatuous, that was the way to get there; but he himself thought constantly about usefulness and from a more inward standpoint.

Then he showed me what kind of concept he had had of the highest deity. He pictured this to himself as having a human face, with the head surrounded by a radiant circle. He now knew that the Lord was that very person and that the radiant circle was the divine from Him, which flowed not only into heaven but also into the universe, arranging and controlling it. He added that whoever arranges and controls heaven arranges and controls the universe because it is impossible to separate the one from the other. He also said that he believed in only one God, and that the names of the many gods people worshiped were signs of attributes and qualities of that God.

I saw a woman who was stretching out her hand and wanted to caress his cheek. When I wondered about this, he said that when he was in the world he often saw a woman like this who seemed to caress his cheek, and that her hand was lovely. Some angelic spirits told me that the early people did sometimes see women like this, and called them the Pallades. They also said that the women appeared to him from the spirits who lived with people in ancient times. They were delighted with concepts and enjoyed thought but lacked philosophy, and since spirits of this sort were with him and were delighted with him when he thought from deeper within, they presented this kind of woman representatively.

Finally, he suggested the kind of idea he had had of the human soul or spirit, which he called the "pneuma." He viewed it as something alive and inconspicuous, like a kind of ether. He said that he knew his spirit would live after death because it was his inner essence, which could not die because it could think. He also said that he could not think clearly about it, only vaguely, because he had no source of acquaintance with it other than himself, plus some brief glimpses from the ancients.

Incidentally, Aristotle is among the sane people in the other life, and many of his following are among the idiots.

4659.

We stated in nn. 4652f. that a person is a spirit and that the body serves the spirit for useful activities in the world, and in many other places we have stated that the spirit is the inner aspect of the person and the body the outer. If people do not grasp the relationship between the human spirit and its body, they may suppose that the spirit lives inside the body and that the body, so to speak, surrounds it and clothes it. But it should be realized that the spirit is in the body—in all of it and in every part of it; that it is the body's purer substance in both the motor and the sensory organs, and the body is a material entity connected with the spirit at every point, suited to the world the person is then in.

This is what it means to say that a person is a spirit, that the body serves the spirit for useful functions in this world, and that the spirit is the inner aspect of the person and the body the outer. We can also see from this that after death people are likewise in possession of active life and sensory life and are also in human form the way they were in the world, albeit a more perfect one.

Section 5.   Taste, the Mouth, and the Face

4791.

The mouth (lit. "tongue") gives access to the lungs and also to the stomach, so it pictures a kind of entryway to spiritual and heavenly things—to spiritual ones because it serves the lungs and consequently aids in speech, and heavenly ones because it serves the stomach, which furnishes nourishment to the blood and the heart. On the correspondence of the lungs with spiritual matters and the heart with heavenly matters, see nn. 3635 and 3883–3896.

For this reason, the mouth corresponds in a general way to an affection for what is true, or to the people in the Universal Human who are involved in affection for what is true, and secondarily in affection for the good that comes from what is true. People who love the Lord's Word, and long for insights from it into what is true and good, belong to this province. But there are distinctions: some belong to the tongue, some to the larynx and windpipe, some to the throat, some to the gums, and some to the lips. For there is not even the smallest part of a person with which there is no correspondence.

I have often been granted experience of the fact that people involved in affection for what is true belong to the province of discernment, in a broad sense. This has happened by an obvious inflow sometimes into my tongue and sometimes into my lips, after which I have been allowed to talk with the people involved. And I have observed that here, too, some spirits correspond to the more inward parts of the mouth and lips, and some to the more outward. If people welcome only more outward truths but not more inward ones without rejecting the latter, I have felt their working not in the inner parts of the mouth but in the outer.

4792.

Since food and nourishment correspond to spiritual food and nourishment, taste corresponds to perception and its affection. Spiritual food is information, discernment, and wisdom. Spirits and angels actually live on these and are nourished by them; they long for them

156

and hunger for them the way starving people long for food. For this reason, appetite corresponds to this longing.

Marvelous as it may seem, they grow on this food. In fact, children who die look exactly like children in the other life and are children as far as their discernment is concerned. But as their discernment and wisdom grow, they do not look like children but like adolescents and eventually like adults. I have talked with some people who died in childhood and looked like youths to me because by that time they were discerning. We can see from this that food is spiritual nourishment.

4793.

Since taste corresponds to perception and to affection for knowing, discerning, and being wise, and since people's life is in that affection, no spirit or angel is allowed to flow into people's taste, for this would mean flowing into the life that is properly theirs. There are, however, wandering spirits from the hellish mob who are more vicious than the rest. Because during their physical life they were absorbed in gaining access to people's affections to do them harm, they keep this craving in the other life as well, and they try by all possible means to gain access to people's taste. If they do gain access, they take over people's more inward reaches, the life of their thoughts and affections. For as stated, they correspond, and things that correspond act as one. Many people nowadays are possessed by them. Obsessions nowadays are relatively inward, not more outward the way they used to be. These inner obsessions are caused by spirits like these. We can tell what they are like by looking at the thoughts and affections, especially the more inward intentions, that people are afraid to have seen. These are so insane in some people that if they were not restrained by outward bonds—prestige, profit, reputation, fear for their lives, and fear of the law—they would rush into acts of murder and plunder faster than madmen. The reader may see in n. 1983 who the spirits are who are laying siege to the inner realms of people of this kind, and what they are like.

To let me know how this worked, they were given permission to try to enter my taste, which they tried to do as hard as they could. Then I was that sure that if they got through into my taste they would also take over my inner reaches, because taste depends on those inner reaches by correspondence with which taste works. They were actually driven off instantly.

EMANUEL SWEDENBORG

These vicious spirits try primarily to loosen all the inner bonds, which are affections for what is good and true or just and fair, fear of divine law, reluctance to harm one's community or homeland. Once these inner bonds are loosened, then the individual is possessed by spirits like these.

If they cannot get themselves into people's inner reaches in this way, by persistence, then they try magical arts, which abound in the other life, arts utterly unknown in this world. They use those to corrupt the information that favors their worst cravings. This kind of possession can be avoided only if people have an affection for what is good and a consequent faith in the Lord.

I have also been shown how they were driven away. When they were thinking of penetrating to the inner parts of the head and the brain, they were brought down through the excretory routes there, and in this way were brought toward the outer layers of the skin. There they seemed to be hurled into a ditch that was bubbling with liquid filth. I was informed that spirits like this correspond to pockets of infection in the surface skin where scabies occurs, so they correspond to scabies.

4794.

Spirits, or people after death, have all the senses they had while they were living in the world—sight, hearing, smell, and taste, that is. They do not, however, really have a sense of taste, but instead something like it that is connected with smell. The reason they do not have taste is that they thus cannot gain access to the taste of people on earth, and in this way take possession of their inner reaches. Then, too, this prevents them from being distracted by this sense from the longing to know and be wise—that is, from spiritual hunger.

4795.

This also enables us to determine why twin functions are assigned to the tongue—the function of assisting in speech and the function of assisting in nutrition. To the extent that it assists in nutrition, it corresponds to an affection for knowing, discerning, and being wise, which is why the words for wisdom and being wise, *sapientia* and *sapere,* come from the word for flavor, *sapor.* And to the extent that it asserts in speech, it corresponds to an affection for thinking and bringing forth these matters.

THE UNIVERSAL HUMAN

4796.

When angels make themselves visible, all their inner affections appear clearly in their faces and radiate from them, as though the face were the outward form and pictorial representation of the affections. To have a face that differs from one's affections does not happen in heaven. If people do feign a different face, they are cast out of the community.

We can see from this that the face corresponds in general to all the more inward elements, affections and thoughts alike, or elements both of intent and of discernment within people. So in the Word too, "the face" and "faces" are used to mean affections, and "the Lord lifting up His countenance" upon someone means that He is merciful out of the divine affection that belongs to His love.

4797.

Changes of affectional state are genuinely visible in angels' faces as well. When they are in their own community, they have their own faces; but when they enter another community, their faces change to accord with that community's affections for what is good and true. But the actual face is still a background that is recognizable throughout the changes. I have seen sequences of changes reflecting the affections of communities with which angels were communicating. For each individual angel is in some province of the Universal Human, and therefore communicates broadly and in a general way with all the angels who are in the same province, even though each one is in the part of that province to which he or she most precisely corresponds.

I have seen their faces altering by variations from one end of their range of affections to the other; but I have observed that the same basic face remained, as though the dominant affection were shining through all its variant forms. So I was shown the faces of a complete affection over its full range.

Marvelously, I have also been shown the changes of affections from early childhood to adulthood by facial variants. I was enabled to recognize how much from childhood was retained in the later age, and to recognize that this was the person's distinctive humanity. There is actually an outward form of innocence in the little child that is the distinctive humanity; and love and charity from the Lord flow into it as into a plane. When the person is regenerated and becomes

159

wise, then the childhood innocence, which was external, becomes internal. This is why true wisdom dwells in no home but innocence (cf. nn. 2305, 2306, 3183, 3994). It is also why the only people who can enter heaven are the ones who have some innocence, in keeping with the Lord's words, "Unless you become little children, you will not enter the kingdom of heaven" (Mt 18:3, Mk 10:15).

4798.

Evil spirits too can be recognized by their faces, for all their cravings or evil affections are written on their faces. One can also tell from their faces which hells they are communicating with. For the hells are many, all distinguished by the genera and species of cravings for evil. In general, when their faces are seen in heaven's light, they are almost lifeless. Some are sallow like corpses, some black, some monstrous. They are actually forms of hatred, cruelty, deceit, and hypocrisy. But to each other, in their own light, they look different because of hallucination.

4799.

There were some spirits with me from another planet, which I have described elsewhere, whose faces were different from those of the people of one planet. Their faces protruded, especially around the lips, and were also open. When I talked with them about their life-style and how they conversed with each other, they said that among themselves they talked primarily by facial changes, especially changes around the lips, expressing their affections with the parts of the face around the eyes, in such a way that their companions could grasp fully both what they were thinking and what they were intending. They also tried to demonstrate this to me by flowing into my lips, using various kinds of folding and curving around them. However, I was not able to receive these changes because my lips had not been devoted to this kind of discipline from early childhood. Still, I could observe what they said through this communication of their thinking.

However, I can confirm the ability of the lips to express speech in general from the multiple sequences of muscle fibers woven together around the lips. If these were individually developed so that they acted articulately and freely, they could express many variant forms that are unknown to people in whom these muscle fibers lie squeezed together.

The reason they have this kind of speech there is that they are unable to pretend, or to think one way and present a face that is at variance. They actually live in such sincerity that nothing whatever is hidden from their companions. Rather, they know instantly what others are thinking, what they are intending and therefore what they are like, and also what they are working toward. In fact, actions accomplished by people who are sincere dwell within the frame of conscience, so other people can tell at a glance what their inner expression or spirit is.

They showed me that they do not control their faces, but let them act freely. It is different for people who from childhood have accustomed themselves to pretending—that is, to speaking and acting differently from their thought and intent. Their faces are tensed in readiness to change as their shrewdness advises. Anything someone wants to conceal does make the face tense; the face expands from this tension when the person is pretending to express something sincerely.

While I was reading about the Lord in the New Testament of the Word, the spirits mentioned above were present, and some Christians were with me as well. I perceived that these latter were cherishing libels against the Lord within themselves and that they also wanted to communicate them silently. The spirits from the other planet were amazed that the Christians were like this. But I was given to tell them that in our world they were not like that out loud, though they were at heart. I also said that there were people like this who preached the Lord, and moved the masses to sighs and even to tears by their pretended pious zeal, conveying absolutely nothing of what was in their hearts. The spirits were speechless that such a discrepancy could exist between inner and outer things, between thought and speech. They said that they had absolutely no knowledge of this kind of discrepancy and that it was impossible for them to say with the mouth or display with the face anything at odds with the affections of the heart. If it were not for this, they would be broken apart and destroyed.

4800.

Very few people can believe that there are communities of spirits and angels that correspond to specific parts of the human being, and that the more communities there are and the more members within a community, the better and stronger the correspondence is. There is actually a strength in numbers when there is one heart.

To teach me this, I have been shown how they activate and flow into the face, how they do so into the muscles of the forehead, the cheeks, the chin, and the throat. Members of the first of these provinces were allowed to flow into me, and then the particular parts were altered according to their inflow. Some of them talked with me as well, but they did not know that they were assigned to the province of the face. The assigned province is kept hidden from spirits, but not from angels.

4801.

One particular person talked with me who during his earthly lifetime had been exceptionally knowledgeable about the more external truths of faith but had not led a life in conformity with the precepts of faith. He actually loved no one but himself, despised others in comparison, and believed that he would be among the leaders in heaven. But since he was like this, the only notion he could have of heaven was that it was like an earthly kingdom. When he discovered in the other life that heaven is utterly different, that the leaders there are the people who have not climbed over others, and especially the people who have believed themselves unworthy of mercy and therefore last as far as earning anything is concerned, then he was highly incensed and rejected those things that had made up his faith during his physical life. He tried incessantly to bring violence on the people who belonged to the province of the tongue. I was allowed to feel his effort deeply for many weeks, and to know in this way the identity and quality of the people who correspond to the tongue, and to know who the ones are who are opposed to them.

4802.

There are also spirits like this who sometimes let in heaven's light and accept true elements of faith, but are still evil. This means that they have some perception of what is true, and also accept truths avidly, but not in order to live by them. Their goal is rather to boast of them and to be seen as exceptionally discerning and sharp-sighted. Human discernment is actually so constituted that it can accept what is true, but true things do not become part of people unless they live by them. If human discernment were not like this, people could not be reformed.

If people were like this in the world—understanding what is true and still living lives of evil—they are the same in the other life as well, but in that life their ability to discern what is true is misused, for gaining control of others. They know there that truth gives them a communication with some heavenly communities, so that they can be with evil people and succeed, since in the other life truths are attended by power. But since they have lives of evil, they are in hell.

I talked with a pair of people who were like this during their physical life, who were astonished to be in hell, since they had quite a convincing belief in the elements of faith. But they were told that for them the light by which they discerned truths was a light like that of winter in the world. In it, things looked just as beautiful and colorful as in the light of summer, but everything becomes numb in that light and nothing seems delightful or glad. Further, since the goal of their discernment of truth was boasting and therefore was selfish, when the sphere of their goals rears itself up toward the more inward heavens, to angels by whom only goals are perceived, this is unbearable. Then they are cast away, which is why they were in hell. It was added that in the olden days people like this were especially called "serpents of the tree of knowledge," because when they debated about life, they spoke in opposition to truths. It was also said that women are like this who have lovely faces but smell foul. They are for this reason rejected wherever they go, cast out of the communities. When people like this come to angelic communities in the other life, they actually do smell, and they sense this themselves as they approach the communities. All this enables us to determine what faith is when there is no life of faith.

4803.

One fact quite unknown in this world is worthy of mention: the fact that the states of good spirits and angels are constantly changing and improving, and that as this happens they move up into the more inward realm of the province they live in, which means moving into worthier functions. In fact, there is in heaven a constant purification, a new creation, so to speak. However, things are so arranged that to eternity, no angel can ever arrive at absolute perfection. The Lord alone is perfect and all perfection comes from Him.

The people who correspond to the mouth constantly want to talk, since they find the peak of delight in talking. As they are being perfected, they reach a point where they say only what benefits their companions, their group, their heaven, and their Lord. Their joy in talking in this manner increases in the measure that the craving dies of focusing on themselves in their talking and of soliciting wisdom on their own account.

4804.

There are many communities in the other life called "friendly societies." They are made up of people who during their physical lives preferred the joy of conversation to all others, and who loved the people they talked with without caring whether they were good or evil as long as they were pleasant. So they were not friends to what is good and true.

People who were like this during physical life are like this in the other life; they apply themselves exclusively to the delight of conversation. Many such communities have been with me, but at a distance, seen primarily a little to the right, higher than my head. I have been enabled to notice their presence by a sluggishness and dullness and by a lessening of the joy I was in. The presence of communities of this sort actually brings these symptoms on. Wherever they come, they take joy away from others. And, remarkably, they make it part of themselves. They actually divert the spirits who are with other people and turn them toward themselves. As a result, they transfer another's joy to themselves. And since they are therefore troublesome and harmful to people involved in what is good, they are barred by the Lord from coming near to heavenly communities. This lets us know how much harm is done to people's spiritual lives by friendship if the focus is on the role (*persona*) rather than on the good. Anyone can of course be a friend to someone else, but must still be friendliest to the good.

4805.

There are also more inward friendly societies which do not take away the outward joy of others and divert it to themselves, but take the inner joy or blessedness that derives from the affection for spiritual things. They are in front, to the right, just above the lower earth, with some of them a little higher. I have sometimes talked with the lower ones, and then the higher ones would flow in, in a general way. They were the sort of people who during their physical life had at heart loved the people who were within their own broader circle and who returned their brotherly embrace. They believed that they only

164

were really alive and enlightened, and that people outside their communion were relatively lifeless, so to speak, and benighted. And since they were like this, they also thought the Lord's heaven would consist wholly of their chosen few.

But I was given to tell them that the Lord's heaven is vast, made up of people from every tribe and tongue, and that in it dwell all the people who were involved in the good of love and faith. They were also shown that there are people in heaven who relate to every province of the body, both external and internal. However, if they aspired to anything but what corresponds to their life, they could not have heaven. Then they were shown that their own community was a more inward friendly society, which by nature, as stated, robbed others of the blessedness of spiritual affections when they approached, that they regarded others as "not the elect" and as lifeless. When this thought was communicated to them, it brought on a sadness, which, nevertheless, by a law of the design of the other life, turns back on themselves.

CHAPTER 5
Hands, Arms, Feet, and Legs

4931.

We have explained above that heaven in its entirety reflects a single person, including the particular organs, members, and viscera. This is because heaven reflects the Lord; the Lord is actually the "all in all" of heaven, to the point that heaven strictly speaking is the Divine-True and the Divine-Good that come from the Lord. This is why heaven is divided into so many so-called provinces, as many as there are viscera, organs, and members in a person, and there is a correspondence with them. Without this kind of correspondence between the human being and heaven, and through heaven with the Lord, humanity would not last even for a moment. All these elements are held together by means of inflow.

But all these provinces relate to two kingdoms, a heavenly kingdom and a spiritual kingdom. The former, that is, the heavenly kingdom, is the kingdom of the heart in the Universal Human; while the latter, that is, the spiritual kingdom, is the kingdom of the lungs in the Universal Human. Just as in a person, the heart dominates and the lungs dominate in each and every detail. These two kingdoms are marvelously united. The union is also portrayed in the union of heart and lungs in the human, and in the union of their functioning in the particular members and viscera.

A person as embryo, or still in the womb, is in the kingdom of the heart, but on being brought forth from the womb, enters the kingdom of the lungs in addition. And if people suffer themselves to be led through by truths of faith into the good of love, then they return from the kingdom of the lungs into the kingdom of the heart within the Universal Human. So they actually reenter the womb and are reborn. Then, too, the two kingdoms are united within them, but in reverse order. Before, the kingdom of the heart was actually under the control of the lungs, but afterward the kingdom of the lungs is under the control of the heart. That is, the truth of faith was dominant in them before, but afterward the good of charity is dominant. On the correspondence of the heart with the good of love and the lungs with the truth of faith, see nn. 3635 and 3883–3896 above.

4932.

The people in the Universal Human who correspond to the hands, arms, and also the shoulders are the ones possessed of power through faith's truth derived from what is good. People who are actually involved in faith's truth derived from what is good are involved in the Lord's power. They ascribe all power to Him and none to themselves; and the more they ascribe nothing to themselves not verbally, but at heart, the more power they have. This is why angels are called powers and strengths.

4933.

The reason hands, arms, and shoulders correspond to powers in the Universal Human is that all the energies and powers of the whole body and of all its inner organs relate to them. For the body exercises its energies and powers through the arms and hands. This is why "hands, arms, and shoulders" are used in the Word to indicate powers (on this use of "hand" cf. nn. 878, 3387). We can see this use of "arms" in many passages, such as the following:

Be our arm each morning (Is 33:2).

The Lord Jehovah is coming in strength, and
His arm will rule for Him (Is 11:10).

He will do this by the arm of his might (Is 44:12).

My arms will judge the peoples (Is 51:5).

Put on your might, O arm of Jehovah (Is 51:9).

I looked about and there was no helper; ... Therefore My own arm brought salvation (Is 53:5).

Cursed be the person who trusts in man, and makes flesh his arm (Jer 17:5).

I made earth, man, and beast, ... by My great power, and by My outstretched arm (Jer 27:5, 32:17).

The horn of Moab is cut off, and his arm is broken (Jer 48:25).

I am breaking the arms of the king of Egypt, ... I will strengthen the arms of the king of Babylon against him (Ez 30:22, 24, 25).

Jehovah, break the arm of the impious (Ps 10:15).

According to the greatness of your arm, make the sons of death remain (Ps 79:11).

They were led out of Egypt by a strong hand and an outstretched arm (Dt 7:19; 11:2, 3; 26:8; Jer 32:21; Ps 136:12).

We can conclude from this also that "the right hand" is used in the Word to mean a higher power, and "sitting on the right hand of Jehovah" to mean omnipotence (Mt 26:63, 64; Lk 22:69; Mk 14:61, 62; 16:19).

4934.

I saw a naked arm, bent forward, that had so much force and at the same time menace in it that I not only began to tremble, I felt as though I could be utterly crushed to the finest powder. It was irresistible. I have seen this arm twice. In this way I was taught that "arms" mean might and "hands" power. I also felt a heat breathing from the arm.

4935.

The naked arm is presented in different positions, which determine how it terrifies. In the position just described, it is beyond belief. It actually seems as though it could instantly shatter bones and marrow. Even people who were fearless during their physical life are struck with utter terror at this arm in the other life.

4936.

Sometimes people have appeared holding staffs, and I have been told that they were wizards. They are in front, a long way to the right, deep in caves. The ones who were more virulent wizards are more deeply hidden away there. They seem to themselves to have staffs. By hallucinations, they form many kinds of staff, and they believe they can do miracles with them. They think there is an energy in their staffs. One reason for this is that staffs are supports for their right hands and arms, which by correspondence are might and power.

I could see from this why people in olden times thought of wizards as having staffs. The early pagans got this from the representative early church in which staffs like hands were signs of power (cf. n. 4876). And since they were signs of power, when miracles were to happen Moses was commanded to stretch out his staff or his hand (Ex 4:17, 20; 8:5–20; 9:23; 10:3–21; 14:21, 26, 27; 17:5, 6, 11, 12; Nm 20:7–10).

4937.

Hellish spirits too sometimes present a shoulder by hallucination, using it to repel forces that are then unable to pass by it. However, this works only for the people who are involved in such hallucinations. They do know that the shoulder corresponds to all power in the spiritual world. "Shoulder" is also used in the Word to mean all power, as we can see in the following passages:

You have shattered the yoke of his burden and the staff of his shoulder (Is 9:6).

You push with side and shoulder, and thrust with your horns (Ez 34:21).

You split his whole shoulder (Ez 29:7).

... that they may serve Jehovah with one shoulder (Zep 3:9).

A boy is born to us ... and the government will be upon His shoulder (Is 9:6).

I will place the key of the house of David upon His shoulder (Is 22:22).

4938.

The people in the Universal Human who correspond to the feet, soles, and heels are people who are nature-centered; so "feet" are used in the Word to indicate things of nature (cf. nn. 2162, 3147, 3761, 3986, 4280); "soles," lower elements of nature (cf. n. 259). Actually, heavenly things in the Universal Human constitute the head, spiritual things the body, and natural things the feet. They also follow in this order. Then, too, the heavenly things, which are highest, are bounded by the spiritual things, which are intermediate; and the spiritual things are bounded by the natural things, which are lowest (*ultima*).

4939.

Just once, when I was raised into heaven, there appeared to me a kind of head on my level, with a body below and with feet still lower down. I perceived from this how the higher and lower elements of human beings correspond to things in the Universal Human, and how the one flows into the other. I perceived, that is, that the heavenly (which is the good that belongs to love and is the first member of the sequence) flows into the spiritual (which is the true derived from it and is the second member of the sequence) and then into the natural, which is the third member of the sequence.

We can see from this that natural things are like the feet that support higher things. It is nature too that bounds the realities of the spiritual world and of heaven. This is why nature in its entirety is a theater that portrays the Lord's kingdom, and why the details of nature are symbolic (cf. nn. 2758, 3483). It is also why nature continues to exist by an inflow that follows this sequence, and why it could not last an instant without this inflow.

4940.

Another time when, surrounded by a column of angels, I was let down into areas of the lower regions, I was enabled to perceive with my senses that the people in the land of the lower realms corresponded to the feet and the soles. Then, too, these areas are underneath the feet and the soles.

I also talked with the people there; they were the kind who were involved in natural pleasure and not in spiritual pleasure. On the lower earth, see n. 4728.

4941.

In these areas also live the people who credited everything to nature and very little to the divine. When I have talked with them and the conversation has turned to the subject of divine providence, they traced everything back to nature. Still, people there who led a good moral life, after being kept there for some time, gradually shed these principles and don true ones.

4942.

While I was there, I heard a noise in one room that sounded as though there were people on the other side of the wall who wanted to break in. This terrified the people in the room, who were convinced that they were robbers. I was told that the people there are kept in this kind of fear to deter them from evils, since for some people fear is a means to improvement.

4943.

In the lower earth under the feet and soles, there also live the people who placed merit in good deeds and works. Many of them seem to themselves to be splitting wood. The place where they are is quite cold, and it seems as though they get some warmth by their work.

I talked to them, too, and I was allowed to ask whether they wanted to leave the area. They said that they had not yet earned this by their work. But when they have completed this stage, they are released.

These people are on the natural level because wanting to earn salvation is not spiritual. Besides, they value themselves more highly than they do others, and some of them even look down on other people. If they do not get more joy than others in the other life, they are angry at the Lord. So when they split wood, it sometimes seems as though something of the Lord's is under the wood, an appearance that stems from their displeasure.

However, since they did lead religious lives and behaved as they did out of an ignorance that contained some innocence, sometimes angels are sent to them to comfort them. Also, something like a sheep appears to them at times, above them and to their left, and they derive some comfort from this sight.

4944.

As for people from our world who came from Christendom, lived good moral lives, and had some charity toward the neighbor but did not care much about spiritual matters, most of them are sent to places under the feet and the soles until they shed the natural concerns they were involved in and absorb as much of spiritual and heavenly matters as they can in view of their former life. Once they have absorbed these, they are brought out and raised into heavenly communities. I have sometimes seen them coming out, and have seen their happiness at entering heavenly life.

4945.

I have not yet been allowed to know the arrangement of the areas under the feet. There are very many of them, and they are quite distinct. Taken together, they are called "the land of the lower regions."

4946.

There are some people who during their physical lives had absorbed the notion that people should not care about matters of the inner person, that is, spiritual ones, but only about matters of the outer person, or natural ones, because deeper matters would disturb the pleasures of their lives and render them unpleasant. They tended

171

to act on my left knee, a little above the knee in front, and also on the sole of my right foot.

I talked with them in their house. They said that during their physical lives they had thought that only outward things were alive, not discerning what the internal was. That is, they knew about natural matters, but they did not know what the spiritual was. But I was allowed to tell them that by doing this, they had shut out countless things that could have flowed in from the spiritual world if they had given recognition to deeper concerns and thus allowed them to enter their thought-concepts.

I was also allowed to say that there are countless elements in each thought-concept that seem like nothing but a simple unit to a person who is primarily nature-centered. Yet there is an unlimited number of things that flow in from the spiritual world, giving spiritual people a higher kind of insight that enables them to see and grasp whether something is true or not.

Since they had doubts about this, it was demonstrated by first-hand experience. A single concept was portrayed for them, which they saw as a simple unit—like a vague point, that is. Things like this are readily portrayed in heaven's light. When this concept was opened and their inner sight was opened at the same time, then it looked like a universe leading to the Lord. They were told that it was like this in every concept of the good and the true—each is an image of the whole heaven because each comes from the Lord, who is the whole of heaven, or the actual essence that is called heaven.

4947.

People also live under the soles of the feet who during their physical lives have "lived the good life" in a worldly sense—gratified by things of a worldly nature, loving to live in luxury, but only from an outward or physical desire and not from an inner or mental one. They have not actually been conceited or valued themselves above others, even though they were established in positions of importance. They lived as they did for physical reasons. So they had not rejected the church's teachings, much less convinced themselves that those teachings were wrong. At heart, they said these teachings were true because people who studied the Word knew they were. In some people like this, the more inward reaches are open toward heaven, and they are gradually sown with heavenly seed—justice, honesty, piety, charity, mercy—and eventually they are brought up into heaven.

THE UNIVERSAL HUMAN

4948.

However, people who during their physical lives have thought about and focused on nothing, inwardly, except selfish and worldly concerns have closed off every path or all inflow from heaven. For love of self and the world is the opposite of heavenly love.

People like this who lived in luxury or in the gracious life, combining this with cunning at a deeper level, are under the sole of the right foot. But they are deep down there, underneath the land of the lower regions, where there is a hell for people of this sort. There is nothing but filth in their homes. They seem to be carrying filth around, because their lives correspond to such stuff. One senses the stench of filth, varied according to their different kinds and types of life. Many people who were celebrities on earth wind up there.

4949.

There are many people who have homes under the soles of the feet, and I have occasionally talked with them. I have seen some of them trying to climb out, and have been allowed to feel their effort to climb. It reached all the way to my knees, but they fell back. This is how it is portrayed to the senses when some of the people from these houses aspire to higher things, as these for example coveted the houses of people in the province of the knees and thighs. I was told that people like this were ones who had looked down on others. This is why they want to get out—not just through the foot into the thigh, but even above the head if they can; but eventually they fall back. They have a particular kind of stupidity, for this kind of arrogance stifles and quenches heaven's light—that is, intelligence. This is why the sphere that surrounds them looks like sediment.

4950.

Under the left foot, a little to the left of center, there are the people who credited everything to nature but nevertheless admitted that there was a "being of the universe" from which all of nature came. They were, however, examined to see whether they believed in any "being of the universe" or "highest deity (*summum numen*)" that had created everything. On the contrary, I perceived from their thinking as it was communicated to me that this was like something soulless, which in their belief had no life. I could conclude from this that they did not acknowledge a Creator of the universe, but acknowledged (only) nature. They even said that it was impossible for them to have a concept of a living deity.

4951.

Under the heel, a little farther back, there is a deep hell. The intervening space looks like a vacuum. The most vicious people are there. They explore spirits furtively with a view to doing them harm, and they slip in furtively in order to destroy. This was their life's delight.

I have often watched them. They pour out the venom of their malice toward people in the world of spirits and they rouse up the people there by various tricks. They are profoundly vicious. They look as though they were wearing cloaks, though sometimes they look different. They are often punished, and when this happens they are sent down deeper and covered with a kind of cloud, which is the sphere of malice that breathes from them. One sometimes hears a kind of murderous roar coming out of that depth.

They can reduce people to tears or strike them with terror. They gained this ability during their physical lives by associating with sickly and simple people in order to get hold of their wealth. They would reduce them to tears and so move them to compassion, and if this did not work, they would strike at their fears. There are many people of this sort who plundered numbers of homes in this way, to enrich monasteries.

I have also noted some in the middle distance, but these seemd to be sitting in a room and talking things over. They are also vicious, but not to the same extent.

4952.

Some people who were nature-centered told me that they did not know what to believe because everyone's lasting lot depended on his life and also on how he thought from confirmed principles. But I answered that it would have been adequate if they had believed that there was a God who governed everything, that there was a life after death, and especially if they had lived not like wild animals but like people—that is, in love for the Lord and in charity toward the neighbor, in what is good and true instead of against it.

They countered that they had lived like this, but I rejoined that they seemed so outwardly, but if the laws had not stood in the way they would have pounced upon the life and wealth of anyone handy more savagely than wild animals.

They came back with the claim that they did not know what charity toward the neighbor was or what "the internal" was. But I answered that they were unable to know because a love of self and the world, and outward concerns, had taken over all their thinking and purposing.

CHAPTER 6
The Loins and Reproductive Organs

5050.

We have in the preceding chapter shown which people in the Universal Human or heaven belong to the province of the hands, arms, and feet. Now we need to tell which communities in heaven or the Universal Human are the ones the loins correspond to, the loins and the connected organs we refer to as the reproductive organs. In general terms, we must realize that the loins and their associated organs correspond to genuine marriage love, and therefore to communities of people characterized by that love. The people in these communities are exceptionally heavenly, and live more than others in the delight of peace.

5051.

In the course of a peaceful dream, I saw several trees set in a woody shelter. One was tall, the second lower, and two were small. The lower tree moved me with an intense delight, and all the while an utterly indescribable charm was touching my mind.

When I woke up, I talked with the people who had been causing the dream. They were angelic spirits (see nn. 1977 and 1979), who told me that what this scene referred to was marriage love: the tall tree referred to a husband, the lower one to a wife, and the two small ones to children. They went on to say that the extraordinarily delightful peace that had touched my mind was indicative of the delight of the peace people have in the other life who have lived in genuine marriage love. They added that people like this belong to the province of the thighs just above the knees, while the ones in a state of still greater delight belong to the province of the loins.

I was also shown that there is a mediating communication

through the feet with the soles and heels. We can see that this communication exists from the large nerve in the thigh. It sends out its branches not just through the loins to the organs assigned to procreation (which are the organs of marriage love), but also through the feet to the soles and heels. This also clarified what is meant in the Word by the hollow and nerve in Jacob's thigh, which was dislocated when he wrestled with the angel (Gn 26:25, 31, 32), discussed above in nn. 4280, 4281, and 4314–4317.

Then I saw a huge dog, like the ones the ancient writers called Cerberus, with its jaws gaping in terrifying fashion. I was told that a dog like this means a guard to prevent people from crossing over from heavenly marriage love to a love of adultery, which is hellish. Heavenly marriage love occurs when spouse loves spouse most tenderly and lives with the children, content in the Lord. This gives an inward delight in this world, and a heavenly joy in the other life. But when someone is crossing over from this love to the opposite one, and it seems to contain a heavenly joy even though it is hellish, then this kind of dog appears as a guard, so that the contradictory pleasures will not make contact.

5052.

The innermost heaven is the one through which the Lord instills marriage love. The people there are in peace more than other people are. Peace in the heavens is quite like springtime in the world, which touches everything with rejoicing: it is utterly heavenly in its origin. The angels in this heaven are the wisest of all. They love little children far more than their own fathers and mothers do. They are present with infants in the womb, and through them the Lord takes care that infants are nourished and developed there. So they superintend the womb during the process of birth.

5053.

There are heavenly communities that correspond to all the organs and members assigned to procreation in each sex. These communities are distinct from others just as this province in the human body is quite distinct and separate from the rest.

The reason these communities are heavenly is that marriage love is the basis of all loves (see nn. 686, 2733, 2737, and 2738). Its use is also the highest of all, which gives it the greatest of joys. For marriage is the seedbed of the whole human race, and also the seedbed of the Lord's heavenly kingdom, since heaven comes from the human race.

5054.

People who have loved little children very tenderly, especially mothers with this love, are in the province of the womb and the surrounding organs, the cervix and the ovaries. The life people there enjoy is the gentlest and sweetest of all, and they have a surpassing heavenly joy.

5055.

But I have not been allowed to know the identity and nature of the communities that belong to the specific organs of generation. They are actually too inward for anyone in a lower sphere to understand. They relate to uses of those organs that are deeply hidden and far removed from knowledge. The reason is providential—to prevent things that are intrinsically most heavenly from damage by foul thoughts, which involve lewdness, promiscuity, and adultery. These thoughts are aroused in most people at the mere mention of these organs, so I am allowed to cite other things I have seen that are less closely connected.

5056.

A spirit from another planet was with me (I will discuss spirits from other planets elsewhere, by the Lord's divine mercy). He asked insistently that I intercede for him so that he could get into heaven. He said that he was not aware of having led an evil life, he had only reproved inhabitants of his planet. There are in fact people who reprove and punish others who do not live rightly, who will be mentioned in the description of inhabitants of other planets. He added that after he reproved them, he taught them. When he talked, his voice seemed to break, and he could arouse sympathy.

But all I could tell him was that I could be no help. Only the Lord could, and there was hope if he was worthy. But then he was sent back into the company of honest spirits from his own planet. They said that he could not join with them because he was not of their kind.

However, since he kept passionately demanding to be let into heaven, he was sent to a community of honest spirits from our planet.

These too, though, told him that he could not stay with them. In heaven's light, he had a black color, but he himself said he was not black, he was the reddish color of myrrh.

I was told that this was the characteristic first stage of people who are later accepted among those who make up the province of the seminal vesicles. The semen collects in these vesicles, with its appropriate fluid. Once they have been combined, the combination is passed on in such a form that after emission, the elements are separated in the cervix of the womb so that the process of conception can take place. There is in this substance an energy, a virtual desire, to perform this use, which means shedding the fluid it has been clothed in.

Something like this appeared in relation to this spirit. He came to me again, but in shoddy clothes, and said that he was longing to get into heaven, and that now he was aware of his own nature. I was allowed to tell him that this might be a sign that he would be accepted soon. Then he was told by angels that he should throw away his clothes. He threw them off eagerly, so quickly that practically nothing could have been quicker. This served to picture the kind of eagerness people have in the province to which the seminal vesicles correspond.

5057.

I saw a mortar, and there was a man standing beside it with an iron tool. In his hallucination, he seemed to be pulverizing people in the mortar, tormenting them cruelly. He was doing this with immense delight. The delight was communicated to me so that I could know what it is like and how strong it is for people like this. It was a hellish delight. I was told by angels that this kind of delight was predominant among Jacob's descendants, and that they found no greater pleasure than in treating unbelievers cruelly, leaving their bodies to the wild beasts and birds, dismembering them alive with saws and axes, throwing them into brick kilns (2 Sm 12:31), beating and hurling their children about. Things like this were commanded and conceded only to people whose thigh nerve was dislocated (cf. n. 5051). They live under the right heel, with adulterers who are also given to cruelty.

I also wondered that anyone believed that this people was chosen in preference to others. This is why so many people convince themselves that life makes no difference, that what matters is election and a consequent admission to heaven from pure mercy, regardless of the quality of one's past life. Yet rational sanity enables anyone to see that this kind of thinking is opposed to the divine. The divine is actually mercy itself, so that if heaven were a matter of mercy alone, regardless of past life, absolutely everyone would be accepted. Sending someone to hell to be tortured when that person could be accepted into heaven would be ruthlessness, not mercy. And choosing one person over another would be injustice, not justice.

So people who have believed and convinced themselves that they are the elect and that other people are not the elect, and that admission to heaven is by mercy, regardless of past life, were primarily people who had lived evil lives. They are told too, as I have heard and seen several times, that heaven is in no way denied to anyone by the Lord, and that if they wish they can learn this from experience. To this end, they are brought up into some community of heaven where there are people involved in an affection for what is good, or who have lived their lives in charity. But when they get there, being evil, they begin to feel pain and an inward torment because the life is opposed to them. And when heavenly light appears, then they look like devils in that light, almost devoid of human form. Some of them have their faces drawn in, some a kind of lattice of teeth, some look like monsters. In these forms they are horrified at themselves and dive headlong into hell, the deeper the better.

5058.

There was one man who had been quite prominent in the world. I had been acquainted with him, but had not known what he was like inwardly. But in the other life, after several cycles of his life state, it became clear that he was treacherous. After he had been with treacherous people for a while in the other life, and had had a hard time of it, he wanted to leave them. At that time I heard him saying that he wanted to get into heaven. He too believed that acceptance was simply a matter of mercy. He was told that if he arrived in heaven he would not be able to stay, that he would be tormented there like people on earth in their death throes, but he still insisted.

He too was let into a community of simple good folk, who were in front above my head. But once he arrived, he began to act deceitfully and treacherously, in keeping with his life. So in less than an hour the good people there, who were simple folk, began to complain that he was taking away their perception of what was good and true. This meant that he was taking away their delight and so ruining their state.

Then a little light from a more inward heaven was let in, in which he looked like a devil. The upper part of his nose had a deep, ugly wound cleaving it. He also began to be tormented inwardly. When he felt this, he made a dive out of the community into hell.

We can see from this that election and acceptance are not from mercy, but that it is a person's life that makes heaven. However, all the elements of a life of mercy and a faith of truth, grounded in mercy, are the elements in this world that are receptive of mercy. These people find acceptance from mercy, and are the ones called "the elect" (see nn. 3755 f., 3900).

5059.

As for people who have lived in patterns contrary to marriage love (in adultery, that is), when they have approached me they have tended to pour pain into my loins, the severity depending on the adulterous lives they had led. I could see from this inflow that the loins did correspond to marriage love.

Their hell, too, is under the back part of the loins, under the buttocks, and they spend their time there in filth and excrement. These materials are delicacies to them as well, since things like this correspond to these pleasures in the spiritual world. But this will need to be discussed when, by the Lord's divine mercy, we deal generally and specifically with the hells.

5060.

I have been able to determine which spirits correspond to the testes in the same way, that is, from people who are opposed to marriage love and afflict the testes with pain. When communities are at work, they act into those parts and members of the body to which they correspond. Heavenly communities do so with an inflow that is soft, sweet, and pleasant: the opposing hellish communities do so with an inflow that is harsh and painful. Their inflow, however, is perceptible only to people whose more inward reaches have been opened, and who have thereby been granted a perceptible communication with the spiritual world.

The people who are opposed to marriage love and affect the testes with pain are people who connive by using love, friendship, and favors. When people like this have come to me, they have wanted to talk to me in secret, with a great fear lest anyone else be present. They were like that during their physical lives; and since they were, they are the same in the other life. Everyone's life follows him.

Something faint and airy was welling up from the region around Gehenna. It was a group of spirits of this sort. At this point, however, it looked to me as though there were only one spirit even though there were many of them. There were bands in the way of this spirit, which he seemed to himself to be removing, meaning that he wanted to remove obstacles. Thought processes and mental efforts do actually appear symbolically in the world of spirits, and when they appear, one notes immediately what they mean.

After that, it seemed as though a small, snowy man came out of his body and approached me. This pictured their thinking and intent, their desire to put on a state of innocence so that no one could have any suspicions of them.

When he reached me, he headed down for my loins and seemed to wind himself around them, which pictured their desire to present themselves as being in chaste marriage love. Then he wound himself around my feet in spiraling curves, which pictured their desire to slip into me through things that are pleasant on the level of nature. Finally, this little man became almost invisible, which pictured their desire to be completely hidden.

I was told by angels that this kind of infiltration is characteristic of people who connive under the guise of marriage love, that is, who have in this world infiltrated with a view to adultery with married women, talking chastely and reasonably about marriage love, being nice to the children, by all means praising the husband, so that eventually they have been trusted as friendly, chaste, and innocent, when in fact they are devious adulterers.

I was shown what they are like as a result. After the events just described, the snowy little man became visible, and then he looked swarthy and very black, and most noticeably misshapen. He was cast into his hell, which was deep beneath the middle of the loins. People there spend their time in the foulest excrement; and in that region they are also with the thieves who relate to general involuntary sensation, described in n. 4327.

I have since talked with people like this, and have been puzzled by the fact that they had some conscience about adulteries. That is, because of conscience they would not sleep with someone else's wife when they were given leave. And when I talked with them about this, they denied that anyone had a conscience. I was told that most such people come from the Christian world, that there is rarely anyone from other regions.

5061.

By way of a corollary, I may add the following matter of interest. There were some spirits who lay hidden for a long while, closed into a private hell. I had occasionally wondered just who they were. Then one evening they were let out; and then I heard a sound coming from them, a rather chaotic murmur, which lasted quite a while. As they gained strength, I heard snide remarks about me coming from them, and perceived an effort toward climbing up and murdering me.

I asked some angels why. They said that these people had hated me during their lifetime, even though I had done them no harm whatsoever. I was also taught that when people like this simply perceive the sphere of someone they hate, they breathe out his destruction. However, they were sent back into their hell.

I could determine from this that people who have hated each other in this world do meet in the other life and try to do each other serious harm. I have learned about this often, from other instances as well. Hatred is in fact the opposite of love and charity, and is a spiritual turning away, a virtual spiritual revulsion. So the moment people like this perceive in the other life the sphere of someone they hate, they fly into a rage. We can see from this what is involved in the Lord's words in Matthew 5:22–26.

CHAPTER 7
The Inner Viscera

5171.

In the other life, one can tell what provinces heavenly communities belong to from their location relative to the human body, and also from their working and inflow. For they work and flow into the organ or member they belong to. However, their inflow and working cannot be perceived except by people who are in the other life. This can be perceived by people on earth only if their inward reaches are adequately opened, and even such people cannot perceive it unless the Lord has granted them the ability to reflect on their sensations and their perceptions at the same time.

5172.

There are some honest spirits whose thinking is not contemplative, and who therefore express what occurs to them quickly and apparently without premeditation. They have a quite inward perception, which is not so much put into visual forms the way it is for other people, since in the course of their lives they have been self-taught, so to speak, more about the goodness of things than about their truth.

It has been pointed out to me that people of this sort belong to the province of the thymus gland. The thymus is actually a gland that is especially important to children, and that is soft at that time of life. In people like this, there is still something soft and childlike into which their perception of the good flows; and a general sense of what is true shines forth from this perception. These people can be surrounded by turmoil and still not be confused, just like the gland in question.

5173.

In the other life, there are many kinds of agitation and also many kinds of leading into spiritual orbits. The blood pictures these agitations, as to the body fluids or lymphs—like the ways the chyle purifies things in the body, which is also accomplished by various violent ways of breaking things down. The leadings into spiral orbits are pictured by the ways these fluids are brought into use after their purification. One of the most common events in the other life is for spirits after they have been agitated to be brought into a peaceful and joyful state, or even into the communities they are to be admitted and joined to.

This correspondence of the breaking down and purifying of the blood, body fluids, and chyle, and the digestive processes in the stomach, with such phenomena in the spiritual world must necessarily seem strange to people who think only about the natural side of such processes. It will seem all the more strange to people who believe only in the natural side, and therefore deny that there is or can be any indwelling spiritual reality that is activating and controlling. Yet that is how things are—there is in each and every phenomenon of the three kingdoms of nature an inherent active force from the

EMANUEL SWEDENBORG

spiritual world. Otherwise, nothing whatever in the natural world would function as a cause or effect. Nothing, by the same token, would produce anything. This reality from the spiritual world that is inherent in natural phenomena is called the force instilled from the beginning of creation, but it is the energy whose cessation would mean the cessation of activity or motion. This is why the whole visible world is a theater symbolic of the spiritual world.

This is the same as with the muscular motions that give rise to activity. Unless there were an energy within, an energy from human thought and intent, action would instantly cease. For according to laws familiar in the scholarly world, if energy ceases, then motion ceases; in energy lies all directiveness; and there is nothing real within motion except energy. It is obvious that this force or energy within activity or motion is a spiritual reality within the natural because thinking and intending are spiritual, while being active and in motion are natural. People who do not think beyond the realm of nature do not grasp this at all, and yet they cannot deny it. However, the productive element in intent and secondarily in thought is not similar in form to the action produced. The action only symbolizes what the mind is intending and thinking.

5174.

It is recognized that nourishment or food is agitated in many ways in the stomach, to extract the contents that are suited to use, and that these are carried off in the chyle and go from there into the blood. It is known that this process continues in the intestines.

Agitations like these are pictured by the first agitations of spirits, all of which are consequent on their lives in the world, with a view to separating out the evil elements and gathering together the good elements that are suited to use. So we can say of souls or spirits that shortly after decease or separation from the body, they enter, so to speak, the region of the stomach and are there agitated and purified. People in whom evil elements have gained the upper hand, after they have been agitated without effect, carried through the stomach into the intestines and then all the way to the end—the colon and rectum —and from there they are discharged into the chamber-pot, that is, into hell. But people in whom good elements have the upper hand, after the processes of agitation and purification, become chyle and are carried off into the blood. This is a longer way for some, a shorter way for others. Some are agitated roughly, some gently, some very

184

little at all. The ones who are hardly agitated at all are pictured by the juices of foods that are absorbed by the blood vessels immediately and carried into the circulatory system all the way to the brain and beyond.

5175.

Actually, when people die and step into the other life, their lives are like something that is gently taken by the lips, and then is channeled through the mouth, throat, and esophagus into the stomach. How this happens depends on the natures they have acquired during physical life by their activities. Many people are handled gently at first, for they are kept in the company of angels and good spirits. This is symbolized by foods' first being handled gently by the lips and then having their quality tasted by the tongue. Foods that are soft—on the sweet side, rich, or spiritous—are taken directly into the blood vessels and carried into circulation. But foods that are hard —bitter, sour, not very nourishing—are handled more harshly. They are taken through the esophagus into the stomach, where they are broken down by various painful means. The ones that are still harder, more sour and barren, are forced down into the intestines and eventually into the rectum, where the first hell is. Eventually they are cast out and become excrement.

Human life after death is parallel. At first, people are kept in their outward concerns, and since they had led civil and moral lives outwardly, they are with angels and honest spirits. But afterward these outward aspects are taken away, and then their inner nature can be seen, what they are like in their thoughts and in their affections, and finally in their goals, which determine the kind of life they will have permanently.

5176.

As long as they are in this state—a state like that of nutrients or food in the stomach—they are not in the Universal Human, but are in the process of admission. But when, symbolically speaking, they are in the blood, then they are in the Universal Human.

5177.

People who have been very worried about the future, especially people who have therefore become grasping and miserly, appear in the region where the stomach is. Many of them have appeared to me there. Their life sphere can be compared to the nauseous smell that comes from the stomach, or to the rank smell of indigestion. People of this sort stay in this area a long time, because their worry about the future, confirmed by their behavior, severely hinders and slows down the inflow of spiritual life. They actually take responsibility for matters of divine providence; and people who do this put obstacles in the way of inflow and move the life of goodness and truth away from themselves.

5178.

Since worry about the future is what causes anxieties in people, and since people of this sort appear in the stomach region, anxieties affect the stomach more than the other inner organs. I have even been allowed to observe how these anxieties are increased and lessened according to the nearness and distance of these spirits. Some anxieties are felt more inwardly, some more outwardly, some higher up and some lower down, depending on the different sources, channels, and boundaries of these worries.

This is also why the region around the stomach is knotted when anxieties like this take possession of the spirit, sometimes painfully so, and why anxieties seem to well up from this region. This is also why the region around the stomach is free and relaxed, with a sense of well-being, when someone stops being worried about the future or when things are going so well that there is no fear of misfortune.

5179.

I once noticed a tension in the lower part of my stomach, from which I could tell that spirits of this sort were present. I talked with them, and said it would help if they went away because their sphere, which brought on anxiety, was not in keeping with the spheres of the spirits who were with me. Then we got talking about spheres, and the fact that there are so many spiritual spheres around a person, and yet people neither know nor want to know that they exist because they deny everything called spiritual, everything they cannot see and touch. We talked about the fact that there are spheres, from the spiritual world, surrounding people, and that through these spheres people are in community with spirits of like affection, and the fact that many things happen as a result that people either ascribe entirely to nature, or deny, or refer to the more mysterious side of nature. Take, for example, what people ascribe to luck. Some people are completely convinced by experience that some mysterious thing called luck is at work, but they do not know where it comes from. At some other time, if the Lord's divine mercy permits, we will explain from the witness of experience that this sort of thing is a result of one's spiritual sphere, and is the outmost aspect of providence.

5180.

There are genii and spirits who affect the head with a kind of suction or drawing, in a way that causes pain at the point where this kind of drawing or suction occurs. I have noted a clear feeling of suction, as though the membranes were being sucked out without anesthetic (*ad plenum sensum*). I doubt that other people could stand the pain, but being used to it, I have often undergone this, eventually without pain. The primary point of suction was the top of my head, and from there it spread toward the area of my left ear and then toward the region of my left eye. The spreading toward the eye was from spirits, while the spreading toward the ear was from genii. The latter and the former are the people who belong to the province of the *reservoirs and ducts of the chyle,* to which the chyle is drawn from all sides, at the same time that it is also being sent out in all directions.

Further, there were other spirits who were active inside my head in almost the same way but with a less forceful suction. I was told that these were people to whom a subtle chyle corresponded, a chyle that is brought toward the brain, and is there combined with fresh spirit of the soul in order to be consigned to the heart.

I first saw the ones who were acting from the outside, in front and a little to the left, and later higher up, as though their visible area was from a plane through the septum of the nose rising toward the plane of the left ear.

Two kinds of people make up this province, one rather unassuming, the other impudent. The unassuming ones are people who wanted to know others' thoughts in order to attract and obligate them to themselves. In fact, if someone knows another's thoughts very deeply, he knows that person's hidden and more inward aspects, which effect a union between them. Their goal is communication and friendship. These people want to know and explore only good things, and they interpret the rest favorably.

But the impudent ones have a craving and drive to catch other people's thoughts with a view either to profiting themselves or to harming others. Because of this kind of craving and drive, they keep the other's mind focused on the subject they want to know about, not letting up, and making connections with points of agreement that stem from affections. In this way, they draw out even secret thoughts. They act the same way in the other life, in the communities there, and even more skillfully. There they do not let the person wander from the concept that they are arousing and thereby drawing out. So afterward they virtually hold their victim in chains, subject to their whim, because they are thoroughly acquainted with their evils. But these spirits are among the wanderers, and are often punished.

5181.

Sometimes the spiral orbits enable one to recognize which province in the Universal Human (and correspondingly in the body) spirits and angels belong to. The orbits of people who belong to the *lymphatic* province are slight and quick, like water flowing gently, so that hardly any orbital motion is noticed.

People who belong to the lymphatic system are later taken to places that they relate to the *mesentery.* I have been told that there are labyrinths there, and that they are taken from the mesentery to various places in the Universal Human in order to serve their uses, like the chyle in the body.

5182.

There are orbits into which newly arrived spirits must be introduced so that they can participate in groups of others, talking and thinking together with them. There needs to be a harmony and agreement of all in the other life so that they may be one, like all the parts of the body, which make a one by their agreement even though there is variety everywhere. The same holds true in the Universal Human, to the end that the thought and speech of one individual may be at peace with that of others. It is a basic necessity that thought and speech within a community be in intrinsic agreement; otherwise the disagreement is perceived as an irritating, harsh noise that wounds the minds of others. Then, too, all disagreement tends to disunite, and it is an impurity that needs to be cast out.

This impurity from disagreement is pictured by the impure matter that is with and in the blood and that needs to be excreted from it. The excretion is accomplished by various kinds of agitation, which are nothing but temptations or tests of various kinds, and later by admission into orbits. The first admission into orbits is to adjust them to each other; the second is to bring agreement in thought and speech; the third is to come to mutual agreement as to thoughts and as to affections; and the fourth is to bring agreement in matters of the good and the true.

5183.

I have been allowed to observe the orbits of people who belong to the province of the *liver,* and this for the space of some hours. Their orbits were gentle, with different circular flows depending on the function of that organ. They moved me with a strong sense of pleasure. Their working varies, but it is generally circular. This diversity of their working is also pictured in the diversity of the functions of the liver. The liver in fact takes in blood and separates it. It discharges the better part into the blood vessels, sends the mediocre part off into the hepatic duct, and leaves the worst part to the gall bladder. This is how it works in adults; but in fetuses the liver receives blood from the mother's womb and purifies it, instilling the purer part into the blood vessels so that it flows into the heart by a shorter route. So it stands guard in front of the heart.

5184.

The spirits who belong to the *pancreas* act in a sharper fashion, rather like sawing, and even with that kind of sound. The sound itself comes audibly to spirits' ears, but not to the ears of physical people unless they are in the spirit while they are in the body. Their region is between the regions of the spleen and the liver, more to the left.

People in the province of the liver are almost directly above the head, but their work comes downward into the spleen.

5185.

There are spirits who relate to the pancreatic, hepatic, and cystic ducts, and therefore to the kinds of bile they contain, which the intestines discharge. These spirits are mutually distinct, but they cooperate in response to the state of the people their work is focused on. They attend particularly to instances of correction and punishment, which they want to direct. The worst of them are so stubborn that they are never willing to leave off unless they are discouraged by fears and threats. They are afraid of humiliation, and in the face of it they promise anything.

They are people who clung stubbornly to their own opinions

during their physical lives, not so much from any evil of their lives as from a natural perverseness. When they are in their natural state, they do not think about anything—thinking about nothing is thinking vaguely about a lot of things at once, with no clear thought about anything. Their pleasures are in correcting people and doing good in this manner: they are not averse to filth.

5186.

The people who make up the province of the *gall bladder* are at the back. They are people who during their physical life looked down on anything honest and to some extent on anything religious. They are also people who treated these matters lewdly.

5187.

A particular spirit came to me asking whether I knew where he could stay. In my judgment he was honest, but when I said that he might be able to stay here, some troublesome spirits of that province came and beleaguered him severely. This distressed me, and I tried in vain to prevent it. Then I noticed that I was in the province of the gall bladder: the troublesome spirits were some of those who despised anything honest and religious.

I was allowed to watch the form of agitation. It was a compulsion to speak faster than the process of thought, which they were effecting by pulling his speech away from his thinking. Then they used a compulsion to follow their speech, a compulsion attended by pain. They use this kind of agitation to train slow people to think and talk more quickly.

5188.

There are people in the world who work by pretense and lying, which are sources of evil. I was shown what they are like and how they work—by using harmless people as means of persuading others, and by casting others in the role of having said some particular thing when in fact they have said nothing of the kind. In short, they use evil means to reach whatever goal they choose. Their means are devious, deceitful, and crafty. People like this relate to the defects known as *false swellings* (*spuria tubercula*), which tend to grow on the pleura and other membranes. If they take root there, they spread widely, so that they eventually weaken the whole membrane.

Spirits like this are punished severely. Their punishment is different from the punishments of other people. It is done by whirling them. They are whirled around from left to right, at first in a circle that seems level. Then as they whirl the circle begins to swell, and then the swelling seems to sink down and become hollow. Then the speed is increased. It is remarkable how like in form this is to the physical swellings or abscesses.

I have noticed that while they were being whirled around, they tried to draw other people, especially sick ones, into their spin—into their ruin, that is, indicating that they did not care whom they lured to destruction when they seemed to themselves to be doomed.

I have also noted that they have exceptionally powerful sight, able to see through things instantly, so to speak, and to seize on favorable things as their means. So they are sharper than other people. They can also be called fatal whenever they occur in the chest cavity, whether in the pleura, in the pericardium, in the mediastinum, or in the lungs.

I have been shown that after their punishment, people like this are cast out to the rear and deep down, and that they lie there on their faces and stomachs with just a trace of human life. They are thus deprived of their sharp-sightedness, which was part of their bestial life. Their hell is in a deep place under the right foot, a little forward.

5189.

Some spirits came in front of me, and before they came I noticed a sphere that stemmed from evils. For this reason, I thought that evil spirits were coming, but it was rather their enemies. I could tell that they were their enemies by the irritated, hostile opposition to them that they instilled. They took up a position over my head and addressed me, saying that they were people. I answered that they were not people equipped with bodies like people in the world, who normally call themselves people because of their physical form. But they were people nevertheless, I said, because a person's spirit is the real person. I did not notice any objection to these statements, because they were supporting them.

They went on to say that they were different from each other, a community in which no one was like any other. Since this seemed impossible to me, they said that there actually is a community of unlike people in the other life. So I talked with them about this, saying that if a common cause united them, they could then associate because this would mean they all had a single goal.

They said that it was characteristic of them that each one spoke in a unique way, and yet they all thought alike. This they then illustrated by examples that showed that a single perception was common to them all, but that their modes of speech were different.

Then they attached themselves to my left ear, and said that they were good spirits and that it was their style to talk in this fashion. I was told that they come in a group, and that no one knows where they come from. I perceived the sphere of the evil spirits as intensely hostile to them, since evil spirits are the subjects whom they harass. Their community, a wandering one, was pictured by a man and a woman in a room, in clothing that changed to a deep blue robe.

I perceived that they related to the isthmus in the brain, between the cerebrum and the cerebellum, through which fibers pass and from which they exit in various directions. They act differently in the outward realms, depending on where they go. They also relate to the ganglia in the body, where a nerve flows in and divides into many fibers, which lead here and there and act differently at their limits even though they come from a single beginning. So at their limits, they are apparently unlike, even though they are alike in fundamental purpose.

It is also recognized that a single active force can take many different forms at its boundaries, depending on the forms it finds there. Then, too, fundamental purposes are pictured by the beginnings that fibers come from, as they exist in the brain: consequent thoughts are pictured by the fibers that come from these beginnings, and consequent actions are pictured by nerves that come from the fibers.

5377.

Having dealt now with the correspondence with the Universal Human of some of the inner organs of the body—the liver, the pancreas, the stomach, and others—we now continue with the correspondence of the peritoneum, the kidneys, the ureters, the bladder, and the intestines.

Absolutely everything in the human body, both outside and in, has a correspondence with the Universal Human. If it were not for this correspondence with that human (that is, with heaven or with the spiritual world, which amounts to the same thing), nothing whatever could come into being or continue to exist, because there would be no link to something prior and therefore with the

First—that is, with the Lord. Anything disconnected and therefore independent cannot continue to exist for even a moment. The very continuance stems from a linking with and dependence on the source of all becoming, for continuing to be is a constant coming into being.

This is why it is not just everything in the human body that corresponds, but everything in the universe as well. The sun itself has a correspondence, and so does the moon, for in heaven the Lord is both the sun and the moon. The sun's flame and warmth, and the sun's light, have their correspondences. The Lord's love for the whole human race is what the flame and warmth correspond to, and the Divine-True is what the light corresponds to. The stars themselves have their correspondence. Heaven's communities and their dwellings are the correspondents of the stars. Not that the communities are in the stars, but that they are in that kind of pattern. Everything we see under the sun has a correspondence, each and every member of the animal kingdom and each and every member of the vegetable kingdom. It is true of each and every one that if there were no inflow into it from the spiritual world, it would instantly collapse and die.

This I have also been taught by an abundance of experience, for I have been shown what many things in the animal kingdom and even more in the vegetable kingdom correspond to. I have also been shown that they could in no way continue to exist without their inflow; for deprived of the necessary antecedent, the subsequent fails, and so does the antecedent if it is separated from its subsequent.

Because the primary correspondence is that of the human with heaven and through heaven with the Lord, the way a person corresponds determines that person's appearance in the other life in heaven's light. So angels appear with indescribable brilliance and beauty, while hellish people appear with unspeakable darkness and deformity.

5378.

Some spirits came to me, some quiet ones. Later they did talk, but not as many individuals, rather all together as one. I observed from what they said that they were the kind that wanted to know everything and were eager to explain everything, and thereby to assure themselves that things were true. They were unassuming, and said that they did not do anything on their own, only from others, even though it seemed to come from themselves.

Then they were attacked by some other spirits. I was told that they belonged to the communities that constitute the region of the kidneys, ureters, and bladder. But the first spirits responded mildly. Still, the latter spirits kept attacking and challenging them, this being in fact characteristic of the kidneys. So since they could not accomplish anything against them by acting mildly, they resorted to a device natural to them, namely, increasing themselves and thereby terrifying their opponents.

As a result, they seemed to grow huge, precisely as though a single individual's body were swelling so as to seem like Atlas, reaching to heaven. A spear appeared in the hand of this individual, but apart from terrifying, there was no intent to do actual harm.

The kidney people fled from this. Then someone appeared who pursued them as they fled, and there was another person who flew between the feet of the huge one, from the front. The huge person seemed also to have large wooden shoes, which he threw toward the kidney people.

I was told by angels that the unassuming spirits who enlarged themselves were ones who related to the peritoneum. The peritoneum is the general membrane that surrounds and encloses all the abdominal organs the way the pleura encloses all the organs of the chest cavity. Because this stretches out so and is relatively vast and capable of swelling, these people may present themselves as seemingly huge when they are attacked, and may strike terror at the same time, especially toward people who make up the region of the kidneys, ureters, and bladder. These organs or vessels lie in a fold of the peritoneum, and are restricted by it. The wooden shoes pictured lowest natural elements like the ones the kidneys, ureters, and bladder carry off (on shoes being lowest natural elements, see nn. 259 and 4938–4952). As to their statement that they did not do anything on their own, only from others, in this respect too they reflect the peritoneum, since it is like this.

5379.

I have also been shown symbolically what happens when people who make up the colon of the intestine attack people who are in the region of the peritoneum. The people who make up the colon of the intestine are swollen, like the intestine by its gas. When they wanted to assault others, a wall seemed to be put in their way, and when they would try to get around that wall, a new wall would spring up. This is how they were restrained.

THE UNIVERSAL HUMAN

It is recognized that there are secretions and excretions in a specific sequence from the kidneys into the bladder. The kidneys have first place in the sequence, the ureters are intermediate, and the bladder has the last place. The people who make up these regions in the Universal Human are likewise in a series, and though they are all of the same general type, they do differ like different species of the same genus. They talk with hoarse voices, as though their tongues were split, and they are eager to get themselves into the body, though this is only an effort.

Their positions relative to the human body are as follows. The ones related to the kidneys are toward the left, close to the body, under the elbow. The ones related to the ureters are toward the left a little farther from the body. The ones related to the bladder are still farther away. Together they form almost a parabola, going toward the front from the left side, since they propel themselves toward the front from the left side on a rather long course.

This route is one general route to the hells, the other being the intestines; for both routes end in the hells. The people who are in the hells do in fact correspond to the kinds of matter excreted through the intestines and the bladder. The false and evil things they are involved in are nothing but urine and excrement, spiritually understood.

The people who make up the region of the kidneys, ureters, and bladder in the Universal Human are the kind that want nothing more than to explore and examine what other people are like, and to chastise and punish as long as some principle of justice is involved.

This is the nature of the particular gifts of the kidneys, ureters, and bladder, since they examine the blood that flows into them to see whether it contains any useless and harmful fluid. This they also separate from the useful part and then chastise, since they send it downward and harass it by various means along the way. These are the particular gifts of the people who make up the region of these parts.

However, the spirits and communities of spirits who correspond to the urine itself, especially to foul urine, are hellish. In fact, the moment urine is separated from the blood, even though it is still in the minute tubes of the kidneys or is contained in the bladder, it is still outside the body. For anything that has been separated no longer makes any circuit through the body, and accordingly contributes nothing to the growth and maintenance of its parts.

5382.

I have often noted from experience that the people who make up the province of the kidneys and ureters are particularly apt at exploring or examining other people's natures, what they think and what they intend, that they have a craving to discover the causes of things and to determine people's responsibility for any fault, with the particular goal of being able to punish them. I have also talked with them about this craving and this goal.

Many people of this sort were judges when they lived in the world, and their hearts' delight was when they found what they believed to be a just reason for penalizing, chastising, and punishing.

The activity of spirits like these is noticed in the area toward the back, where the kidneys, ureters, and bladder are. The people who belong to the bladder stretch toward Gehenna, where too some of them sit as though it were a court of law.

5383.

The means they use to explore and examine other people's spirits are many, but I may relate only this one. They induce other spirits to talk, which is done in the other life by an inflow that I cannot effectively describe. If the implications of what they say are simple, they judge their quality on that basis. They also induce particular states of affection. But the spirits who use this type of examination are some of the cruder ones: others use other means. There are some who note other people's thoughts, desires, and deeds the moment they come near, and note also any past behavior that they find painful to think about. They catch hold of this, and if they think their case is just, they punish them.

A remarkable feature of the other life, which scarcely anyone in this world can credit, is that the moment one spirit approaches another (even more so when a spirit approaches a person on earth), that spirit knows the other's thoughts and affections, and what the other has done. There is consequently a knowledge of the whole present state exactly as though the first had been associating with the second for a long time. There is this kind of communication, but there are differences in what spirits notice. There are some who perceive more inward matters, and some who perceive only more outward ones. If these latter have a craving for information, they use various means to explore the more inward things.

5384.

The means of punishment used by the people who make up the region of the kidneys, ureters, and bladder in the Universal Human are also varied. For the most part, they take away whatever is pleasant and happy and bring on discomfort and grief. In their appetite for doing this, these spirits are communicating with the hells. However, in the justice of the case they have established by their previous examination, they are communicating with heaven, so they are kept in this region.

5385.

We can determine from all this the meaning of statements in the Word that "Jehovah tests and searches the kidneys (AV "reins")" and "the heart," and that "the kidneys punish," as in Jeremiah:

Jehovah *searches the kidneys* and the heart (11:20),

and again,

Jehovah searches the righteous, *seeing the kidneys* and the heart (20:12).

In the Psalms,

You search the hearts and *the kidneys,* O righteous God (7:9),

and again,

Jehovah, *examine my kidneys* and my heart (26:2),

and again,

Jehovah, you possess my kidneys (139:13).

In Revelation,

> I am the one who *examined the kidneys* and the heart (2:23).

In these passages, "kidneys" are used to denote spiritual elements and "heart" heavenly ones. That is, "kidneys" are used to denote matters of truth, and "heart" matters of goodness. The reason is that the kidneys purify the serum while the heart purifies the blood itself. So "searching, exploring, and examining the kidneys" means searching, exploring, and examining the extent and quality of what is true—that is, the extent and quality of a person's faith. We can see this meaning in Jeremiah also:

> Jehovah, you are near their mouths but far *from their kidneys* (12:2),

and In Psalms,

> Jehovah, behold, you desire *truth in the kidneys* (51:6).

We can also see in the Psalms that punishment too is predicated of the kidneys:

> By night, *my kidneys punish me* (16:7).

5386.

There are also organs of secretion and excretion elsewhere in the body. In the brain there are the ventricles and the mammillary processes that carry off the phlegms. And further, there are little glands everywhere—mucous and salivary ones in the head, and a great many in the body, tens of thousands in the skin, through which sweat and subtler wastes are excreted. Generally speaking, these correspond to different ways of being opinionated in the spiritual world, and also to different forms of conscientiousness in things that do not matter. Some of these appear above the head in the middle distance. It is characteristic of them that they arouse scruples in matters where there should be none. So since they burden the consciences of simple folk, they are called "overconscientious." they do not know what conscience is, since no matter what occurs, they make it a matter of conscience. Actually, once some scruple or doubt has been raised, if the mind is anxious and dwells on it, there is never any lack of supporting and therefore burdensome data.

When spirits like this are present, they also bring on a palpable anxiety in the abdominal area, right under the diaphragm. They are also present with people during temptations. I have talked with them, and have noted that they have no breadth of thought that would enable them to rest content in more useful necessary concerns, since they are unable to give their attention to due proportions because they cling so tenaciously to their own opinions.

5387.

The people who correspond to the urine itself, however, are hellish, because as already stated, urine is outside the body, having already been separated from the blood. In itself, it is nothing but an unclean waste fluid that is discharged.

I am allowed to relate the following information about these people. I perceived a spirit, at first apparently within my body, but soon outside on the right. When he took his position there, he was inconspicuous—he had a gift for making himself unnoticed. When I questioned him, he gave no response. I was told by others that he had practiced piracy during his physical life. It is obvious in the other life, in fact, from the sphere of life affections, who someone was and what that individual was like, since everyone's life persists.

He kept changing his position, appearing now on the right and now on the left. I perceived that he was doing this to avoid my knowing who he was and his being compelled to speak. Other spirits told me that his kind was extremely fearful of the slightest danger, extremely bold when there was no danger, and that they were the opposite of the spirits to whom the process of discharging urine corresponded. These latter try by all available means to inflict harm on him; and to remove all doubt about this, I was shown by experience. When the spirits corresponding to the discharge of urine drew back a little and the pirate was present, the flow of urine was stopped completely and there was a reflexive sense of danger. But when they were recalled, the flow of urine was intensified in proportion to their presence.

He later admitted that he was a pirate, saying that he was clever at hiding himself and had a studied skill at misleading the pursuit. He said that now he loved stale urine far more than clear water, that the odor of foul urine was utterly delightful to him, so delightful that he wanted to make his home in swamps or even casks of stale urine.

I was also shown what his face was like. He had no face, only something black and bearded in its stead.

Later, some less accomplished pirates were summoned. They too talked very little; and strange to say, they kept gnashing their teeth. They also said that of all liquids, they loved urine best, especially if it was cloudy. These spirits, however, did not have the bearded something for a face like the former one, but rather a fearful tangle of teeth. Both beards and teeth are indicative of the lowest elements of nature. Their lack of faces indicated that they had no rational life, for the absence of any visible face is a sign that there is no correspondence of the more inward reaches with the Universal Human. In the other life, everyone actually appears, in heaven's light, according to correspondence, which means that hellish people appear horribly deformed.

5388.

A particular spirit was with me and talked with me, who had had no faith during his physical life and had not believed in any form of life after death. He had also been one of the diligent types. He had an ability with his words to trap people's spirits into supporting and agreeing with him, so his actual nature was not immediately noticeable in his conversation. He could talk as flowingly as a river, like a good spirit. But first his unwillingness to talk about matters of faith and charity was recognized, and then his inability to follow in thought, withdrawing instead. Then it was perceived by closer examination that he was agreeable in order to deceive. Agreements do vary, depending on their objectives. If the goal is sociability or pleasant conversation or something like that, or even legitimate profit, it is not so bad. But if the goal is the hidden one of enticing and thus manipulating someone else into some evil undertaking—broadly speaking, if the goal is to do harm—then it is evil.

This was the kind of objective the spirit in question had. He too was in opposition to the ones who were in the region of the kidneys and ureters. He also said that of all odors, he loved the stench of urine best, and he caused a contraction, a painful tension, in the lower area of my belly.

THE UNIVERSAL HUMAN

5389.

There are bands of spirits who wander around and come back from time to time to the same places. Evil spirits are deathly afraid of them, since they torture them with a specific kind of torment. I was told that they correspond to the fundus or the upper part of the bladder in general, and to the muscular ligaments that spiral in toward the sphincter, where urine is expelled by a kind of twisting. These spirits attach themselves to the back area where the *cauda equina* is. Their modus operandi is by rapid alternation that no one can restrain. There is a squeezing and restraining means directed upward, coming to a point in the shape of a cone. Evil spirits who are thrown into this cone, especially from above, are cruelly tortured by alternating stresses.

5390.

There are also other spirits who correspond to unclean excretions, namely the kind who were relentlessly vengeful in the world. They have appeared to me in front, toward the left. People also correspond to these unclean excretions who bring spiritual matters down to unclean earthly ones. Spirits like this have appeared to me too, bringing filthy thoughts with them, which lead them to talk filth as well. They also twisted and transformed clean things into unclean ones. Many of these people come from the dregs of society, while some of them had been highly esteemed in the world. These latter did not talk this way in public, but they still thought this way. They restrained themselves from talking the way they thought so that they would not be disgraced and lose their friendships, profits, and prestige. However, with people like themselves, in freedom, their conversation was like that of the dregs of society—even filthier, because they were more gifted intellectually, which gifts they used to pollute even the holy elements of the Word and of doctrine.

5391.

There are also kidneys called the subsidiary kidneys or renal capsules. Their gift is to separate not the serum so much as the blood itself, and to send it on in purer form in a brief circuit toward the heart. In this way they also prevent the nearby spermatic ducts from taking all the purer blood. They serve their primary function, however, in the fetus and in newborn infants.

There are chaste virgins who make up this region in the Universal Human, sensitive to anxiety and fearful of disturbance. They lie quietly, lower down on the left side. If there are thoughts of heaven involving some change in their state, they become worried and sigh, as I have often been allowed to sense quite clearly. When my thoughts were led toward little children, they felt an extraordinary inner comfort and joy, which they also expressed openly. Then when I was thinking about something with unheavenly implications as well, they were worried. Their anxiety stemmed primarily from their basic inclination to keep their thoughts centered on a single subject and not to dispel their worries by changing the subject.

The reason they belong to this region is that they keep other people's thoughts steadily centered in definite concepts in this manner. As a result, the connected sequence of these thoughts stands out clearly, highlighting the things that need to be removed, the things an individual needs to be purified from. In this way, too, angels have a better view of inner things, since once the elements that becloud and distract have been removed, both insight and inflow are clarified.

5392.

We can in some measure determine which spirits make up the region of the intestines in the Universal Human by reference to the ones that relate to the stomach, since the intestines are an extension of the stomach, and the stomach's functions are augmented and intensified there. This goes on all the way to the last intestines, the colon and the rectum. For this reason, the people in these areas are close to the hells called "fecal."

In the area of the stomach and intestines dwell people who are in the lower earth. Because these people have brought with them from the world unclean things that cling to their thoughts and affections, they are kept here for some time, until these matters are wiped away—that is, cast aside. Once these matters have been cast aside, these people can be raised into heaven. The people here are not yet in the Universal Human. They are in fact like foods that have been forwarded into the stomach, which are let into the blood and therefore into the body only when they have been cleansed of impurities. As for people who have been defiled by the more earthly impurities, they are down below these people, in the intestinal area, while the actual excrement that is discharged corresponds to the hells that are called "fecal hells."

5393.

It is known that the colon of the intestines stretches wide, and so do the people in that area. They stretch forward and leftward in a curved line leading to a hell. The people in that hell are people who were devoid of compassion and had no qualms of conscience about wanting to destroy the human race. That is, they wanted to kill and plunder, utterly heedless of resistance or compliance, men and women alike. A high percentage of soldiers and officers exhibits this fierce spirit, savaging the vanquished and defenseless after battle, not during it, killing and robbing them violently.

I have talked with angels about people like this, what they are like when they are left to their own devices and allowed to act freely, outside the law. They are far more savage than the worst of wild animals, who do not revel in the murder of their own kind like this. They only defend themselves, and they are content with what is allotted to them for food. Once they are full, they do not go on acting in the same way.

Humans are different, because their behavior springs from cruelty and savagery. The angels were aghast at this quality of the human race. The human heart rejoices and the human spirit exults at the sight of a whole landscape of military columns and rivers of blood. It is not a joy in the liberation of the homeland, only as being acclaimed great and heroic. Yet they call themselves Christians and actually believe they will wind up in heaven, where there is only peace, compassion, and charity. People like this are in the hell of the colon and rectum.

However, people with some humanity in them appear toward the left in front, in a curved line, inside a kind of wall. There is still a great deal of selfishness in them. If people have some respect for the good, this is sometimes pictured by little stars—not brilliant, almost fiery.

A wall once appeared to me near my left elbow, with a kind of plaster relief on it. The wall grew longer and higher, with the color of the upper part tending toward a deep blue. I was told that it symbolized the better of people of this type.

5394.

People who were cruel and adulterous love nothing more than filth and excrement in the other life. The stenches of such matters are wholly gratifying and delightful to them, and they prize them above all other pleasures. This is because they correspond. Their hells are in part under the buttocks, in part under the right foot, and in part deep down in front. These are the hells reached via the rectum of the intestines.

A particular spirit was transferred there, and talked with me from there. He said he saw nothing but outhouses there. Some of the residents talked with him and took him to some of these many outhouses. Later on he was taken to another location, a little to the left. While he was there, he said that an incredibly foul stench was drifting from some caves in the region, and that he dared not move a foot for fear of falling into some cave. The smell of corpses also drifted from the caves. This was because their inhabitants were cruel and devious people, to whom the smell of corpses is quite delightful. But we will discuss them later, when we describe the hells, and specifically the fecal and carrion hells.

5395.

There are people who do not live for any use to their country or community, but only for the sake of living there. They find no pleasure in holding office except to be honored and respected, and they campaign for office for this purpose. They enjoy food, drink, recreation, and conversation with no purpose but pleasure. In the other life, there is no way they can be in the company of good spirits, let alone angels. For good spirits and angels, usefulness is the cause of pleasure, and the nature and extent of their pleasure depends on their usefulness. In fact, the Lord's kingdom is nothing but a kingdom of uses. If people are valued and respected according to their usefulness in an earthly kingdom, why not in a heavenly kingdom?

People who lived solely for themselves and their pleasures, with no intent to be useful, are also underneath the buttocks. Depending on the kinds and the goals of their pleasures, they live in filth.

5396.

I may relate the following as a kind of appendix. There was a great crowd of spirits around me, which sounded like some chaotic flow. They complained that they were being completely destroyed, for there appeared to be nothing in the crowd holding them together, and this made them fearful of extinction. They thought this would be a complete extinction, as happens in such events.

But in their midst I noticed a gentle sound—sweet, angelic —whose whole content was structured. There were angelic choirs within, and the chaotic crowd was outside. This angelic stream lasted a long while. I was told that this was symbolic of the way the Lord governs surrounding dissonant and chaotic elements from a core of peace, so that the peripheral chaos settles out of the randomness of its own nature into a pattern.

CHAPTER 8
The Skin, Hair, and Bones

5552.

The way correspondences work, the human functions that have the most life in them correspond to the communities in the heavens that have the most life and consequently the greatest happiness. This means, for example, the communities to which the outer and inner human sensory functions correspond and which have to do with discernment and intent. In contrast, the human functions that have the least life in them correspond to communities there that have less life. This means, for example, the layers of skin that enclose the entire body, and the cartilages and bones that stiffen and support everything in the body. It also means the hairs that grow out of the skin.

We need now to state what communities these parts correspond to, and what these communities are like.

5553.

The communities the skin corresponds to are in the entryway of heaven. They are given a perception of the quality of spirits who are reaching the first threshold of heaven, whom they either turn away or let in. So they can be called the thresholds or vestibules of heaven.

5554.

The communities that make up the body's outer coverings are many. They vary between the face and the soles of the feet, since there is variety everywhere.

I have talked with them a great deal. As to their spiritual life, they were the kind of people who let themselves be convinced by others that something was true, and once they had heard support for it from the literal meaning of the Word, believed it without reservation. They then held to their opinion, and led not too bad a life in accord with it. However, interaction between them and people of unlike dispositions is not easy, because once they have adopted an opinion, they cling to it tenaciously and do not let themselves be swayed by rational considerations.

Many people from our planet are like this, because our world is involved in outward concerns, and even reacts against inner ones the way the skin does.

5555.

There are people who knew only the general principles of faith during their physical life—for example, that they should love the neighbor—and who from this general principle helped evil and honest people indifferently, claiming that everyone was their neighbor. While they lived in the world, they were very susceptible to devious people, hypocrites, and confidence men. The same thing happens to them in the other life; and they do not heed what other people tell them because they are focused on their senses and do not enter into rational considerations. These people too make up the skin, but the outer, less sensitive layer.

I have talked with people who made up the skin of the pate. There are, however, many different kinds of these spirits, just as the skin varies from place to place. It varies, for example, in different regions of the pate, toward the back, front, or sides, on the face, or on the chest, abdomen, legs, feet, arms, hands, and fingers.

5556.

I have also been granted to know what spirits make up the scaly layer of the skin. Compared with the other layers, this is the least sensitive, since it is covered with scales that are very much like thin cartilage. The communities that make up this layer are communities of people who constantly debate whether things are true or not, and never get beyond that point. When I talked with them, I was granted a perception that they have no grasp whatever of what is true and what is not. In fact, the more they debate, the less they grasp. To themselves, they seem wiser than other people, since they place wisdom in debating. The are utterly unaware that the very essence of wisdom lies in perceiving without debate whether something is true or not.

Many of these were people who got that way in the world by being confused about the good and the true by philosophical arguments. As a result, they have less common sense.

5557.

There are also spirits through whom others talk, while they themselves scarcely understand what they are saying. They have admitted this, but they still talk a lot.

This is what becomes of people who only chattered during physical life, without thinking at all about what they were saying—they simply loved to talk more than anything else. I have been told that they occur in groups, some related to the membranes that cover the body's viscera, some to the layers of skin that are only slightly receptive to sensation. They are actually only passive forces: they do not do anything on their own, only from others.

5558.

There are spirits whose method of learning is to claim one after another in their community that a given proposition is true. Then once they have made this claim, they watch to see whether it flows freely, without any spiritual resistance. If in fact the claim is not true, they immediately feel a resistance from within. If they do not feel a resistance, then they decide that it is true; and this is the only way they know. This is characteristic of the people that make up the glands of the skin; but there are two kinds of them. There is one that affirms things because they seem to flow, as described. They presume that the claim is harmonious with heaven's form because there is no resistance. So it must be harmonious with the truth, and has therefore been affirmed. The other kind rashly asserts that things are true even though they do not know.

5559.

I have been shown symbolically the symmetry with which elements are woven together in the skin. For people in whom these outermost elements were responsive to inner ones, or whose material aspects were subservient to spiritual ones, there was a lovely symmetry of spirals marvelously interwoven, rather like a lacework that is quite beyond description. Afterward, forms still more coherent, subtle, and harmonious were pictured. This is how the skin of a regenerate person looked.

But for people who were devious, their outermost levels looked like tangles of snakes, while for people involved in witchcraft, they looked like disgusting intestines.

5560.

There are many communities that the cartilages and bones correspond to. Characteristically, though, they have very little life in them, just as bones have very little life in comparison to the softer tissues around them. The skull and the bones of the head are like this, for example in comparison to the two lobes of the brain and the medulla oblongata, and to the sensitive substances they contain. So too are the vertebrae and ribs in comparison with the heart and lungs, and so on.

5561.

I have been shown how little life there is in people who relate to the bones. Other people talk through them, and they scarcely know what they are saying. But still they talk—it is their sole delight.

People settle into this kind of state who led evil lives but still had some remnants of goodness hidden away inside. These remnants make a little spiritual life, after many centuries of devastation (on "remnants," see nn. 468, 530, 560, 561, 660, 1050, 1738, 1906, 2284, 5135, 5342, and 5344).

I have been told that they have very little spiritual life. "Spiritual life" means the life angels have in heaven. People are led into this life in the world, through elements of faith and charity. It is the actual affection for the good, which is a matter of charity, and the affection for the true, which is a matter of faith, that are spiritual life. Without this, human life is a nature-bound, worldly, carnal, earthly life, which is not a spiritual life unless this latter life is within it. It is rather the life characteristic of animals in general.

5562.

People that come out of devastation and serve the uses that the bones serve do not have any focused thought, but a general, almost unfocused thought. They are the people we call "withdrawn," because they are not present in their bodies. They are slow, sluggish, and dull, behind schedule in everything. Still, their lot is sometimes not without its restfulness, since cares do not get through to them—they just vanish in the general fog.

5563.

Sometimes pains are felt here and there in the skull, and it feels as though kernels that are separate from the other bones are in pain. I have been granted to know from experience that this arises from false elements that stem from cravings. Remarkably enough, different kinds and species of falsity have their specific locations on the skull: this I have also become familiar with from a great deal of experience.

Kernels like this, which are hardened, are broken up and rendered soft in people who are being reformed. This happens in various ways. In general, it happens by instruction in what is good and true, by sharp inflows of truths accompanied by inner pain, and by an actual tearing apart accompanied by outward pain.

A natural characteristic of false elements from cravings is that they harden. They are actually opposed to truths, and since truths are patterned after the form of heaven, they flow willingly, freely, gently, softly. But since false things tend to the opposite, they have opposing patterns. This means that the fluidity characteristic of heaven's form is arrested, and this means a hardening.

This is why people who were involved in murderous hatred, in the vindictiveness of that hatred, and in their consequent falsities have skulls that are absolutely hard. Some are like ebony, which no rays of light (which are truths) penetrate: they all bounce off.

5564.

There are some spirits, quite small, who thunder when they talk, so that one of them may sound like an army. This way of speaking is inborn. They are not from our planet but from another, which I will describe when, by the Lord's divine mercy, I describe the inhabitants of various planets.

I was told that they relate to the scutiform cartilage, which is at the front of the chest cavity, acting as a support for the ribs in front, and also for various muscles involved in producing sound.

5565.

There are also people who relate to the harder bones, like the teeth, but I have not been granted much knowledge about them. I know only that they have scarcely any spiritual life left. When they appear to view in heaven's light, they seem not to have any face, but only teeth instead. The face actually pictures the more inward aspects of a person, the person's spiritual and heavenly elements—that is, elements of faith and charity. So if people have not acquired any of this life during their physical lives, this is what they look like.

5566.

A particular spirit came to me, looking like a black cloud with wandering stars around it. Wandering stars mean false things, while fixed stars mean true ones. I noticed that he was a spirit who wanted to beset me. When he did, he aroused fear. Some spirits, especially robbers, can do this. I could tell from this that he was a robber. When he was near me, he wanted to attack me full force, with witchcraft, but it was fruitless. He stretched out his hand to wield some imaginary power, but nothing whatever happened.

Then I was shown what his face was like. He had no face, only something utterly black instead. In it was a mouth, opened threateningly and savagely like a maw, with teeth set in rows. In short, he was like a rabid dog with jaws agape, so much so that he was all gape and no face.

5567.

One spirit attached himself to my left side. At that point, I did not know where he was from or what his nature was: he acted obscurely. He wanted to penetrate more deeply into me, but he was turned back. He imposed a general sphere of thought-concepts that I cannot describe: I do not remember ever before observing a similar kind of general sphere. He was loyal to no principles, but he was generally against everyone he could refute and disparage by his skill and inventiveness, even though he did not know what was true. I was amazed that he was so inventive, that he could refute others so cleverly while he had no ability to recognize the truth.

After a while he left, but he came back shortly with a clay flask in his hand, and wanted to give me a drink from it. It contained a kind of hallucination that took discernment away from the people who drank it. This was portrayed, because if people attached themselves to him in the world, he took away their discernment of what was true and good; yet they still stayed with him.

In heaven's light, he seemed to have no face, only teeth, because he had the ability to ridicule others, and still had himself no knowledge of what was true. I was told who he was. While he lived, he was renowned, and some people realized what he was really like.

5568.

Sometimes teeth-gnashers have been with me. They came from hells where people live who have not only led evil lives but have convinced themselves against the divine and traced everything back to nature. They do gnash their teeth when they talk. It is a ghastly sound.

5569.

As bones and skin have their correspondence, so too do hairs. They sprout from roots in the skin. Anything involving correspondence with the Universal Human applies to individual angels and spirits, for each one reflects the Universal Human as a specific image. Angels have hair that is becomingly and properly arranged. Hair represents their natural life and its correspondence to their spiritual life. On "hair" or "hairs" meaning matters of natural life, see n. 3301; and on "haircuts" as adjusting natural matters to a suitable propriety, see n. 5247.

5570.

There are many people, mainly women, whose whole emphasis was on beauty. They had given no thought to deeper matters, scarcely any to eternal life. This is overlooked in women up to the age of early maturity, when the eagerness wanes that normally precedes marriage. But if they keep up this absorption in later years when they are able to understand things differently, then they acquire a characteristic that remains after death. In the other life, people like this have long, thick hair covering their faces. They keep combing it, too: it is a matter of elegance for them. For "combing hair" means adjusting natural things to seem beautiful (see n. 5247). Other people recognize what they are like from this behavior. Spirits can actually tell from the color, length, and distribution of someone's hair what that person was like as to natural life in the world.

5571.

There are people who have believed that nature was everything, and have convinced themselves of this. They have led secure lives on this basis, without recognizing the reality of a life after death—a heaven, then, or a hell. Since people like this are wholly nature-bound, in heaven's light they seem not to have any face. In its place they have something like a beard, hairy and ragged. For as already stated, the face pictures the spiritual and heavenly elements deeper within people, while the hair pictures natural elements.

5572.

There are many people in Christendom nowadays who ascribe everything to nature and almost nothing to the divine. More of these are in one nation than another, however. I may therefore relate a conversation I had with some members of the larger nation.

5573.

A spirit was unobtrusively present above my head, but I was enabled to perceive that he was present from a smell of burnt horn or bone and the odor of teeth. Later came a great crowd like a cloud, upward from below, behind me. They were unobtrusive too, and they took a stance over my head. I thought they were unobtrusive because they were subtle, but I was told that they were unobtrusive in a spiritual sphere but obvious in a natural sphere. They are called "unobtrusive natural people."

The first thing I discovered about them was that they used every effort, skill, and art to see that nothing about them was made public. To this end, they skillfully stole other people's concepts away and imposed others, which made it hard for people to discover them. This lasted quite a while. I could tell from this that during their physical lives they had been people who did not want any of their actions or thoughts made public. They presented some other face and speech instead. Still, they did not so much pretend things as deceive other people by lying.

I perceived that the people with me had been businessmen during their physical lives, but the kind who found more pleasure in the actual transaction of business than they did in wealth, so that business was virtually their soul. So I talked business with them, saying that it was no obstacle to their entrance to heaven, and that there were both rich and poor people in heaven. They rejoined that they had thought that they would have to give up business in order to be saved, giving everything to the poor and making themselves destitute.

But I was given to answer that this was not the way it was. Business-men who were in heaven because they had been good Christians and were still rich thought differently. Some of them were actually among the wealthiest of all. These people had as their goal the common good and a love for the neighbor. They plied their trades because of the roles these trades had in the world, and did not put their whole heart in them.

I said that the reason the spirits I was talking to were lower down was that they had been completely nature-bound. They had therefore not believed in life after death, heaven, hell, or the spirit. It did not matter to them if they used any means at all to deprive others of their goods: they could see entire households destroyed, without compassion, for the sake of their own profit. They had therefore ridiculed everyone who talked about spiritual life.

I was also shown what kind of belief they had about life after death, heaven, and hell. We saw a spirit who was raised into heaven from left to right. We were told that he was someone who had just died, and that he had been brought by angels directly into heaven. We talked about this, but even though they had seen it too, they still had a very strong sphere of disbelief, and tried to spread it wider. They wanted to convince themselves and others in opposition to what they saw.

Since they had such a strong disbelief, I was given to tell them that if they had happened to see someone revived who was lying dead on a mortuary table, they would say that they would believe only if they saw large numbers of people revived. And if they had seen this happen, they would still attribute it to natural causes.

Later, when they had been left to think it over for a while, they said that at first they believed the scene was a fake. Once they were convinced that it was not a fake, they said they believed that the dead person's soul had some secret connection with the one who revived it. There was still something secret about it that they did not under-stand, because there were many incomprehensible things in nature. At any rate, there was no way they could believe that it had happened by any supernatural force.

This revealed the quality of their belief—they could never be led to believe in any life after death or hell or heaven. They were entirely nature-bound.

When people like this are seen in heaven's light, they seem to have no face, only something thick and hairy in its place.

CHAPTER 9

The Correspondence of Diseases with the Spiritual World

5711.

Since we are to discuss the correspondence of diseases, we need to know that all the diseases people have also have a correspondence with the spiritual world. In all nature, nothing happens that does not have a correspondence with the spiritual world. If something has no correspondence, it has no cause that makes it happen, that therefore makes it exist. The things that occur in the realm of nature are nothing but effects. Their causes are in the spiritual world, and the causes of those causes, which are "ends," are in the more inward heaven. An effect cannot be maintained unless its cause is constantly within it, for when the cause ceases, the effect ceases. Seen in its own right, the effect is nothing but a cause, but it is so clothed outwardly that it enables its cause to act as a cause in a lower sphere.

A cause relates to an end in the same way that an effect relates to a cause. Unless a cause too is happening from its cause (which is an end), it is not a cause. For a cause without an end is a cause with no design, and where there is no design, nothing happens.

So now we can see that, seen in its own right, an effect is a cause, and seen in its own right, a cause is an end; and we can see that the end proper to the good exists in heaven and emanates from the Lord. So an effect is not an effect unless its cause is within it and constantly within it, and a cause is not a cause unless its end is within it and constantly within it. An end is not an end proper to the good unless the divine that emanates from the Lord is within it. We can also see from this that as each and every thing in the world has come into being from the divine, each and every thing is maintained in being from the divine.

5712.

We have mentioned this to let it be known that diseases too have a correspondence with the spiritual world. It is not a correspondence with heaven, the Universal Human, but with people in its opposite, with people in the hells. By "the spiritual world" in the broadest sense we mean heaven and hell. When people die, they cross from the natural world into the spiritual world.

The reason diseases have their correspondence with these people is that diseases correspond to cravings and passions of the spirit (*animi*), these being their source. In general, the sources of diseases are excess, various kinds of extravagance, pleasures merely physical, and also hatred, vengefulness, licentiousness, and the like. These are destructive of people's inner reaches, and as these are destroyed, the more outward elements are affected, bringing people into disease, and by disease to death. It is recognized in the church that death is the human lot because of evils, or on account of sin. So too are diseases, because these are part of death.

We can conclude from this that diseases too have a correspondence with the spiritual world, but it is a correspondence with impurities there, since diseases are intrinsically impure. They actually well up from impurities, as we have already stated.

5713.

All hellish people impose diseases, in different ways, because all the hells are involved in cravings and longings for evil. Their cravings are therefore against heavenly things, so they act in people from the opposite direction. Heaven, the Universal Human, holds everything together in connection and in health. Hell, being in the opposite state, destroys and severs everything. So if hellish people attach themselves, they bring on diseases and ultimately death.

However, they are not allowed to flow into the actual solid parts of the body, the parts that make up human viscera, organs, and members, but only into cravings and falsities. It is only when someone is declining into death that they flow into the impurities characteristic of disease. For as stated, nothing ever occurs in a person unless its cause exists in the spiritual world. If a person's natural level were severed from its spiritual level, it would be separated from its whole cause of being, and therefore from its whole vital force.

This does not, however, hinder people from being healed by means on the natural level. This is actually in harmony with the means of divine providence.

I have been taught that this is how things work by a great deal of experience, so often and for so long that there is no doubt left. Evil spirits have in fact attached themselves to me often and for long periods of time. They have brought on pain and disease proportional to their presence. I have been shown where they were and what they were like, and told where they came from as well.

5714.

There was a particular spirit who had been a consummate adulterer during his physical life. He had taken the greatest delight in adulterous relationships with many women, rejecting and loathing them immediately afterward. He maintained this practice right into old age. Besides, he was devoted to pleasures, did not help anyone or perform any duty except to advance himself and especially his adulterous ventures.

He was with me for several days. I saw him under my feet, and when his life sphere was communicated to me, wherever he moved he caused pain in the membranes around the bone and the nerves—in the lower surface of the toes of my left foot, for example. And when he was allowed to get out, he caused pain in the parts where he was, especially in the membranes around the bones in my thighs, and also in the membranes in my chest under the diaphragm, and in my teeth, from within.

When his sphere was at work, he also brought on a very severe pain in my stomach.

5715.

A large rectangular opening appeared to me, leading diagonally downward to a great depth. In the depth, I saw a round opening that was open at first, but soon closed. There was an alarming heat breathing out of it that was gathered from different hells, stemming from various kinds of craving, like arrogance, lasciviousness, adultery, hatred, vindictiveness, quarrelsomeness, and belligerence. These are the sources of the heat in the hells that breathes forth from them. When this heat was active in my body, it brought on an instantaneous disease like a burning fever, but when it stopped flowing in, this symptom suddenly stopped.

When someone gets this kind of disease because of the way he has lived, then an impure sphere corresponding to the disease immediately attaches itself, and it is present as an aggravating cause.

To let me know for certain that this was how it worked, there were spirits with me from many hells, affording a communication with the sphere of exhalations from them. As these were allowed to be active in the solid parts of my body, I was seized by tension, pain, and even corresponding disease, which suddenly stopped as these spirits were driven out. To leave no room for doubt, this has happened thousands of times.

5716.

There are also spirits not far away who bring on sickly chills like the ones that come with a feverish cold. This too I have been taught by experience. They also bring on states that cause mental disturbance, and bring on fainting spells as well. The spirits from this region are particularly vicious.

5717.

There are some spirits who not only relate to the thickest substances of the brain—its wastes—but also know how to infect it with a kind of poison. When spirits like this approach, they rush into the skull and keep going all the way to the medulla spinalis. People cannot sense this unless their more inward reaches have been opened. I have been enabled to sense their approach very clearly, and also to sense their effort, an effort to destroy me. But it was fruitless because I was kept safe by the Lord. They were trying to rob me of all intellectual ability. I felt their working very clearly, and felt the pain of it too, though this soon stopped.

Later I talked with them, and they were forced to admit where they came from. They told me they lived in dark forests where no one dared mistreat friends, because if anyone did, it was a license to their friends to treat them savagely. For this reason, they are kept chained. They are misshapen, with brutal faces, and hairy.

I was told that these are the kind that slaughtered whole armies in the olden days, as we read in the Word. They do rush into the recesses of a person's brain and strike a terror so insane that one person will butcher another. Nowadays, people like this are kept locked in their hell and not let loose. They relate to fatal head tumors inside the skull.

I mentioned that they rush inside the skull and keep going all the way to the medulla spinalis, but it should be realized that this rush of the spirits is an appearance. They move outside, along a route that corresponds to the locations inside the body. This is felt as though the process were happening inside, which is due to the correspondence. As a result, their working is readily channeled into the person it is focused on.

5718.

There are spirits of a particular kind who, out of a desire to control and rule everyone by themselves, stir up enmity, hatred, and strife among others. I have seen the strife that results, and been amazed. I asked who they were, and was told that they were spirits of this sort, who stirred up these conflicts on the "divide and conquer" principle, because they wanted to be the only rulers.

I was also allowed to talk with them. They immediately stated that they ruled everyone. I was given to answer that they were mad if they tried to gain control by means like that.

They talked with me from a middle height above my forehead. Their speech was flowing, because they had been skillful speakers during their physical life. I was taught that people like this are the ones related to the third phlegm of the brain, which robs it of vitality and brings on a sluggishness by its presence. This is the source of the blockages that cause the beginnings of many diseases, including various kinds of dullness.

I noticed that they were entirely devoid of conscience, and that they thought of human prudence and wisdom as the stirring up of enmity, hatred, and murderous strife, in order to gain control. I was allowed to ask them whether they realized that they were now in the other life, and would live there to eternity, and that there were spiritual laws that absolutely prohibited this kind of behavior. Did they realize that in the world they might have been esteemed as wise among stupid people, but that they were madmen among the wise? This displeased them. I went on to state that they should know that heaven consists of mutual love, the love of one person for another. This was the source of order in heaven, and this was how such multitudes could be ruled as one. But the opposite held true for them, because they communicated nothing but hatred, vengefulness, and cruelty to others: they plotted against their own companions.

They answered that they could not be anything but what they were, to which I was given to reply that they could realize from this that everyone's life follows him.

5719.

There are people who cheapen and ridicule the Word in its letter, and, even more, people who do so to its deeper meaning. They therefore cheapen and ridicule the teachings that stem from the Word, and are at the same time without any love for the neighbor, being involved in self-love instead. They relate to impurities in the blood that travel through all the veins and arteries and thereby defile the whole mass.

To keep them from causing this kind of disease in people by their presence, they are kept separate from others, in their own hell. They communicate only with people like themselves, because these people cast themselves into the steam and sphere of that hell.

5720.

I have had the company of hypocrites, people who talked piously about divine matters, with loving affection about the public and the neighbor, affirming justice and right, while at heart they scorned and ridiculed these values. When they were allowed to flow into the parts of my body to which, by the law of opposites, they corresponded, they caused pain in my teeth. When they were very near, the pain was so severe that I could not stand it; and as they moved away, the pain subsided. This was demonstrated to me repeatedly so that there would be no doubt left.

One of them was a man I had known during his physical life, so I talked with him. In this case, too, there was pain in my teeth and gums in proportion to his presence. When he rose up toward the left, the pain spread to my left jawbone and the bone of my left temple, all the way to my cheekbones.

5721.

The most obstinate people of all are the ones who seemed more righteous than others during their worldly lives and also had secure positions of considerable dignity. For these two reasons, they had both an authority and a weightiness; and yet they believed in nothing, and lived lives of utter selfishness. They burned with a raw hatred and vengefulness toward people who did not support them and who did not revere them, and even more toward people who opposed them in any way. If they discovered a blemish on any such person, they made it into a monstrous evil and told everyone about it, even though their target was one of the finest of citizens.

In the other life, people like this talk the way they did in the world—authoritatively and ponderously, apparently from righteous principles—so that many people believe they are especially trustworthy. However, they are extremely vicious. When they attach themselves to someone, they cause an intense pain through a weariness they breathe in and constantly amplify to an unbearable peak. This brings on such a weakness of spirit, and consequently of body, that the person can scarcely hoist himself out of bed. This has been demonstrated to me by the fact that in their presence, this kind of weakness came over me, while it subsided in proportion to their departure.

They use many ways of instilling weariness and weakness, especially censure and defamation among their own number: they cast a general sphere of these attitudes.

When they are debating in their own councils about divine worship, faith, and eternal life, they reject them absolutely, and they do this as though they had some special wisdom. In the other life, they are willing to be counted devils if only they are allowed to rule the hells, and thus to have the power, so they believe, to counteract the Divine.

Inwardly, they are foul, because they especially are involved in self-love and therefore in hatred and vengefulness, and in cruelty toward anyone who does not support them. They suffer severe punishments, I have heard, until eventually they stop trying to mislead others with their simulation of righteousness. Once this simulation is taken away from them, they talk in a different tone. Afterward they are cast out of the world of spirits, then toward the left, and are thrown into a deep hell. This hell is toward the left in the middle distance.

5722.

There are other spirits who were the foulest of all during their physical lives, so foul that decency forbids description. By their presence and their inflow into the solid parts of the body, they bring on a weariness with life and such a listlessness in the limbs and joints that a person cannot hoist himself out of bed.

They are exceptionally obstinate, undeterred by punishment like other devils. They appear near the head, and seem to be lying down there. When they are driven away, it does not happen quickly but slowly, and then they gradually spiral down toward the lower regions. And when they reach the bottom, they are so tormented that they cannot restrain themselves from lashing out at others. Their joy in doing evil is so great that nothing is sweeter to them.

5723.

There were spirits with me who brought on such severe pain in my stomach that it seemed I could not go on living. The pain was so severe that I would cause unconsciousness in other people. However, they were moved away, and it stopped. I was told that spirits like this were people who during their physical lives had not devoted themselves to any discipline, not even homemaking, but had devoted themselves wholly to pleasure. Further, they had lived in shameful idleness and sloth, utterly heedless of other people. They were also scornful of faith. In brief, they were animals, not people. The sphere of spirits like this brings a numbness of limbs and joints to people who are sick.

5724.

There are thick fluids in the brain that have something more volatile or living mixed in. When these thick fluids are discharged from the blood there, they settle among the meninges first, and then among the fibers, part of them into the large ventricles in the brain, and so on. There are spirits who relate by correspondence to these thick fluids in which there is something volatile, some trace of life. They appear above the middle of the head, almost straight in front, in the middle distance. It was characteristic of them in physical life to arouse pangs of conscience and slip them into matters of no conscience. In this way, they troubled the consciences of simple folk, without knowing what ought to stir one's conscience, since they made everything that happened a matter of conscience.

Spirits like this cause a constriction in the part of the abdomen under the area of the diaphragm. They are also present in temptations, and bring on anxieties that are sometimes unbearable. The ones that correspond to the thickest, least living fluid keep the person's thought stuck in these anxieties.

I engaged in conversation with them to find out what they were like. They tried in various ways to trouble my conscience. This was the delight of their life; and I was enabled to note that they could not pay attention to rational considerations and had no broader view of things from which to see details.

5725.

I have been allowed to learn from experience what a deluge or flood is, spiritually understood. There are two kinds of flood, one involving cravings and the other involving falsities. The flood of cravings is a flooding of the voluntary part, the right side of the brain, while the flood of falsities is a flooding of the cognitive part, which involves the left side of the brain.

When a person who has lived in goodness is let back into his self-image (that is, into the sphere of his self-life), something like a flood seems to occur. While he is in this flood, he is resentful and touchy, his thoughts are restless, and his cravings are violent. This varies, depending on whether the left side of the brain where false things are is flooded, or the right side where evil things are.

But when the person is kept in the sphere of the life received from the Lord through rebirth, then he or she is completely separate from any flooding like this. Such people are, so to speak, in a calm and sunny spot, happy and blessed—far removed, then, from resentment, anger, restlessness, cravings, and the like. This is the morning or springtime of spirits: the former is their evening or autumn. I have been allowed to perceive being apart from the flood for a considerable stretch of time, while I was seeing other spirits in it. Later, though, I myself was submerged in it, and then I noticed what the flood was like. People in the process of temptation are in states of this sort.

This also taught me the meaning of the flood in the Word. That is, the last descendants of the earliest people, who belonged to the Lord's heavenly church, were completely flooded by evil and false things, and thus perished.

5726.

Since the only source of death is sin, and sin is whatever is contrary to the divine design, evil therefore closes the smallest, quite invisible vessels that combine to make the next larger ones. These smallest, quite invisible vessels are extensions of the more inward elements of the person. This is what causes the first and most inward blockage, and the first and most inward impurity in the blood. As the impurity increases, it causes illness and finally death.

But if people had lived good lives, then their more inward

elements would be open to heaven, and through heaven to the Lord. So the smallest, invisible, miniature vessels (because of their correspondence, we can call these outlines of the first fibers "miniature vessels") would be open, too; so people would be free of disease. There would be only a decline in extreme old age, when they became children again, but wise children. And then when the body could no longer serve the inner person, the spirit, people would cross without illness from their earthly bodies into the kind of bodies angels have —straight from this world into heaven.

Soul-Body Interaction

There are three opinions and traditions—three hypotheses—about the interaction of soul and body, or the way one works in the other and with the other. The first is called "physical inflow," the second "spiritual inflow," and the third "preestablished harmony."

The first, called physical inflow, is based on sense-impressions and misconceptions derived from them, since it looks as though the objects of sight that affect the eyes flow into the thought and produce it. In similar fashion, it seems as though the words that stimulate the ears flow into the mind and produce concepts in it, and it seems much the same with smell, taste, and touch. Since the organs of these senses do first receive the stimuli from the world that brush against them, and since the mind seems to think and even intend in response to affections proper to these stimuli, early philosophers and scholastics believed that an inflow derived from them into the soul. In this way, they arrived at a hypothesis of physical or natural inflow.

The second hypothesis, called spiritual inflow (some people call it "opportune ["occasional"] inflow"), is based on order and its laws. Since the soul is spiritual substance, and by reason of order is more pure, more primary, and more inward, while the body is material and therefore more crude, more secondary, and more outward, and since it is in keeping for the more pure to flow into the more crude, the more primary into the more secondary, and the more inward into the more outward, it is therefore in keeping with order for the spiritual to flow into the material, and not the reverse.

This means that the thinking mind flows into the sight, subject to the state imposed on the eyes by the things that are being seen—a state that that mind, further, arranges at will. In the same way, the perceiving mind flows into the hearing, subject to the state imposed on the ears by words.

The third hypothesis, called preestablished harmony, is based on appearances and misconceptions of reason, because even as the mind operates, it acts in unison with the body. However, every operation is first sequential and afterward simultaneous (sequential operation is inflow and simultaneous operation is harmony), as when the mind thinks and then speaks, or intends and then does. So it is a rational misconception to support the simultaneous aspect and rule out the sequential.

There can be no fourth opinion about the relationship of soul and body beyond these three. Either the soul will operate into the body, or the body into the soul, or the two will constantly be working in parallel.

2.

Since spiritual inflow, as stated, is based on order and its laws, it has been recognized and accepted by wise people in the learned world in preference to the other two views. Whatever is based on order is a truth, and a truth makes itself known by its own intrinsic light, even within the shadow of truth where hypotheses dwell.

But there are three shadows that envelop this hypothesis: ignorance of what the soul is, ignorance of what the spiritual is, and ignorance of what inflow is like. So these three shadows need to be dispelled before reason sees the actual truth. For a truth posited is not an actual truth, but only a guess at the truth. It is like a mural seen by starlight, with the mind imaginatively projecting some other form on it. It is different after daybreak, when the sunlight strikes it, revealing not just its general outlines but its details as well, and presenting them to view. So open truth emerges from the shadow of truth where this hypothesis dwells, once it is realized what are the nature and quality of the human soul and what is the quality of the inflow into it, through it into the thinking and perceiving mind, and from that mind into the body.

But no one can convey this except a person granted by the Lord to associate with angels in the spiritual world and at the same time with people in the natural world. Since this has been granted to me, I have been able to describe each of these matters, having done so in the book *Marriage Love* (the spiritual is there treated in the Noteworthy Account in nn. 326–329, the human soul in n. 315, and inflow in n. 380 and more extensively in nn. 415–422).

Is anyone unaware, or incapable of being aware, that the good of love and the truth of faith flow into us from the Lord? That they flow into our soul, become conscious in our mind, and flow out from thought into speech, from intent into deed? We shall proceed to show that this is the source of spiritual inflow, its origin, and its course, in the following sequence:

I. There are two worlds—a spiritual world where spirits and angels are, and a natural world where people are.

SOUL-BODY INTERACTION

II.   The spiritual world arose and endures from its sun, and the natural world from its sun.

III.   The sun of the spiritual world is pure love from Jehovah God, who is at its center.

IV.   Warmth and light go forth from that sun, the essence of the outgoing warmth being love, and the essence of the outgoing light being wisdom.

V.   Both that warmth and that light flow into human beings, the warmth into our intent, producing the good of love, and the light into our discernment, producing the truth of wisdom.

VI.   These two elements (warmth and light, or love and wisdom) flow united into our souls, through them into our minds, our affections, and our thoughts, and from these into our physical senses, words, and deeds.

VII.   The natural world's sun is pure fire, and the world of nature arose and endures from that sun.

VIII.   Consequently, everything that comes from that sun is intrinsically dead.

IX.   The spiritual "puts on" the natural the way a person puts on clothes.

X.   It is spiritual elements clothed in this fashion that enable a person to live as a rational and moral being—that is, a spiritually natural being.

XI.   The acceptance of this inflow depends on the state of love and wisdom within the individual.

XII.   The discernment in a person can be raised into the light or wisdom heaven's angels are in, in proportion to the individual's rational development, and the intent can likewise be raised into their warmth or love depending on the individual's life deeds. But the love within the intent is not raised except as the person intends and does what the wisdom of discernment teaches.

XIII.   It is quite different with animals.

XIV.   There are three levels in the spiritual world and three in the natural world, unrecognized until now, which determine how all inflow occurs.

XV.   Purposes exist on the first level, means on the second, and results on the third.

XVI.   We can see from this what spiritual inflow is like, from its source to its results.

We must now briefly explain the details.

I.   There are two worlds—a spiritual world where spirits and angels are, and a natural world where people are.

3.

In Christendom to date, there is a thick fog about the existence of a spiritual world, an abode of spirits and angels, distinct from the natural world where people are. This is because no angel has come down and taught us in so many words, nor has any human gone up and seen. To prevent ignorance of that world, and a consequent wavering faith about heaven and hell, from making such fools of us that we become materialistic atheists, the Lord has graciously opened the sight of my spirit. He has thus raised me into heaven and lowered me into hell, and has shown me visually what each is like.

So I have been able to see that there are two worlds distinct from each other—one where everything is spiritual, which is therefore called the spiritual world, and one where everything is natural and which is therefore called the natural world. I have seen that spirits and angels are alive in their world and we in ours, and that everyone crosses over by means of death from our world into the other, where we live to eternity. Acknowledgment of each world must be presupposed in order to explain inflow from the ground up, which is our present task. For the spiritual world actually flows into the natural and activates it, even in detail. This takes place with human beings and animals alike, and constitutes also the life force of trees and plants.

II. The spiritual world arose and endures from its sun, and the natural world from its sun.

4.

The reason the spiritual world has one sun and the natural world another is that these worlds are wholly distinct, and a world traces its beginning to a sun. A world where everything is spiritual cannot in fact be born from a sun whose derivatives are wholly natural. This would be physical inflow, which is disorderly.

The emergence of a world from a sun (and not the reverse) follows from the result of means. A world in all respects endures by means of a sun, and its enduring points to its emergence. So people say that enduring is a constant emergence. We can see from this that if a sun were taken away, its world would collapse into chaos, and this in turn into nothing.

I can bear witness to the existence of a sun in the spiritual world other than the one in the natural world, because I have seen it. It looks fiery like our sun, about the same size, and as far from angels as ours is from us. It does not rise or set, though, but stays halfway between the zenith and the horizon, so that angels have a constant light and a constant springtime.

If a rational person did not know anything about the spiritual world's sun, he or she could readily accept some wild notion about the creation of the universe, on deep reflection being able to see only that the universe exists from nature, and that since the sun is the source of nature, the universe comes from the sun as its creator.

Further, no one can grasp spiritual inflow without an awareness of its source as well. For every inflow is from a sun—spiritual inflow from its sun and natural inflow from its sun. Our inner sight, which is a property of our minds, receives an inflow from the spiritual sun; while our outer sight, which belongs to our bodies, receives an inflow from the natural sun. They are united in their functioning like the soul and the body.

We can see from this what blindness, darkness, and folly afflict people who do not know anything about the spiritual world and its sun: blindness, because a mind that relies on eyesight alone is, in its logical processes, like a bat flitting erratically and abruptly toward hanging curtains at night; darkness, because when things flow into the mind's sight from the eyesight, the mind's sight loses all illumination and becomes like an owl's; and folly, because the person is still thinking, but is thinking from natural matters about spiritual ones and not the reverse, which means thinking mindlessly, obtusely, and foolishly.

III. The sun of the spiritual world is pure love from Jehovah God, who is at its center.

5.

Spiritual things cannot come from any source but love, and love cannot come from any source but Jehovah God, who is love itself. So the sun of the spiritual world, from which all spiritual things flow as from their source, is pure love that comes from Jehovah God, who is at its center. That sun itself is not God, but it is from God, being the sphere from Him that most closely surrounds Him.

The universe—meaning all worlds taken together, as many as there are stars in the sky—was created by Jehovah God by means of that sun.

The reason creation was accomplished by means of that sun, which is pure love (by Jehovah God, that is), is that love is the very Reality (*Esse*) of life and wisdom is the consequent Emergence (*Existere*) of life; and all things were created out of love by means of wisdom. This is the meaning of these words in John:

The Word was with God, and God was the Word; all things were made through Him, and without Him nothing was made that was made; and the world was made through Him (1:1, 3, 10).

Here "the Word" is the Divine-True, which also means divine wisdom. So, too, the Word is there referred to as the light that enlightens everyone (verse 9), just as divine wisdom does by means of the Divine-True.

If people trace the origin of worlds to any other source, they perceive distortedly, like deranged people who see masks as men, illusions as lights, and logical constructs as substantial images. Actually, the created universe is a coherent work out of love by means of wisdom. This you will see if you are capable of surveying its connections from first things to last.

In the same way that God is one, the spiritual sun is one as well. This is because spatial extension cannot be attributed to the spiritual things that derive from that sun; and a spaceless "Reality-Emergence complex" occurs at all points in space, unlimited by space. The same holds true for divine love, then, from the point of origin of the universe to its boundaries. Reason sees remotely that the Divine fills everything, and by so doing maintains everything as it was created. Reason sees this close at hand to the extent that it recognizes what love is like intrinsically, how it is united with wisdom so that goals are perceived, how it flows into wisdom so that means are produced, and how it works through wisdom so that results are achieved.

IV. Warmth and light go forth from that sun, the essence of the outgoing warmth being love, and the essence of the outgoing light being wisdom.

6.

In the Word, and consequently in the usual ministerial sermon, the portrayal of divine love through fire is familiar. For example, people say that heavenly fire fills the heart and kindles a holy longing to worship the Lord. This is because fire corresponds to love and consequently refers to it. This is why Jehovah God appeared to Moses as fire in the bush, and to the Israelites in similar form on Mount Sinai. This is also the reason for the command to keep a perpetual fire on the altar, and to light the lamps of the Menorah in the tabernacle every evening. This is because fire indicated love.

We can see clearly from the effects of love that there is a warmth from this fire. People are kindled, heated, and fired up as their love rises into zeal, or into blazing anger. The source of the blood's warmth, the vital heat of the human being and of animals in general, is nothing but the love that constitutes their life. Hell fire is nothing but the love that is set against heavenly love. This, then, is why divine love looks like a sun to angels in their world, fiery like a sun, as already stated; and this is why angels are in warmth in proportion to their acceptance of love from Jehovah God through that sun.

It follows naturally that the essence of light in heaven is wisdom. For love and wisdom are inseparable, like Reality and Emergence, with love actually emerging by means of wisdom and in keeping with it. This is like the situation in the world, where in springtime warmth is one with light and makes things sprout and bear fruit. Besides, everybody knows that spiritual warmth is love and spiritual light is wisdom. People do grow warm as they love, and are in light as they are wise.

I have seen that light very often. It vastly surpasses natural light both in clarity and in brilliance. In fact, it is intrinsic clarity and brilliance, so to speak, looking like gleaming, glistening snow, the way the Lord's clothes looked when He was transfigured (Mk 9:3; Lk 9:29). Since light is wisdom, the Lord calls Himself the light that enlightens everyone (Jn 1:9), and elsewhere states that He is the light itself (Jn 3:19; 8:12; 12:35, 36, 46). That is, He calls Himself the very Divine-True that is the Word, meaning wisdom itself.

People believe that the natural lighting (*lumen*) that is an attribute of rationality comes from the light of our world. However, it comes from the light (*lux*) of the spiritual world's sun. For the mind's sight flows into the eye's sight—into the light rays, then—and not the other way around. If it were the other way around, that would be physical inflow, not spiritual inflow.

V. Both that warmth and that light flow into human beings, the warmth into our intent, producing the good of love, and the light into our discernment, producing the truth of wisdom.

7.

We do know that everything everywhere goes back to the good and the true, that nothing whatever exists that does not contain some referent to these two. This is why two recipients of life exist in us, one a recipient of the good, called "intentionality," and one a recipient of the true, called "discernment." Since good is a matter of love and true a matter of wisdom, intentionality is a recipient of love and discernment a recipient of wisdom.

The reason good is a matter of love is that we intend what we love, and when we accomplish it, we call it good. The reason true is a matter of wisdom is that all wisdom is made up of true elements. In fact, the good that a wise person is considering is true, and becomes good when he or she intends and does it.

If we do not duly make the distinction between these two recipients of life, intentionality and discernment, and form ourselves a clear concept of them, our struggles to understand spiritual inflow are fruitless. For there is one inflow into intentionality and another inflow into discernment—an inflow of the good of love into our intentionality and one of the truth of wisdom into our discernment. Both come from Jehovah God, directly through the sun He is at the center of, and indirectly through the angelic heaven.

These two recipients, intentionality and discernment, are as distinct as warmth and light, since intentionality receives heaven's warmth, which in essence is love, and discernment receives heaven's light, which in essence is wisdom, as stated above.

There is one inflow that occurs from the human mind into words, and another that occurs into deeds. The inflow into words comes from intentionality through discernment, while the inflow that occurs into deeds comes from discernment through intentionality. People who are familiar only with the inflow into discernment, and not with the inflow into intentionality at the same time, and who build trains of thought and draw conclusions on this basis, are like one-eyed people who see things one-sidedly, not simultaneously from both sides. Or they are like cripples, who use only one hand awkwardly, or like lame people, who walk haltingly on one foot, with a cane.

It is clear from these few facts that spiritual warmth flows into our intentionality and produces the good of love, and that spiritual light flows into our discernment and produces the truth of wisdom.

VI. These two elements (warmth and light, or love and wisdom) flow united into our souls, through them into our minds, our affections, and our thoughts, and from these into our physical senses, words, and deeds.

8.

Until now, the spiritual inflow taught by astute and brilliant minds has been one from the soul into the body. It has not been any inflow into the soul, and through it into the body, even though people have known that every good element of love together with every true element of faith flows into us from God, with nothing of it being from ourselves. Further, the things that flow in from God flow first of all into our souls, through our souls into our rational minds, and through these into the elements that constitute our bodies. If we try to trace spiritual inflow in some other way, we are like people who stop up the channel of a spring and still expect a steady flow of water from it, or like people who trace the beginning of a tree back to its root but not to its seed, or like people who review corollaries apart from their premise.

The soul is not life itself, but a recipient of life from God, who is life in itself. Every inflow is an inflow of life, and is therefore from God. This is the meaning of the statement "Jehovah God breathed into the man's nostrils the breath [lit., "soul"] of lives, and the man became a living soul (Gn 2:7)." "Breathing the breath of lives into the nostrils" refers to granting a perception of what is good and true. Further, the Lord says about Himself, "As the Father has life in Himself, so He has granted the Son to have life in Himself (Jn 5:26)." "Life in oneself" is God; and the soul's life is a life flowing in from God.

Granting then that every inflow is an inflow of life, that this works through its recipients, and that the central or first of these recipients in us is our soul, then for a fitting perception of this inflow we must begin from God, and not from some halfway point. For unless we do begin from God, the doctrine of inflow is like a carriage without wheels or a ship without sails.

It is because of this that we dealt in the foregoing pages with the sun of the spiritual world, in whose midst is Jehovah God (n. 5), and with the inflow of love and wisdom, and consequently of life, from that sun (nn. 6–7).

Life flows from God into us through the soul, through the soul into the mind (that is, affections and thoughts), and out of these into our physical senses, words, and deeds, because these are matters of life in its sequential arrangement. The mind is in fact subject to the soul, and the body subject to the mind. Further, there are two lives to the mind, one involving intentionality and one involving discernment. The life of the mind's intentionality is the good of love, and its offshoots are called affections. The life of its discernment is the truth of wisdom, and its offshoots are called thoughts. The mind is alive by means of these two complexes. The senses, words, and deeds, on the other hand, are the body's life. It follows from their sequence of occurrence that these exist from the soul through the mind: they demonstrate their origin to a wise person quite plainly, even without research.

The human soul, being a higher spiritual substance, receives its inflow directly from God. The human mind, being a lower spiritual substance, receives an inflow indirectly from God, through the spiritual world. The body, being made out of nature's substances, which are called "matter," receives an inflow from God indirectly through the natural world.

We will see below that the good of love and the truth of wisdom flow united (that is, coalesced into a one) into our souls from God, but that as they proceed they are separated by us, and are brought back into union only by people who allow themselves to be led by God.

VII.   The natural world's sun is pure fire, and the world of nature arose and endures from that sun.

9.

We turn our attention to nature and the world of nature, meaning the atmospheres and the earths we call planets, including this globe of lands and seas we live on and all the things that adorn its surface every year. Everybody knows perfectly well from personal observation, and from the story of how the earth came to be inhabited, that all of these owe their existence to the sun alone, which constitutes the center point and which is everywhere present by means of its light rays and its graduations of warmth. And in view of the fact that it is the source of their continuing existence, reason can know perfectly well that it is also the source of their emergence. For constant existence is constant emergence parallel to original emergence.

From these premises, it follows that the natural world was created by Jehovah God in a second phase, by means of this sun.

We have already presented the existence of spiritual and natural things completely distinct from each other, and the origin and maintenance of spiritual things from and by a sun that is pure love, with the creator and preserver of the universe, Jehovah God, in its midst. It follows naturally that the origin and maintenance of natural things rests in a sun that is pure fire—as naturally as a deduction follows from a given, or a given from a first.

The sun of nature and its worlds is pure fire, as all its effects join in demonstrating. We have, for example, the focusing of light rays in a hearth by optical means, producing both violently consuming fire and flame. Its warmth has a nature like that of simple fire: its temperature gradations depend on its angle of incidence, producing various climates and the season of the year. And there are many other matters that enable the reason to use the physical senses to establish the fact that the natural world's sun is nothing but fire, and that it is fire in its very own purity.

People who have no knowledge of the origin of spiritual things from their sun, only about the origin of natural things from theirs, can hardly help jumbling spiritual and natural things together, and deciding on the basis of sensory deceptions and derived trains of thought that spiritual things are nothing but pure natural things, and that love and wisdom arise out of their activity, roused by light and warmth. Because nature is all they see with their eyes, perceive with their nostrils, and breathe with their chests, they give nature credit for all rational processes, and thereby soak up materialism the way a sponge soaks up water. We may liken them, though, to drivers who put the cart before the horse.

It is different with people who draw a distinction between spiritual and natural things, and derive the latter from the former. For they perceive that the soul's inflow into the body is spiritual and that the natural things pertaining to the body are of service to the soul as vehicles and means for it to achieve its results in a natural world. If you come to some other decision, you can be compared to a crab who progresses by pushing stepwise with his tail and twists his eyes backward as he goes. And your rational sight may be compared to Argus's eyesight, in the back of his head while the eyes in front were asleep. These people believe they are as sharp-sighted as Argus when they reason, for they say, "Doesn't everyone see the beginning of the universe in nature? What is God, then, but the most inward plane of nature?"—and other irrational things, in which they take more pride than wise people do in rational statements.

VIII. Consequently, everything that comes from that sun is intrinsically dead.

10.

If anyone lifts the reasoning of his understanding a little bit above matters of the physical senses, will that person not see that love in its own right is alive, that its visible, fiery form is life? Will that person not see conversely that simple fire in its own right is relatively dead, and that therefore the spiritual world's sun is alive because it is pure love, while the natural world's sun is dead because it is pure fire? The same holds true for everything that emanates and emerges from them.

There are two things that bring about all the results in the universe—life and nature. They accomplish these results in orderly fashion when life energized nature from within. It is different when nature from within prompts life to act, which happens with people who place an intrinsically dead nature above and within life, giving their whole devotion to sense pleasures and physical cravings, and giving no weight to the spiritual elements of the soul and really rational elements of the mind.

Because of this inversion, these people are called "the dead." All materialistic atheists in the world are like this, and all satans in hell. They are given the name "the dead" in the Word. See, for example, the Psalms: "They clung to Baal-Peor, and devoured the sacrifices of the dead" (106:28); "The enemy persecutes my soul, he makes me sit in shadows, like the world's dead" (143:3); "To hear the groan of the prisoner, and to free the sons of death" (102:20); and in the book of Revelation "I know your works, your having a name of being alive; but you are dead: be watchful, and strengthen the remnants that are about to die" (3:1, 2).

They are called "the dead" because spiritual death is damnation, and damnation happens to people who believe that life comes from nature, and that nature's light is the light of life. In this way, they hide and stifle and smother any idea of God, heaven, and eternal life. As a result, they are like owls, who see light in darkness and darkness in light. That is, they see false things as true, and evil things as good. And since for them the heartfelt pleasures are pleasures in what is evil, they are rather like those birds and animals that feed on corpses as delicacies, and savor the stenches from tombs as sweet fragrances.

Besides, they see no other inflow than a physical or natural one. If they do support spiritual flow, it is not from any actual concept of it, but only because some teacher told them about it.

IX. The spiritual "puts on" the natural the way a person puts on clothes.

11.

It is recognized that there is something active and something passive in every event, and that nothing emerges either from the active alone or from the passive alone. It is like this with the spiritual and the natural. The spiritual, being a living force, is the active; while the natural, being a dead force, is the passive. So it follows that anything that has emerged in this subsolar world from its beginning, and has kept on emerging moment by moment, exists out of the spiritual by means of the natural. This holds true not only for members of the animal kingdom, but for members of the vegetable kingdom as well.

Something similar is also recognized—namely, that there is something original and something instrumental in everything that is accomplished; and that when something happens, these two look like one, even though they are distinguishably two. So one of the rules of wisdom is that the original cause and the instrumental cause, taken together, make one cause. This is the way it is with the spiritual and the natural, too. In actual accomplishments, these two look like one because the spiritual is inside the natural like a fiber inside a muscle or like blood inside arteries, or like thought inside words and affection inside sounds, making itself felt by means of the natural through these agencies. Still we can see, albeit dimly, that the spiritual puts on the natural the way a person puts on clothes.

We can compare the organic body that the soul dons to clothes, because the soul does put it on. Further, the soul takes it off and throws it away like old clothes when it crosses over from the natural to the spiritual world through death. The body does grow old like a garment. But the soul does not, since it is a spiritual substance that has nothing in common with natural changes that go from beginnings to endings, and regularly finish.

If people do not think of the body as clothing or a covering of the soul, intrinsically dead, simply fitted to receive the living energies that flow in through the soul from God, then they cannot help deciding on the basis of their errors that the soul lives on its own and the body on its own, with a preestablished harmony between the two lives. Or they may decide that the soul's life flows into the body's life, or the body's life into the soul's life, thus imagining either a spiritual or a natural inflow. However, a truth to which every created thing here bears witness is that the "later" does not act on its own, but from something previous, a source, which in turn does not act on its own, but from something earlier still. So nothing acts except from a First One, who does act on His own—that is, from God. Beyond this, life is unique, and cannot be created. But it is most perfectly capable of flowing into organic forms fitted to receive it. Each and every thing in the created universe is this kind of form.

Many people believe that the soul is life, and that because we live from our souls we live from our own life, on our own, and not from any inflow of life from God. These people, however, accomplish nothing but the snarling up of a Gordian knot made up of illusions, entangling all their mental judgments in it. Or they devise a labyrinth such that the mind can never retrace its way by any threads of reason, and get out. Effectively, they lower themselves into underground caverns, so to speak, where they spend their time in eternal darkness. For countless illusions result from this, with ghastly details, such as the notion that God has transferred and transcribed Himself into people so that every individual is a kind of demigod who lives self-sustaining and therefore does what is good and what is wise independently. There is the similar notion that we own faith and charity in our own right, obtaining them from ourselves and not from God. There are many other abnormalities like the ones that occur among people in hell, who believed during their lives on earth that nature was alive, or produced life by its own activity. When these people look at heaven, they see its light as utter darkness.

Once I heard a voice from heaven, saying that if a glimmer of the life within us were ours, and not God's within us, neither heaven nor anything in it would exist. Consequently, there would be no church on earth, and therefore no eternal life.

The reader is referred to further information on this topic in the Noteworthy Occurrences in the book *Marital Love*, nn. 132–136.

X.   It is spiritual elements clothed in this fashion that enable a person to live as a rational and moral being—that is, a spiritually natural being.

12.

The premise just established—that the soul puts on a body the way a person puts on clothes—leads to the corollary that the soul flows into the human mind, and through it into the body, bringing with it a life that it is constantly receiving from the Lord. So it conveys this life indirectly into the body, where by a very intimate union, it creates the appearance that the body is alive. We can see, both from this and from a thousand testimonials of experience, that it is the spiritual united to the material, like a living force to a dead one, which causes a person to speak rationally and to act morally. It looks as though the tongue and lips spoke from some intrinsic life, as though the arms and hands acted in similar fashion. But it is intrinsically spiritual thought that does the speaking and intrinsically spiritual intent that does the acting. Each does so by means of its own organs, which are intrinsically material because they are assembled from the natural world.

The truth of this is seen in broad daylight as long as one bears the following in mind. Take the thought out of speaking—is not the mouth instantly mute? Take the intent out of acting—is not the hand instantly still?

We can compare the union of spiritual and natural elements, and the consequent lifelike look of the material elements, to fine wine in a clean sponge, or the sweet juice in a grape, or the pungent smell of cinnamon. In all these instances, the containing fibers are materials with no taste of their own, no odor. The taste and odor come only from the fluids in and among the fibers, so that if you squeeze out the moisture, they are stringy and lifeless. It is like this with the organs of the body proper if the life is extracted.

We can see from the logical processes of our thought that we are rational, and from instances of upright behavior and propriety that we are moral, out of a union of both spiritual and natural elements. We have these qualities from our capacity to receive an inflow from the Lord through the angelic heaven, the site of the actual home of wisdom and love, consequently of rationality and morality. On this basis, we see that the spiritual and the natural united within us make us live as spiritually natural beings.

The reason things are both similar and different after death is that a person's soul is clothed with a substantial body after death the way it was clothed with a material body in the natural world.

Many people believe that the mind's perceptions and thoughts, being spiritual, flow in uncovered, not by means of structured forms. But these people are just dreaming, these people who have not seen what lies within the head, where perceptions and thoughts occur in their fundamental forms. They have not seen, for example, that the brains are there, interlaced and interwoven out of gray matter and medullary matter, or that there are little glands, cavities, and sections, all enclosed by the meninges and the matters. They have not seen that people think and intend sanely or insanely depending on the sound or disturbed condition of all these elements. Consequently, they have not seen that our rationality and morality depend on the organic constitution of our minds. For without forms structured to receive spiritual light, our rational sight (which belongs to our discernment) would have no attributes, like natural sight without any eyes, and so on.

XI. The acceptance of this inflow depends on the state of love and wisdom within the individual.

13.

In the preceding pages, we have set forth that the human being is not life, but an organ that receives life from God. We have set forth that love united with wisdom is life, and further that God is love itself and wisdom itself, which means life itself. It follows from this that we are images of God—recipient vessels of life from God—to the extent that we love wisdom, or the extent that wisdom embosomed in love dwells within us. Conversely, to the extent that we are in the opposite love and consequent madness, we receive life not from God but from hell—the life that is called death.

Love and wisdom themselves are not actually life. They are rather the essential reality of life, while the delights of love and the pleasures of wisdom constitute life. Actually, life's essential reality emerges by means of these delights and pleasures. The inflow of life from God brings these delights and pleasures with it, like an inflow of springtime light and warmth into human minds, into all kinds of birds and animals, even into plants, which then sprout and grow. For love's delights and wisdom's pleasures open up spirits and make them fit to receive, the way joy and happiness open up faces and make them fit for the inflow of the soul's gaiety.

A person touched by the love of wisdom is like a Garden of Eden where there are two trees, one the tree of life and the other the tree of knowledge of good and evil. The tree of life is the acceptance of love and wisdom from God. The tree of knowledge of good and evil is acceptance of these elements from oneself. This latter person is mad, even to the point of believing himself to be as wise as God. But the former person is truly wise, believing that no one is wise save God alone, and that people are wise to the extent that they believe this— even more to the extent that they are conscious of wanting this to be true. But there is more material on this in the Noteworthy Occurrences included in the book *Marital Love*, nn. 132–136.

I should like to append an arcanum from heaven that corroborates this. All heaven's angels turn their foreheads toward the Lord as the sun, while all hell's angels turn the backs of their heads toward Him. These latter receive His inflow directly into their intentions, which are intrinsically lusts, and make their discernment give assent. But the former receive the inflow into the affections of their discernment, and make their intentions give assent. As a result, they are in wisdom, while the others are in madness. Actually, human discernment resides in the cerebrum, which is behind the forehead, and human intentionality resides in the cerebellum, which is in the back of the head.

Everyone knows that a person crazed by false notions gives in to the passions of his evil side and supports them by chains of reasoning from his discernment. Everyone knows, too, that a wise person sees from true notions what the nature of his intention's passions are, and holds them in check. A wise person does this because he or she is turning to face God—that is, believing in God and not in self. Insane people, on the other hand, do what they do because they turn their faces away from God—they believe in themselves and not in God. Believing in oneself is believing that one is loving and wise on one's own, not because of God. "Eating from the tree of knowledge of good and evil" refers to this state. But believing in God is believing that one is loving and wise because of God, not on one's own. This is "eating from the tree of life" (Rv 2:7).

On this basis, it is possible to grasp (still only by moonlight at night, so to speak) that the acceptance of life's inflow from God depends on the state of love and wisdom within the individual.

We can draw further illustrations of this inflow from the inflow of light and warmth into plants, which bloom and bear fruit depending on the way their constituent fibers are joined together—that is, depending on how they receive. We can draw illustrations too from the inflow of light into gem stones, which alter the rays into colors depending on the set of their component parts—that is, on how they receive the light. Or we could look at prisms and raindrops, which give rise to rainbows depending on the incidence, refraction, and therefore the reception of light. It is like this with the human mind in relation to the spiritual light that comes from the Lord as the sun, and flows in constantly, but is received in different ways.

> XII. The discernment in a person can be raised into the light or wisdom heaven's angels are in, in proportion to the individual's rational development, and the intent can likewise be raised into their warmth or love depending on the individual's life deeds. But the love within the intent is not raised except as the person intends and does what the wisdom of discernment teaches.

14.

We use the term *the human mind* to mean our two capacities, called discernment and intentionality. Discernment is what receives heaven's light, which essentially is wisdom; and intentionality is what receives heaven's warmth, which essentially is love, as we have already explained. These two elements—love and wisdom—come forth from the Lord as the sun, and flow into heaven in both a general and a detailed manner. This is where angels get their wisdom and love. They also flow into this world in a general and a detailed manner, which is where people get their wisdom and love.

However, while these two elements come forth from the Lord as a single entity and flow into the souls of angels and people as a single entity, they are not received as a single entity in their minds. The light that produces discernment is received first, and the love that produces intentionality is received step by step. This is a matter of deliberate arrangement, since every individual needs to be created anew—that is, reformed—and this is accomplished by means of our discernment. From the cradle, we absorb insights into what is true and good that teach us how to live well, that is, how to intend and behave properly. In this way, intentionality is shaped by discernment.

This is the purpose for which we have been granted the ability to raise our discernment almost into the light angels are in—in order to see what we need to intend and do if we are to thrive in this world, for time, and be blessed after death, for eternity. We will thrive and become blessed if we get ourselves wisdom and keep our intentionality submissive to it. We will become thwarted and miserable if we make our discernment submissive to our intentionality. This is because our intentionality leans toward evil things from the moment of birth, even toward terrible things. So unless it were held in check by means of discernment, we would plunge into unspeakable things. As a matter of fact, we would out of our instinctive savage nature exterminate and butcher everyone who did not support and indulge us, all for our own sake.

Further, if discernment could not be perfected separately, and intentionality perfected by that means, we would not be people but animals. In fact, we would not be able to think if it were not for this separation and the raising of discernment above intentionality. All we could do would be to vocalize our affections. Nor could we act on the basis of reason, only on the basis of instinct; to say nothing of being able to recognize the things proper to God, to recognize God by means of them, to be united to Him in this way, and to live to eternity. Actually, the human being thinks and intends in apparent independence, and this apparent independence is the mutual element of a union. For a union without a mutual element is an impossibility, just as there is no union of something active with something passive unless there is a reaction. God alone is active: the human being lets himself be acted upon, and reacts to all intents with apparent independence, though this too, more inwardly, comes from God.

Once these principles are properly perceived, we can see from them the nature of love proper to our intentionality if it is raised up by means of our discernment. Then we can see what it is like if it is not raised up; and, as a result, we can see what human nature is.

But let us use some comparisons to illustrate a person's nature when intentionality is not raised up by means of discernment. This person is like an eagle soaring in the heights who plunges down and starts gorging himself the moment he sees his prey—objects of his appetite like hens, cygnets, or even lambs. Or he is like an adulterer who hides his paramour down in the cellar, coming upstairs now and again to talk wisely about chastity with his guests, and occasionally tearing himself away from his companions and fulfilling his lust with his paramour. Then, again, he is like a thief in a castle tower who acts like one of the watchmen there, but dashes outside the moment he sees something that could be his prey, and plunders it. He could also be compared to swamp insects that hover like a cloud over the head of a running horse, but settle down when the horse rests and dive into their swamp. This is what people are like if their intentionality or love is not raised up by means of their discernment. They stay down below, at the bottom, immersed in nature's impurities and in the desires of their senses. It is quite different with people who tame the enticements of their intentionality's cravings by means of wisdom in their discernment. For them, discernment enters a marriage contract with intentionality, and they live a delightful life on high.

XIII.   It is quite different with animals.

15.

If people pass judgment solely on the basis of the way things look to their physical senses, they will reach the conclusion that animals have intentionality and discernment just the way people do, the only difference being that people can talk and can therefore express what they are thinking and intending, while animals can only make noises about these things. However, animals do not have intentionality and discernment, but only some image of each, which scholars call an analogue.

People are human because their discernment can be raised above the longings of their intentionality, and can therefore identify and see them and even temper them. But an animal is an animal because its longings impel it to do what it does.

So people are human by virtue of the fact that their intentionality is in submission to their discernment, while an animal is an animal by virtue of the fact that its discernment is in submission to its intentionality. This leads to the following conclusion: because people's discernment receives the light that flows in from heaven, because it grasps and identifies this light as its own and consequently thinks analytically in a wide variety of ways, with apparent independence, it is alive, and is therefore a real discernment. And because people's intentionality receives heaven's inflowing love and acts because of it with apparent independence, it is alive and is therefore real intentionality. The situation with animals is completely different.

It is for this reason that if people do their thinking on the basis of the cravings of their intentionality, they become like animals. In the spiritual world, they even look like animals from a distance: what is more, they act like animals. The only difference is that they could act differently if they wanted to. But if people have controlled the cravings of their intentionality by means of discernment and have thereby behaved rationally and wisely, they look like people in the spiritual world and are angels of heaven.

In short, intentionality and discernment in animals always go hand in hand: and since intentionality is intrinsically blind (being a function of warmth rather than of light), it makes the discernment blind as well. This means that an animal does not know or discern what it is doing. Even so, it does act, since it acts out of an inflow from the spiritual world. This kind of behavior is instinct.

People believe that animals think about what they are doing on the basis of discernment, but there is no shred of such thought. They are impelled to activity simply out of a natural love inherent in them from creation, with their physical senses falling in line. Our thinking and speaking result solely from the separability of our discernment from our intentionality, and from its ability to be raised all the way into heaven's light. For discernment thinks, and thought speaks.

The reason animals act by laws of order engraved on their natures (some with apparent morality and rationality, unlike most people), is that their discernment is a blind submission to the desires of their intentionality and cannot therefore be corrupted by perverse quibbles the way humans' discernment can.

It does need to be borne in mind that by "the intentionality and discernment of animals" in the discussion above, we mean an image or analogue of these capacities. We use these names for the analogues because that is what they look like.

The life of an animal can be compared to that of a sleepwalker who moves around and does things as a result of an intentionality whose discernment is asleep, or to a blind person who follows paths with a dog leading him. So, too, it is like the life of a retarded person who does his task according to set standards as a result of practice and consequent habit. Or it is like the life of an amnesiac who has thereby lost his intellect. He still knows—or learns—how to get dressed, eat fine foods, make love, walk the streets from his house and back again, and to do the sorts of things that gratify his senses and make his body comfortable, and is guided by these enticements even though he is not thinking and therefore cannot talk.

We can see from this how wrong people are when they believe that animals enjoy rationality and are distinguished from man only by their outward form and their inability to express rational things that lie within. These errors lead many people to conclude that if man lives after death, so will animals, or, conversely, that if animals do not live after death, neither will humans. And then there are other dreams that arise out of ignorance about intentionality and discernment, and about the levels through which, like a ladder, the human mind climbs toward heaven.

XIV. There are three levels in the spiritual world and three in the natural world, unrecognized until now, which determine how all inflow occurs.

16.

Searching out causes from their effects, we discover that there are two kinds of levels. One involves things that are prior and posterior; the other involves things that are greater and less. The levels that mark off prior and posterior things should be termed "vertical levels" or "discrete levels." The levels that serve to mark off greater and lesser things should be termed "horizontal levels" or "continuous levels."

Vertical or discrete levels are like levels of one thing's production or composition from something else—for example, a particular nerve from its fibers, a particular fiber from its fibrils, a particular piece of wood or stone from its parts, and a particular part from its particles. In contrast, horizontal or continuous levels are like increases and decreases in width, height, and depth within the same vertical level —for example, larger or smaller volumes of water or air or ether, or greater or lesser masses of wood or stone or metal.

Each and every item in the spiritual and the natural worlds is involved in these two kinds of levels from its creation. The whole animal kingdom in this world is in general and in detail involved in these levels. So are the whole vegetable kingdom and the whole mineral kingdom; and so is the atmospheric space between the sun and our planet.

For this reason, there are three precisely distinguished atmospheres both in the spiritual world and in the natural world, since there is a sun in each. However, the atmospheres of the spiritual world are by virtue of their source substantial, while the atmospheres of the natural world are by virtue of their source material. Since the atmospheres do descend from their sources by these levels, and since they serve light and warmth as containers and transmission media, it follows that there are three levels of light and warmth. Further, since light in the spiritual world is essentially wisdom, and warmth there is essentially love (as explained in the appropriate section above), it also follows that there are three levels of wisdom and three levels of love—in fact, three levels of life. They are separated into their levels by the media through which they travel.

This is why there are three heavens. There is a highest one (also called the third heaven) where angels of the highest level live; there is an intermediate one (also called the second heaven) where angels of the intermediate level live; and there is a lowest one (also called the first heaven) where angels of the lowest level live. These heavens are marked off by levels of wisdom and love. People in the lowest heaven are involved in a love of knowing what is good and true; people in the intermediate heaven are involved in a love of understanding these things, and people in the highest heaven are involved in a love of being wise—that is, of living by the things they know and understand.

Since the angelic heaven is marked off into three levels, the human mind is marked off into three levels, being an image of heaven, that is, a heaven in smallest form. This is why a person can become an angel of one of these three heavens. It happens according to the individual's acceptance of love and wisdom from the Lord. We become angels of the lowest heaven if we accept only a love of knowing what is true and good, an angel of the intermediate heaven if we accept a love of understanding these things, and an angel of the highest heaven if we accept a love of being wise—that is, of living by these things (on the division of the human mind into three regions responding to the heavens, see n. 270 of the Noteworthy Occurrences included in the book *Marital Love*).

We can see from this that all the spiritual inflow from the Lord and into the human being comes down through these three levels, being accepted by the individual according to the level of wisdom and love he or she is involved in. A recognition of these levels would be very useful indeed nowadays, since many people, unacquainted with these levels, stay stuck on the lowest level where their physical senses are. Because of their ignorance (which is a darkness of their discernment), they cannot be lifted up into the spiritual light overhead. So a naturalism invades them spontaneously, so to speak, the moment they get thoroughly involved in prying into matters of the soul, the human mind, and its rationality, and looking at them closely. This applies even more forcefully to inquiry into heaven and life after death. They become consequently like people standing outside with telescopes in their hands, looking at the sky, spouting idiotic predictions, or like people who chatter on and quibble about everything they see or anything they hear, beyond the point where there is any rational content from their discernment. But they are like butchers who think they are skilled anatomists because they have examined the entrails of cattle and sheep as they appear from the outside, but not as they appear from the inside.

The truth of the matter is, however, that thinking on the basis of an inflow of natural light that is not brightened by the inflow of spiritual light is nothing but dreaming, and talking on this basis is babbling. For more on these levels, see the book *Divine Love and Wisdom*, nn. 173–281.

XV.   Purposes exist on the first level, means on the second, and results on the third.

17.

Is there anyone who fails to see that the purpose is not the means, but rather produces the means? Or that the means is not the result, but produces the result? So there are three distinguishable elements that follow in a sequence.

In the human being, the purpose is the love of our intentionality, for we suggest to ourselves and intend what we love. Our means is the capacity of our discernment to calculate, since our purpose seeks out through this ability the intermediate or effective means. And the result, finally, is the activity of the body as a result of these factors and in accordance with them. These are, then, three elements within us that follow in a sequence the way the vertical levels do. When these three are present, then the purpose is within the means, and through the means the purpose is within the result. This is why it is said in the Word that everyone must be judged by his works—within the results, our physical deeds, are our purpose or the love of our intentionality, and our means or the calculation of our discernment. This then involves our whole nature.

If people are unaware of this and do not segment objects of rational consideration in this way, they cannot help limiting their thought to the atoms of Epicurus or the monads of Leibniz or the simple substances of Wolff. This blocks off their understanding like a wall, making it impossible even to think rationally about spiritual inflow because there is no way of thinking about any sequence. For Wolff says of this simple substance that if it is divided it collapses into nothing. In this way, then, the understanding stays in its first light, derived from the senses alone, without advancing a step further. This is why people know the spiritual only as a refined natural, know the rational only as something possessed by animals as well as humans, know the soul only as the kind of breath of wind breathed from the lungs at death—along with other opinions that are matters of darkness rather than of light.

Since (as stated above) all processes in the spiritual world and in the natural world occur in conformity to these levels, we can see that real intelligence is recognizing and discriminating these levels and seeing them in their sequence. They are the means by which every individual can tell what he or she is like, given a knowledge of his or her love. For as already stated, our purpose (which belongs to our intentionality), our means (which belong to our discernment), and our results (which belong to our bodies) follow from our love, like a tree from its seed and a fruit from its tree.

There are three kinds of love: love of heaven, love of the world, and self-love. Love of heaven is spiritual, love of the world is material, and self-love is physical. When a love is spiritual, then all the elements that follow from it, the way forms follow from an essence, derive a spiritual nature from it. The same principle applies if the love is for the world or for wealth and is therefore material. All the elements that follow from it, the way corollaries follow from a premise, derive a material nature from it. In the same way, if the chief love is self-love, or a love of being exalted above everybody else, then all the elements that follow from it derive a carnal nature from it. This is because the individual characterized by a given love focuses solely on himself and therefore stops the mind's thoughts in the body. For this reason, as we have just stated, if we recognize someone's ruling love and also the sequences of purposes to means to results (which three elements follow in a sequence according to the vertical levels), then we recognize the whole person.

This is how heaven's angels recognize everyone they talk with. They perceive people's love from the tone of voice, they see their likeness in their faces and their nature from their physical carriage.

SOUL-BODY INTERACTION

XVI. We can see from this what spiritual inflow is like, from its source to its results.

18.

To this point, we have followed spiritual inflow down from the soul into the body, but not from God into the soul and thus into the body. This we have done because no one knew anything about the spiritual world or its sun, from which spiritual elements flow as from their wellspring, which has prevented them from knowing anything about the inflow of spiritual elements into natural ones.

Now, since I have been allowed to be present in the spiritual world and the natural world at the same time, I am bound by conscience to present these things. What good is it to know something unless someone else knows it too? It is nothing but gathering wealth and hiding it in a safe, only occasionally checking and counting it with no intention of using it. This, plainly and simply, is what spiritual avarice is.

But for a full knowledge of the nature and quality of spiritual inflow, one needs to know what, essentially, "the spiritual" is, what "the natural" is, and what the human soul is. To prevent these candlelight jottings from being handicapped by ignorance of these points, it would be well to refer to particular Noteworthy Occurrences in the book *Marital Love*. On the spiritual, see nn. 326–329; on the human soul, see n. 315; and on the inflow of spiritual elements into natural ones, see n. 380. See also nn. 415–422.

19.

I append the following matter of interest. After the above manuscript was written, I prayed to the Lord and was allowed to talk with some disciples of Aristotle, together with some disciples of Descartes and some disciples of Leibniz. My purpose was to draw out their minds' opinions on soul-body interaction. After my prayer, nine men arrived, three Aristotelians, three Cartesians, and three Leibnizians. They stood around me, Aristotle's admirers on the left, Descartes's adherents on the right, and Leibniz's supporters behind. Quite a way off, rather apart from each other, I could see three men apparently crowned with laurel. I recognized by an inflowing perception that they were the leaders or masters themselves. There was a single man standing behind Leibniz and holding the hem of his robe in his hand: I was told that this was Wolff.

253

When these nine men looked at each other, they started greeting each other courteously, and chatting. But a spirit rose up from the lower regions with a little torch in his hand. He kept waving it in front of their faces, and they became hostile, three against three, looking at each other with forbidding expressions. In fact, an urge to argue and quarrel had taken over.

Then the Aristotelians, who were also scholastics, stepped forward and said, "Is there anyone who does not see that objects of perception flow into the soul through the senses like a person entering a room through a door, and that the soul's thinking depends on this inflow? When a lover sees his beautiful virgin or bride, don't his eyes light up and carry his love to his soul? When a miser sees purses of money, doesn't he burn for them with all his senses, which then carry this craving to his soul and arouse lust for possessing them? When a proud person hears himself praised by someone else, doesn't he prick up his ears, which transmit the praises to his soul? Aren't the senses like entryways, the only entrances to the soul? What conclusion can anyone draw from these and countless other such facts, except that inflow is from nature, or is physical?"

In response to these declarations, Descartes's adherents, who were holding their fingers beneath their brows, now pulled them away and answered, "We are afraid that you talk on the basis of the way things seem. Don't you realize that the eye does not love the virgin or bride on its own, but as a result of the soul? Nor do the physical senses desire the purse on their own, but as a result of the soul. Similarly, this is the only reason the ears seize on the praises of sycophants. Isn't it perception that makes people sensate? And perception is a function of the soul, not of the physical organ. Tell us—if you can—what else but thought makes the tongue and lips talk, and what else but intentionality makes the hands work? Yet thought and intentionality are matters of the soul and not of the body. So what makes the eyes see, the ears hear, the other organs sensate, if not the soul? On the basis of these and countless other similar facts, anyone at all whose sensitivity is higher than physical sense impressions will come to the conclusion that there is not an inflow of the body into the soul, but an inflow of the soul into the body, which we call opportune inflow, or spiritual inflow."

On hearing these presentations, the three men who were standing behind the other trios, Leibniz's supporters, spoke up and said, "We have heard the arguments on each side: we have compared them and perceived that the second are better than the first in many respects, and the first better than the second in many respects. So if we may, let us resolve the dispute." When they were asked how, they answered, "There is no inflow of the soul into the body or of the body into the soul. Rather, there is a perfectly coordinated, moment-by-moment, simultaneous working of the two, to which our noted founder has given a lovely name, calling it 'preestablished harmony.' "

After all this had happened, the spirit appeared again with the little torch in his hand. But now it was in his left hand, and he waved it toward the bases of their skulls, which resulted in a confusion of concepts for all of them. They kept exclaiming, "Neither our souls nor our bodies know where we are heading. So let us cut this dispute short by casting lots. We will agree with the lot that comes out first." They took three slips and wrote "physical inflow" on one, "spiritual inflow" on the second, and "preestablished harmony" on the third. They mixed these three slips in an empty hat and chose one person to do the drawing. He put his hand in, and took out the slip with "spiritual inflow" written on it. When they had seen it and read it, they all declared (some with clear and fluent voice, some with indistinct and uncontrolled voice), "We agree with this, because it came out first."

Suddenly, an angel was standing there, who said, "Do not believe that the slip favoring spiritual inflow came out by chance. It came out by arrangement. In fact, since you are caught up in confused concepts, the truth itself offered itself to your hand so that you would agree with it."

20

I was once asked how I, a philosopher, became a theologian. I answered that this happened in the same way that fishermen were made disciples and apostles by the Lord, that I too was a spiritual fisherman from my youth. When my companion heard this, he asked what a spiritual fisherman was. I answered that in the Word, a fisherman in the spiritual meaning indicated a person who hunts out and teaches natural truths. I quoted the following passages from the Word. "Then the waters will be lacking from the sea, and the river will fail and dry up, and all the men who cast hooks into the sea will be sorrowful" (Is 19:5, 8). Elsewhere, "Over the river whose waters will be healed, fishermen will stand from En-gedi; net spreaders were there to spread their nets; their fish were like the fish of the great sea, very many" (Ez 47:9–10). And elsewhere, "Behold, I will send, saith Jehovah, for many fishermen, who will fish the children of Israel" (Jer 16:16).

We can see from these passages why the Lord chose fishermen for disciples, and said, "Follow Me, and I will make you fishers of men" (Mt 4:18–19; Mk 1:16–17), and why He said to Peter, after he had caught a vast number of fish, "From now on you will catch men" (Lk 5:9–10).

Afterward, I showed him the source of this meaning of fishermen from the *Apocalypse Revealed*—that is, because "water" means things that are true on the natural level (nn. 50, 932), so also does a river (nn. 409, 932), "fish" means people who are involved in things that are true on the natural level (n. 405), and therefore "fishermen" means people who hunt out and teach truths.

On hearing these statements, my questioner said quite loudly, "Now I understand why the Lord chose fishermen to be His disciples! So it does not surprise me that he has chosen you as well, since as you have said, you have been a fisherman in a spiritual sense from your early youth, that is, a hunter of natural truths. Your present occupation of pursuing spiritual truths is because these latter are based on the former." Being a person of rational ability, he added only that the Lord can tell who is suited to perceive and teach these things that have to do with His new church. It might be one of the primates, or it might be one of his servants. Besides, what Christian theologian is there who has not studied philosophy in his school days? Where else would he gain discernment?

Finally he said, "Since you have become a theologian, explain what your theology is." I answered, "These are its two premises: that God is one, and that there is a union between charity and faith." He responded, "Who denies that?" I answered, "Contemporary theology, if it is examined in depth."

Annotated Bibliography

Benz, Ernst. *Dreams, Hallucinations, and Visions.* New York: The Swedenborg Foundation, 1982. Explains the psychic and religious significance of these three phenomena.

Bigelow, John. *The Bible That Was Lost and Is Found.* New York: The Swedenborg Press, 1979. A fascinating account of how one man discovered the meaning of the Bible.

Keller, Helen. *My Religion.* New York: The Swedenborg Foundation, 1980. A personal account of her faith. Available in large-print edition and cassette tape.

King, Thomas. *Allegories of Genesis.* New York: The Swedenborg Foundation, 1982. This book demonstrates the correspondence between the outer world, the realm of nature, and the inner world of the spirit.

Sechrist, Alice S. *Dictionary of Bible Imagery.* New York: The Swedenborg Foundation, 1981. Reveals symbolic meaning of thousands of words in the Bible.

Swedenborg, Emanuel. *The Apocalypse Explained.* 6 vols. Trans. J. Whitehead. New York: The Swedenborg Foundation, 1982. Swedenborg's symbolic interpretation of the Book of Revelation and other parts of the Bible, particularly the Psalms, the Prophets, and the Gospels.

———. *The Apocalypse Revealed.* 2 vols. Trans. J. Whitehead. New York: The Swedenborg Foundation, 1975. A study that concentrates on the spiritual (symbolic) sense of the Book of Revelation.

———. *Arcana Coelestia.* 12 vols. Trans. J. F. Potts. New York: The Swedenborg Foundation, 1978. Swedenborg explores the spiritual sense of the myth and history of the books of Genesis and Exodus.

———. *Charity.* Trans. W. F. Wunsch. New York: The Swedenborg Foundation, 1982.

———. *Divine Love and Wisdom.* Trans. J. C. Ager. New York: The Swedenborg Foundation, 1982. An interpretation of the universe as a spiritual-natural, or psycho-physical, world. This work describes the creation of the universe and the three discrete degrees of mind.

———. *Divine Providence.* Trans. J. C. Ager. New York: The Swedenborg

BIBLIOGRAPHY

Foundation, 1982. This sequel to *Divine Love and Wisdom* describes how God cares for the individual and for the human race.

———. *The Four Doctrines.* Trans. J. F. Potts. New York: The Swedenborg Foundation, 1981. Swedenborg interprets four leading doctrines of Christianity: The Lord, The Scriptures, Life, and Faith.

———. *Heaven and Hell.* Trans. G. F. Dole. New York: The Swedenborg Foundation, 1979. On the basis of his visionary experiences, Swedenborg gives a comprehensive account of our entry into the next world and life after death. Available in large-print edition.

———. *Marital Love.* Trans. W. F. Wunsch. New York: The Swedenborg Foundation, 1975. An ethical discussion of the relation of the sexes and the origin and nature of marriage love.

———. *Miscellaneous Theological Works.* Trans. J. Whitehead. New York: The Swedenborg Foundation, 1976. A collection of brief works, ranging from doctrinal summary to Scripture interpretation.

———. *Posthumous Theological Works.* 2 vols. Trans. J. Whitehead. New York: The Swedenborg Foundation, 1978. A collection of material left by Swedenborg in manuscript form, including extracts from his correspondence.

———. *The Spiritual Diary.* 5 vols. Trans. A. W. Acton. London: The Swedenborg Society, 1978. A storehouse of spiritual facts, phenomena, and principles noted by Swedenborg at the time of his experiences in the spiritual realm.

———. *True Christian Religion.* 2 vols. Trans. J. C. Ager. New York: The Swedenborg Foundation, 1980. Swedenborg's teachings for the New Christian Era, dealing with a broad spectrum of concerns relevant to the contemporary reader.

Synnestvedt, Sig, ed. *The Essential Swedenborg.* New York: The Swedenborg Foundation, 1981. Presents the basic elements of Swedenborgian thought.

Van Dusen, Wilson. *The Natural Depth in Man.* New York: The Swedenborg Foundation, 1981. A psychologist explores man's inner state, expansion of awareness through drugs, mystical experience, dreams and their significance, and other realms of the psyche.

———. *The Presence of Other Worlds.* New York: The Swedenborg Foundation, 1981. An account of Swedenborg's inner journey of the mind with spiritual and psychological findings.

———. *Uses.* New York: The Swedenborg Foundation, 1981. This small book demonstrates in practical terms how we can find our individual way to personal and spiritual growth.

Zacharias, Paul. *Celebrate Life.* Newton, Mass.: Swedenborg Press, 1981. A devotional book of meditations drawing on the Bible and the works of poets and philosophers.

Index to Introduction

INDEX

INDEX

Quakers, 25

Raphael, 7
Redon, Odilon, 25
Regnum Animale (Swedenborg), 10
Retzius, Gustav, 29*n*10
Reynolds, Elizabeth, 31*n*24
Romantic movement, 19
Ruling Love, 23–24

Scandinavia, 4
Scriptures, 8, 11, 18, 27–28
Seneca, 17
Shakers, 25
Shamans, 4, 23, 30*n*15
Sigstedt, 9
Smith, Samuel, 14, 31*n*24
Soul, 8–9, 24
Spirit, 8, 15
Spirit of Realm, 23
Spiritual Diary, The (Swedenborg), 11
Strindberg, August, 15
Swedberg, Jesper, 3–4
Swedenborg, Emanuel: his *Apocalypse, Explained and Revealed*, 28; his clairvoyant experiences, 13; cognitive systems of, 7; his crisis period, 10–13; his "Doctrine of Correspondences," 25; and dreams, 2, 10; early life of, 3–5; "enlightenment" of, 12; influence of, 22–29; his *Journal of Dreams*, 10–11; and knowledge, 1–2; at Leiden, 10; as "the man who had to know," 1–2; his "Most Ancient Church," 26; philosophy of, 1; his *Regnum Animale*, 10; and Ruling Love, 23–24; his sanity, 12–18; and science, 1–2, 4–8; and self-actualization, 15–17; and sexuality, 23; and Soul-Body Interaction, 15; spiritual crisis of, 2; his *Spiritual Diary*, 11; on the Swedish Board of Mines, 7; theological works of, 18–22; and John Wesley, 14; writings of, 2
Swedish Board of Mines, the, 7
Swedish Lutheran Church, 3

Tessin, Count, 20, 32*n*44
Toksvig, Signe, 15, 28, 29*n*2
Troilus, Archbishop Samuel, 21
Tübingen, 18
Tuxen, General, 21, 32*n*44

Uffizi Gallery, 6
Uppsala University, 3, 4, 32*n*39

Van Dusen, Wilson, 6, 16
van Gogh, Vincent, 15
Vatican, 7
Vedantism, 24
Virgin Birth, 12
von Knobloch, Fraulein, 13

Wakan Tanka, 27
Wesley, John, 14, 18, 32*n*50
Whitmont, Edward, 15
Wolff, Christian, 16

Index to Texts

INDEX

INDEX

INDEX

Judaism, 61
Judgment, Last, 135

Kidneys, 194–200
Kingdom(s): of animals, 115, 193, 240, 249; of discernment, 90; of the heart, 165–66; the heavenly, 73, 79, 165, 177; of intent, 90; of the Lord, 39–40, 41, 56–57, 59, 64–65, 77, 79, 92, 112, 125, 169, 204; of the lungs, 165–66; mineral, 249; of nature, 183–84; spiritual, 73, 89–90, 165; union among, 166; of vegetables, 79, 193, 240, 249

Land of the lower regions, 171
Last Judgment, 135
Leibniz, 252–54
Leviticus, Book of, 63
Life: after death, 213; essential reality of, 243; of evil people, 129–30; from hell, 243; of the Lord, 42, 65, 80, 113, 133; and wisdom, 243
Light: angels of, 128, 139; and animals, 77–78; of heaven, 47, 48–49, 50, 74, 113, 123; kinds of, 127–28; from the Lord, 126, 134; the Lord is, 128, 234; opposite of, 50–51; spiritual, 77–78; and truth, 130; and wisdom, 229, 234–35; of the world, 47, 48–49, 74, 123, 127
Liver, 189
Loins, 88, 175–81

Lord: dependence upon, 112; divine nature of, 65; dwells within, 114; is heaven's sun, 74; kingdom of, 39–40, 41–42, 56–57, 59, 64–65, 77, 79, 92, 112, 125, 169, 204; life of, 42, 65, 80, 113, 114, 133; love for, 48, 73–74, 80, 117; love of, 80, 113, 193; mercy of, 80; is perfect, 163; is the Universal Human, 74; will of, 80; Word of, 82
Lord's Prayer, 99
Love: for children 177; effects of, 233; good of, 228, 234; of heaven, 252; heavenly, 173; kinds of, 252; and life, 243; for the Lord, 48, 73–74, 80, 174; of the Lord, 80, 113, 193; in marriage, 175–81; for neighbor, 74, 104, 174, 206, 213, 219; pure, 229, 232–33; of self, 48, 80, 85, 105, 173, 175, 219–20, 252; and wisdom, 234–45; of the world, 48, 175, 252. *See also* Charity
Luke, Gospel of, 167, 234, 256
Lungs, 73–74, 86–89, 91, 156

Man, 105–06, 108, 114
Marital Love, 241, 244, 251, 253
Mark, Gospel of, 160, 167, 234, 256
Marriage love, 175–81
Matthew, Gospel of, 160, 167, 182, 256
Means, 230, 251–52
Menorah, the, 233

INDEX

Moses, 168, 233
Mouth, 156

Nature: and the hair, 211–12;
and the Lord's kingdom,
41–42; of man, 104; realm
of, 39, 111, 113, 125, 133,
149, 183–84; and the
spiritual world, 37–38,
169–72, 237–39, 242
New Jerusalem, 44, 64
Nose, 146–47
Numbers, Book of, 168

Obedience, 151–52
Odors, 145–48
Order, 228
Organs, human, 70–71
Outer person, 82–83, 103, 121–22,
171–72

Pallades, 155
Pancreas, 189
Peritoneum, 192, 194
Peter, St., 85, 256
Philosophy, 153–55
Pleura, 190
Pneuma, 155
Power, 166–67
Pretending, 161
Providence, 152, 170, 186–87, 215
Psalms, Book of, 167, 197, 198,
239
Purposes, 230, 251–52

Reality-Emergence complex, 233,
234
Rectum, 203
Representations and
correspondences, 37–66, 97

Results, 230, 251–52
Revelation, Book of, 138, 139,
198, 239, 244
Rituals, church, 61

Salvation, 171
Samuel, Book of, 178
Scabies, 158
Scholastics, 154
Self, love of, 48, 80, 85, 105, 173,
175, 219–20, 252
Sensation: involuntary, 115–18;
voluntary, 115–16, 118–19,
120–21
Senses: of angels, 141–44; in
general, 111, 115–16;
nonreal, 143–44; real,
143–44; mentioned, 158
Shoulders, 165–67
Sight: physical, 123–24, 125, 231;
spiritual, 123–24, 125, 133,
136, 231
Silver Age, 117
Sin, 222
Sinai, Mt., 233
Sincerity, 161
Skin, 205–07
Skull, 209
Smell, sense of, 144–45, 147
Soul: and the body, 149, 227–56;
and heaven or hell, 77; as
the inner person, 40–41,
108; receives life, 236
Speech, 105, 150, 161
Spheres, spiritual, 145–46, 186–87
Spirit (of man), 150, 155–56
Spirits: communities of, 103, 121,
161, 186, 195–96; from
another planet, 54; can be
recognized, 84; speech of,

266

Other Volumes in this Series

Jacopone da Todi • THE LAUDS
Fakhruddin 'Iraqi • DIVINE FLASHES
Menahem Nahum of Chernobyl • THE LIGHT OF THE EYES
Early Dominicans • SELECTED WRITINGS
John Climacus • THE LADDER OF DIVINE ASCENT
Francis and Clare • THE COMPLETE WORKS
Gregory Palamas • THE TRIADS
Pietists • SELECTED WRITINGS
The Shakers • TWO CENTURIES OF SPIRITUAL REFLECTION
Zohar • THE BOOK OF ENLIGHTENMENT
Luis de León • THE NAMES OF CHRIST
Quaker Spirituality • SELECTED WRITINGS